Introduction

This Children's Encyclopedia has been designed to help you to find interesting information quickly and easily. The topics are arranged in alphabetical order starting with Aardvark and finishing with Zoology with a whole variety of exciting topics in between.

If you're looking for information on a special topic for homework or for a project you should find lots to help you in these pages. You may just want to browse through the pages and see what topics you want to find out more about. Whatever you're looking for you're sure to find something in this encyclopedia.

We've enjoyed writing this for you and hope that you'll enjoy reading it!

Contents

Children's Encyclopedia

igloo

igloo

Published in 2006
by Igloo Books Ltd
Cottage Farm,
Sywell,
NN6 0BJ.
www.igloo-books.com

A copy of the British Library Cataloguing-in-Publication Data is available from the British Library

10 9 8 7 6 5 4 3 2 1

ISBN: 1 84561 391 0

Packaged by HL Studios, Long Hanborough, Oxon

Printed in Dubai.

Contents

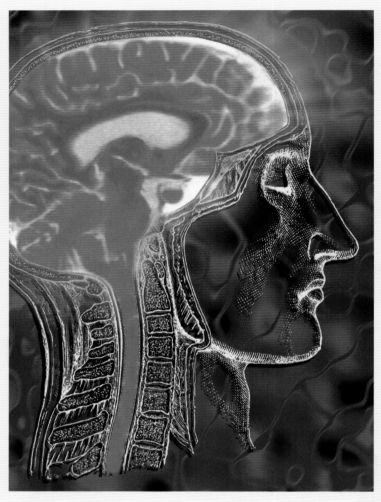

How to use this encyclopedia

Layout – every topic is spread across a double page to provide lots of information and photographs.

Contents – full contents list to help you find the topic you want.

Introduction to topic – every spread has an introduction to open the topic.

Abbreviations – for measurements there are abbreviations used for metres, centimetres, feet, inches, yards, litres, kilometres etc.

Question and answer – whatever the topic you'll find questions and answers to help you find out more.

Key facts – towards the back of the encyclopedia you'll find a comprehensive reference section. If you want to know about the fastest animal or the highest mountain this is where to look.

Insects

Insects make up the largest group of animals on the planet. They first appeared on Earth more than 500 million years ago and exist in almost every part of the world. There are at least a million species of insect ranging from ants, beetles and butterflies to bees and wasps. They can vary in size, from the very smallest which are almost invisible to humans to some very large beetles.

Development

Most insects hatch from eggs, and all go through different stages of development to become adults. In some species an egg hatches to become a larva, which is something like a worm. The larva grows and becomes a pupa, sometimes sealed up in a cocoon or chrysalis. After further changes, the adult emerges. The butterfly is one insect that follows this type of development.

How do insects affect human life?

Some insects are considered pests, for example termites, lice and flies. Some are merely nuisances, although others can cause many problems by spreading disease to crops and humans. Many insects, however, are very beneficial to both people and the environment. Some insects are very important because they pollinate flowers to produce seed and fruit. We have always relied on honeybees for honey, and the silk produced by silkworms played an important role in opening up trade with China many years ago.

What is the most dangerous insect?

The mosquito is probably the most dangerous insect because it carries deadly diseases such as malaria.

How many species of insect are there?

There are probably at least a million different species of insect ranging from ants and butterflies to bees and wasps. Not all species have been identified, so there could be as many as 30 million!

Photographs – lots of colourful photographs for every topic, carefully chosen to illustrate the subject.

Maps – for every country or region topic there's a detailed map showing all the important places there.

The insect body

The usual insect body is made up of three distinct parts.
- **Head** – the head, at the front, contains the brain, eyes, mouth, and antennae.
- **Thorax** – The thorax is the middle part, where the six legs are joined to the body. This is also where the wings are located, in insects that have them.
- **Abdomen** – The abdomen, at the back, contains the organs for breathing, digestion and reproduction.

Some features of an insect's body

- **Antennae** – These are sense organs which allow insects to sense smells and vibrations in the air and in solid matter. Sensing smell is important for insects at mating time and therefore for reproduction.
- **Exoskeleton** – This is a hard outer skeleton which protects an insect's inner organs.
- **Tracheae** – These are a series of fine tubes through which most insects breathe. Insects that live in water breathe through gills.
- **Compound eyes** – These are very different from a human's eyes. They are made up of many thousands of ommatidia, or rod-shaped structures, each of which detects the amount of colour and light going into the eye. Together all these ommatidia produce a view of the world which looks like a mosaic of light and dark.
- **Mandibles** – These are hard jaws which insects use for biting and chewing. The mouths of different insects are adapted to biting, piercing, sucking and scraping. Different insects are well adapted to eating different things, anything from wood, paper, nectar, blood, plants and even other insects!
- **Six legs** – All insects have six legs. That is why spiders, with their distinctive eight legs, are not insects but arachnids.

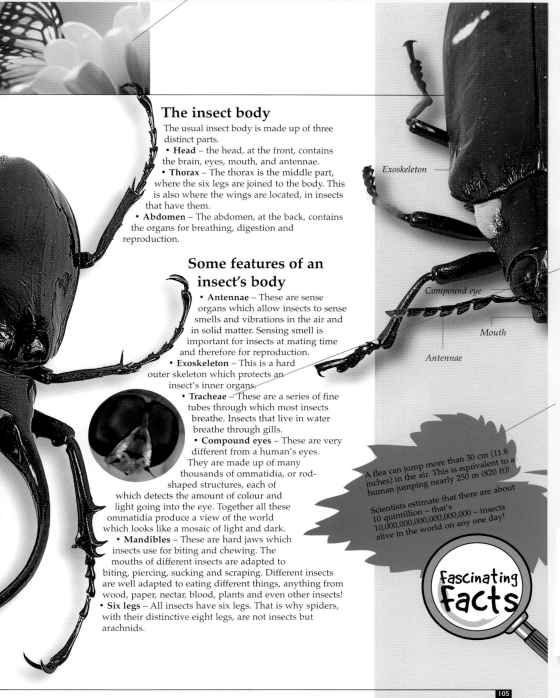

Exoskeleton

Compound eye

Mouth

Antennae

Technical terms – specialist words are always explained to help you learn the technical terms.

Fascinating facts – for every topic you'll find some really interesting and unusual facts in brightly-coloured boxes so that they're easy to find.

A flea can jump more than 30 cm (11.8 inches) in the air. This is equivalent to a human jumping nearly 250 m (820 ft)!

Scientists estimate that there are about 10 quintillion – that's 10,000,000,000,000,000,000 – insects alive in the world on any one day!

Fascinating facts

A timeline of transport:
1783 ➔ The first hot–air balloon invented by the Montgolfier brothers.
1895 ➔ First human glider flown by Otto Lilienthal.
1899 ➔ The first successful airship, the Zeppelin, invented by Ferdinand von Zeppelin.
1903 ➔ The first airplane flown by the Wright brothers (first powered flight).
1907 ➔ First helicopter invented by Paul Cornu.
1926 ➔ First liquid-propelled rocket launched by Robert H. Goddard.
1940 ➔ Modern helicopters invented by Igor Sirkorsky.
1947 ➔ First supersonic (faster than the speed of sound) flight.

Timelines – for some historical topics there are timelines to show the place in history.

105

Index – right at the end there's a detailed index, set out in alphabetical order, to help you find everything you need about all the topics in the encyclopedia.

Aardvark *and other unusual animals*

The aardvark is an African mammal. It uses its strong sense of smell and long, sticky tongue for feeding on large quantities of ants and termites. They are nocturnal animals, which means they feed in the evening and at night.

Hyrax

A hyrax is a small stocky mammal living in Africa and the Middle East. It enjoys basking in the sunshine but in cold weather they huddle together in groups for warmth. They graze on coarse leaves and grass. It weighs between 4.4–11 lbs (2–5 kilos) and measures about 11.8–27.5 inches (30–70 cms) in length.

The pangolin has no teeth and so it cannot chew. However, it has very strong front claws which it uses to rip open anthills and termite mounds. It can then lick up the ants or termites with its long sticky tongue.

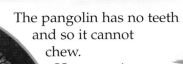

How big is an aardvark?

An aardvark weighs between 88 and 143 lbs (40 and 65 kilos) and measures up to 6.5 ft (2 m) in length. They have long ears, an arched back, and their sharp claws allow them to dig out their food very effectively from hard, dry earth.

Why does a pangolin have scales?

The overlapping scales act like a suit of armour to protect the animal from attack by predators. When threatened the pangolin will curl up like a ball, rather like a hedgehog does.

Pangolin

A pangolin is a scaly anteater, a large mammal measuring anything from 11.8 to 39.4 inches (30 to 100 cms), depending on which species it belongs to. It has quite short legs and a long tail. It is covered in large, hard, plate-like scales.

Porcupine fish

The porcupine fish swallows water or air and swells into a ball shape with its spines poking outwards to frighten its attacker if it feels threatened. This almost doubles its size so only predators with large mouths can attack it successfully.

Porcupine fish have few predators, being mainly eaten by sharks and orcas. Young porcupine fish are sometimes caught by tuna and dolphins. Pufferfish, which are closely related to porcupine fish, are eaten in Japan but as they have poisonous spines they must be prepared very carefully before being eaten to remove all the poison.

Unicorn

A unicorn looks like a slim white horse with a single forward-pointing horn on the centre of its head. Its name derives from the Latin 'cornu' meaning 'horn', so unicorn means 'single horn'.

Do unicorns really exist?

Ancient pictures of unicorns have been found all over the world in countries as far afield as France, India, China and Japan. In a cave deep in the Harz mountains in Germany the skeleton of a unicorn was thought to have been discovered in 1663. Later, however, this alleged discovery was found to be an elaborate hoax.

So sadly you can only see pictures and tapestries of this mythical creature. Some of the most famous unicorn tapestries are a set of six tapestries of La Dame à La Licorne (The Lady and the Unicorn), which were woven in the Netherlands in the early 16th century. They are displayed at the Musée national du Moyen-Age in Paris, France.

Early European settlers thought aardvarks looked like pigs so the Afrikaans name is 'earth pig' from aarde meaning earth and varken meaning pig, although aardvarks are not actually related to pigs at all!

Although a hyrax looks rather like a rabbit, DNA evidence shows that it may be related to the elephant. Despite the difference in size modern hyraxes share the same sort of toenails, sensitive foot pads and small tusks as elephants. Even the shape of some of their bones is similar.

fascinating facts

Acids *and* Alkalis

Lots of everyday substances contain acids or alkalis. Acids are found in citrus fruits (lemons, limes), vinegar, car batteries, even in your stomach! Acids are corrosive – this means that they react with metals and other types of chemicals to form substances called salts (table salt, sodium chloride). Any chemical that reacts like this with an acid is called a base (a neutral substance). If it also dissolves in water then it is called an alkali. Soap is a very common alkali. Alkalis are found in oven cleaners (sodium hydroxide), soap, and cleaning fluids containing ammonia.

The pH scale

The strength of an acid or alkali is determined using the pH scale, which measures the concentration of hydrogen ions in a solution. The scale ranges from 0 to 14, with 0 being the most acidic and 14 the least acidic (or most alkaline). Water, which is neutral (neither acidic nor alkaline) has a pH of 7, a concentrated solution of sulphuric acid has a pH of 1, and a concentrated solution of sodium hydroxide (a strong alkali) has a pH of 14.

Measuring pH

The pH of a solution can be measured using a special chemical called an indicator, which changes colour when exposed to acids or alkalis. Indicator paper is an absorbent paper similar to blotting paper that has had an indicator soaked into it. An example is litmus, a very simple indicator that will go red in an acidic solution or blue in an alkaline solution. With litmus you can tell whether something is acidic or alkaline but not how strong or weak an acid or alkali it is. A more accurate indicator is universal indicator. This is made of a mixture of different indicators and so can show many more colours than litmus – strong acids show as red, weaker acids as yellow-orange, very weak acids as pale green, neutral solutions (like water or blood) as green, weak alkalis as dark green and strong alkalis as dark blue or purple.

Some acids and alkalis

Sulphuric acid – A very strong acid, this can be formed when sulphur is burned and the gas produced dissolves in water. It is one of the causes of acid rain.

Hydrochloric acid – This is another strong acid and is found in your stomach, where it breaks down foods to allow them to be digested.

pH	Example
0	Battery acid
1	Sulphuric acid
2	Vinegar, Lemon juice
3	Sodas, Orange juice
4	Acid rain. No fish can survive in a pH lower than about 4.2
5	Clean rainwater, Black coffee
6	Milk
7	Pure water
8	Sea water
9	Baking soda
10	Milk of magnesia
11	Ammonia
12	Soapy water
13	Bleach
14	Sodium Hydroxide

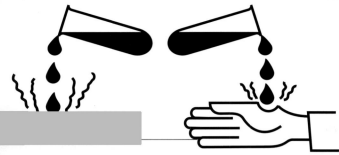

Nitric acid – A strong acid, formed when nitrogen dioxide is dissolved in water.

Ethanoic acid – This is the main ingredient in vinegar. It is a weak acid and, not surprisingly, smells strongly of vinegar!

Ammonia – This is a gas that dissolves in water to form a weak alkali. It is found in many household bleaches and cleaning products.

Sodium bicarbonate (sodium hydrogen carbonate) – Also known as baking soda, this is another weak alkali. It reacts with acids to give off carbon dioxide.

Sodium hydroxide – This is a very strong alkali, also called caustic soda. It can be used (with great care!) for clearing outside drains but is mainly used in industry for removing unwanted acids.

DANGER ACID

Q&A?

When was the pH scale invented?

It was first introduced in 1909 by a Danish chemist named Søren Peder Lauritz Sørensen (1868–1939).

How long have we known about acid rain?

Acid rain was first reported in the 1852s by Robert Angus Smith, a Scottish chemist working in Manchester (England). Smith first used the term 'acid rain' in 1872.

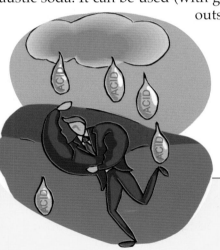

Acid rain

Acid rain is produced when acidic gases (such as sulphur dioxide and nitrogen oxide) enter the atmosphere. These gases react with the oxygen and water vapour in the atmosphere to form dilute solutions of sulphuric and nitric acids. When this acidic solution falls as rainwater it can cause serious damage to plants and animal life as well as corroding stone buildings and monuments. Fish and other aquatic life can be particularly badly affected – besides falling directly into the water they live in, acid rain falling over a wide area will naturally be channelled into rivers, lakes and streams! The principal cause of acid rain is acknowledged to be the pollutants given off from industrial processes, particularly the burning of fossil fuels like oil and coal in power stations. These fuels contain sulphur and will produce sulphur dioxide when burned.

Fascinating facts

Many species of fish cannot survive if their environment falls below a pH of about 4.2

As you move down the pH scale from 14, each level is 10 times more acidic than the one before – so a concentrated solution of a strong acid (pH 0) is 10 million times more acidic than water!

Africa

Africa stretches from the Mediterranean in the north to the South Atlantic Ocean. The human race almost certainly began in East Africa and Africa was, for over 5,000 years, home to one of the greatest civilisations – the Egyptians. First the Arabs and then the Europeans colonised parts of Africa; the French settled in Algeria and the northwest, the Dutch settled in South Africa, and the British settled in the west and in central Africa.

Borders

Before the colonisation of Africa in the 19th century there were no rigid national borders, as the population was largely nomadic, that is, they move from place to place in communities rather than settling in one place. Borders were created to separate the territories of the different European groups. That's why there are so many straight lines. As the nations gained independence during the 1950s and 60s these borders remained and have been the source of some problems as they do not necessarily match the natural ethnic make-up of the people who live within them.

The Sahara

The Sahara desert's boundaries are constantly shifting. As the climate becomes drier the desert continues to expand southward, making it impossible for farmers to sustain a living. Consequently there is a lot of

Is Mt Kilimanjaro a volcano?

Mt Kilimanjaro, the highest point in Africa, is volcanic. Although it is not currently active, it does emit gas though fumaroles (vents) on the main summit of Kibo.

Where is the Blue Nile?

The Blue Nile has its source in Lake Tana in Ethiopia. The White Nile begins much further south in Uganda. The two rivers meet near Khartoum in the Sudan, and from there it is called the River Nile.

0	300	600	900	1200 miles
0	500	1000	1500	2000 kilometres

The giraffe is an African mammal with a very long neck and legs. It is the tallest land animal, often reaching a height of around 17 ft (5 m).

The great Mosque of Djenné in Mali is the largest mud structure in the world. Every year a fresh coat of mud is applied after the rainy season.

poverty and starvation. The Sahara is the largest desert in the world. Many of its inhabitants are nomadic. One reason for not staying in one place is so that their animals will have sufficient food, as the pastures become depleted rapidly in the desert.

The Tuaregs of the southern Sahara wear cloth around their faces to protect them from the sand. This is believed to originate from the belief that such action wards off evil spirits, but more probably relates to protection against the harsh desert sands.

The Nile Delta

The fertile Nile Delta (a delta is the area where a river flows into the sea or a lake – often called the mouth of a river) is home to the densest population in Africa, i.e. Cairo and Alexandria. Cairo has a population of over 7 million and almost 4 million people live in Alexandria.

Kenya

Two tectonic plates have separated and formed this great valley which extends from Tanzania in the south, through the whole of Kenya and into Ethiopia in the North. Tectonic means that there is a structural deformation of the Earth's crust, such as the area is on an earthquake line. This area is still susceptible to earthquakes.

Kenya is one of the most fertile countries in Africa. It is the third largest producer of tea in the world, and tea is a major source of the country's income. Tea is grown mainly in the Kenyan Highlands, west of the Rift Valley, and exports raise around $350 million (190 million GBP) each year.

Ethiopia

Ethiopia is the birthplace of coffee. More than 1,000 years ago, a goatherd in Ethiopia's highlands plucked a few red berries from the Kafa tree and tasted them. He liked the flavour, and the pleasant effect that followed. Today the same berries, dried, roasted and ground, have become the world's second most popular non-alcoholic beverage after tea. Coffee accounts for 63% of Ethiopia's exports and about 25% of the population depends on coffee for its livelihood.

Alexander the Great

Alexander the Great lived from 356 BC to 323 BC. He was King of Macedon, a city-state in Ancient Greece. A city-state is a big city that is run like a country. Alexander was King of Macedon for 13 years, and during this time he became one of the most successful military commanders in world history.

The Gordian knot

Alexander invaded Persia with a massive army. He entered cities and ports, which surrendered one by one. At the city of Gordium, Alexander undid the famous Gordian Knot. In Greek legend, the Gordian knot was the name given to the complex knot used by Gordius to secure his oxcart. Gordius, a poor peasant, arrived in Phrygia (now Turkey) in an oxcart. An oracle had informed the populace that their future king would come riding in a wagon. Seeing Gordius, the people made him king. In gratitude, Gordius dedicated his oxcart to Zeus, tying it up with a peculiar knot. An oracle said that whoever untied the knot would rule all of Asia. One story tells how Alexander proclaimed that it did not matter how the knot was undone, so he cut it with his sword. Another version claims that he did not use the sword, and instead worked out how to untie the knot.

Darius

Next, Alexander's army passed through the

What was Alexander's mother's name?

Olympias.

Can you think of a modern day example of a city-state?

A good example of one today is Vatican City, which is where the Pope lives.

Cilician Gates and met and defeated the main Persian army under the command of Darius III at the Battle of Issus. Darius fled the battle in fear for his life. He was so scared that he left behind his wife, his children, his mother and his treasure.

Alexander then followed Darius, who was kidnapped and then murdered by followers of Bessus. Bessus then declared himself Darius' successor as Artaxerxes V and retreated into Central Asia to launch a campaign against Alexander. Alexander fought a three-year campaign against Bessus. He captured more cities, and also founded a series of new cities, all called Alexandria.

India

By 326 BC Alexander was able to conquer India. He fought the Battle of Hydaspes against Porus, a ruler of a region in the Punjab. After he had won the battle, Alexander made an alliance with Porus and appointed him as satrap (ruler) of his own kingdom. However, Alexander's army was tired out after many years of campaigning, and they mutinied (refused to fight). He had to lead them back to Persia.

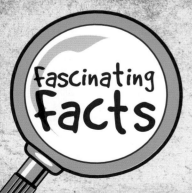

After travelling home with the Persian treasure, his best friend Hephaestion died of an illness. Alexander was deeply upset, and returned to Babylon, a city he had conquered during his campaign against Darius. Babylon is in Mesopotamia, (now part of Iraq). Whilst there Alexander fell ill and died.

It is not clear how Alexander died, but we know he was very young, – only 32. Various causes of his death have been suggested. He might have been poisoned as he had made many enemies he might have died of an illness caused by drinking too much alcohol, or he might have died of malaria. However, in his short life he achieved an amazing amount, conquering most of the known world. By the end of his life, he fully deserved the name Alexander the Great.

fascinating Facts

Alexander the Great made his soldiers shave regularly, so that the enemy couldn't grab them by the beard and stab them with their swords.

Alexander the Great was taught by the famous philosopher Aristotle. Aristotle gave Alexander a copy of Homer's poem The Iliad, which Alexander kept with him all the time. He even slept with it under his pillow!

Animals _and_ Birds

The animal kingdom is enormous; about 1.5 million species of animal have been named and described by scientists, and over a million of these are insects. Many animals, especially in the tropical rainforests and oceans, are yet to be discovered and named.

Mammals

Mammals range from tiny bats to huge whales, and include humans. They have hair, are warm-blooded, and feed their young with milk. They eat a lot to maintain their body temperature. Some eat plants but most are meat-eaters.

Cetaceans

This group of mammals includes dolphins and whales. The blue whale is the biggest animal ever and is thought to live for over 100 years. Dolphins, like humans, have large brains for the size of their bodies.

Primates

There are about 233 species of primate, including lemurs, apes and humans. The largest of the primates is the gorilla, which lives in Africa in groups made up of a dominant male, one or two other males, several females and their young. The males are bigger than the females, and older males are called 'silverbacks' due to their silvery grey hair. Gorillas are intelligent, gentle and sociable animals.

Marsupials

A marsupial is an animal whose young develop in pouches. There are 289 species of marsupials, most of them

Which is the fastest animal in the world?

Peregrine falcons are the fastest birds in the world. They achieve speeds approaching 125 mph (200 km/h) when plunging from the sky after prey.
The cheetah is the fastest mammal in the world, reaching speeds of over 62.5 mph (100 km/hour).

Which mammal feeds exclusively on blood?

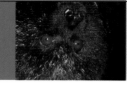

Vampire bats are the only mammals that feed exclusively on blood. They are found in Central and South America. Some bats feed almost entirely on bird blood, but the common vampire bat feeds on the blood of mammals.

in Australia. Red kangaroos are the largest marsupials in Australia. An adult kangaroo can grow to over 5.9 ft (1.8 metres) tall!

Big cats

Cats are found on all continents except Antarctica and Australia, and include the tiger, lion and leopard. Lions are the only social wild cats; they live in family groups. The main role of male lions is to protect the family group and the females do most of the hunting. They usually hunt during the day and prey on mammals like antelope and zebra.

Extinct animals

Thousands of animals that once walked the Earth have become extinct, such as the woolly mammoth and the dodo. Evidence of prehistoric animals comes from fossils, skeletons, preserved hair and dung. Dinosaurs are the best-known example of natural extinction. These reptiles appeared on Earth about 200 million years ago and dominated both land and sea for almost 100 million years.

birds and small mammals. The golden eagle is one of the most magnificent birds of prey. When they spot prey they dive down to seize and kill the victim with their curved talons.

Colourful bills

The puffin is known as the 'clown of the sea' and is easy to recognise: its beak is multicoloured in spring, but turns grey during autumn and winter. The toucan's most prominent feature is also its bill, or beak, which is often very colourful and very large compared to its body.

Birds of prey

There are almost 250 species of bird in the UK, and about 21 of these are birds of prey. These tend to be large birds with forward-facing eyes, hooked beaks and sharp talons to enable them to hunt other animals, including fish,

Red kangaroos can jump more than 6 metres in a single hop.

Chimpanzees are our closest relatives, sharing 98.4 % of our genes.

Male humpback whales have the longest and most complicated song in the animal kingdom. A single song can last for 30 minutes, and be repeated for hours on end.

fascinating **facts**

Antarctica

A ntarctica is home to penguins, almost completely covered by ice, and is the continent that is seeing the greatest increase in temperature caused by global warming.

Antarctica is the coldest and driest place on Earth. It is considerably colder than the Arctic because so much of it is very high, over 9,840 ft (3,000 m) and temperature decreases with increased altitude. During the winter the temperature plunges to between –121°F and –130°F (–85°C and –90°C). In summer it is a little warmer, between –67°F and –130°F (–55°C and –90°C). Because the snow reflects back 90% of the sunlight, sunburn is a major problem to the visiting human population.

If the vast ice cap melts, world sea levels will rise by up to 230 ft (70m) enough to flood London, New York, almost all of Holland and Bangladesh, and completely submerge the Maldives, East Anglia and Florida. If you live in Inverness, Belfast, Dublin, London, York, Liverpool, Southampton or Norwich, then the melting Atlantic ice cap could cause your home to be under the sea in several hundred years' time!

Very little wild life can survive the extreme conditions on the land except various types of penguin and a few insects. The Emperor penguin is the only penguin to breed during the winter. In the surrounding ocean, blue whales and seals thrive, feeding on the abundant krill (small shrimp-like creatures). The only plants on the land are hardy mosses and lichens that can be found in some of the coastal regions.

The aurora australis, sometimes known as the southern lights, is a glow seen

Do polar bears live in Antarctica?

No. Polar bears live in the Arctic region near the North Pole, and penguins live in Antarctica, although not near the South Pole. They live nearer to the edges of the continent.

Antarctica contains 90% of the world's ice. Much of the Antarctic is covered in a sheet of ice, some of it thousand of metres thick. If the Earth's temperature rises and the ice begins to melt, sea levels will rise, causing flooding.

The first person to reach the South Pole was Roald Amundsen in 1911.

Apart a few scientists (4,000 in summer, 1,000 in winter), no people live in Antarctica; however, it is home to some land and sea animals, and birds.

Fascinating facts

in the night sky near the South Pole. It is very similar to the aurora borealis that is observed in the Arctic region (North Pole).

A hole in the ozone layer

Above the earth is the ozone layer which absorbs dangerous rays from the sun. Pollution is causing holes to appear in this layer over the Antarctic. There is the danger that this will affect the ocean and will kill the krill. Without krill, whales and sea birds will not survive.

INDIAN OCEAN

RCTICA

Pole

● Vostok

Who claims Antarctica?

A number of countries claim parts of Antarctica however, in October 1991 it was agreed that no attempts would be made to discover or remove the rich minerals which lie under the ground of Antarctica. This agreements lasts until the year 2041.

A number of countries have set up research stations in Antarctica. The different countries represented are Australia, Britain, France, Germany, Russia, South Africa and

the United States. Antarctica has the cleanest air anywhere in the world and this benefits all types of research because the scientists don't need to worry about pollution. Antarctica is also the darkest place on earth, so it's an excellent setting for the study of the stars.

Archaeology

A rchaeology is the study of human cultures through remains. Remains are all the things left behind after a culture has died out or changed, like buildings, burial sites and everyday objects like tools and cooking-pots. Archaeologists try to work out what life was like for people in the past based on these remains.

What is archaeology?

Archaeology is a very important way of finding out about the past, as there are a lot of things that books and other written evidence cannot tell us because these facts were never written down. For example, when only the rich could read and write they did not write about the lives of the poor. Also, people lived on earth for many thousands of years before learning how to write. Archaeologists have found out what we know about these 'prehistoric' people by discovering and studying remains like stone arrowheads.

Excavation

When an archaeologist digs in the ground it is called an 'excavation' and any object found which was made by a person is called an 'artefact'. Excavations in Britain have found Roman towns and medieval English villages. Ancient tombs have been excavated in Egypt, as well as the famous pyramids, and the ancient cities of Herculaneum and Pompeii (both buried by volcanoes) have been studied in Italy.

Houses, temples, clothing and tools give archaeologists clues as to how people lived in the past. Food remains and artefacts like cooking equipment and 'potsherds' (pieces of broken pottery) can tell us a lot about what people ate and how they prepared their food.

A loaf of bread was found in Egypt that is approximately 4,000 years old! The bread had bits of sand and even stones in it – the Ancient Egyptians must have had very bad teeth! Underwater archaeologists studying ships that have sunk in oceans or lakes can use a special kind of underwater metal detector called a 'magnetometer' to help find shipwrecks.

From human remains (usually bones) archaeologists can find out how tall and how healthy people were, learning even more about how well they ate and what kind of lives they led.

Treasure-hunters or historians?

Early archaeologists were not like the ones we have today, but were more like treasure-hunters. They were not interested in learning facts about the past but just in finding beautiful or expensive objects!

Nowadays, archaeologists are a bit like historians and a bit like scientists. They are interested in discovering and recording the past, but instead of books they use tools and equipment and follow strict methods.

One of the first people to act like this was an Englishman, William Pitt Rivers (1827–1900). He is called 'The Father of Scientific Archaeology' because he collected and catalogued (recorded) all the artefacts he dug up, not just the beautiful ones, and he saw the importance of studying everyday objects to understand the past.

Planning an excavation

When archaeologists excavate a site, they first mark out the area into squares using flags, stakes and string. This is so they can record exactly where everything is found. They dig very carefully using trowels and hoes, and draw plans and take photographs to record what they find. Tools like spoons, dental picks and small brushes are used to make sure nothing is damaged as it is dug from the ground. But the most important tools an archaeologist uses are their notebook and pencil to write down what they find!

Radio Carbon Dating

In 1960, an American scientist called Willard F. Libby won the Nobel Prize for Chemistry for inventing a process called 'Radio Carbon Dating'. Radio Carbon Dating measures how much 'carbon-14' there is in plant or animal remains – the older something is, the less carbon-14 there will be. By measuring the age of remains discovered on a site, archaeologists can work out when the site was inhabited. This is very useful, especially as many people throughout history have lived in the same places and the artefacts they leave behind can get muddled up sometimes!

Aerial survey

Modern archaeologists can use technology to help them in their work. An example of this is an aerial survey, when pictures of an area are taken from high above it (from a plane or helicopter). Remains under the ground can cause changes above the ground. For example, plants growing above a buried wall may grow more slowly than usual. These differences can be seen from above. An aerial survey can help archaeologists plan where to dig or to see the layout of entire houses or cities.

Why do archaeologists use metal detectors?

These can find things like old jewellery and belt-buckles, and can be used to find cannonballs on an old battlefield.

What do we sometimes call an excavation?

A dig.

Architecture

Architecture and the built environment is the art and science of designing buildings and structures. Architecture is also a general word for the human-built environment. People design buildings such as houses, schools and hospitals, but they also design street signs and roads and all the different things that make up our towns and cities. A builder builds a house using many different materials and tools, but the architect designs it. The architect makes the plans for what the building will look like and how it will be built. Buildings all over the world and throughout history have been built in lots of different materials and a wide variety of styles.

Ancient buildings

Most early architecture which still survives today is of buildings like temples and tombs. A good example of this are the pyramids in Egypt. The pyramids were built to house the mummies (bodies wrapped in bandages to preserve them) of the Ancient Egyptian pharaohs (kings) and everything they would need in the afterlife – jewellery, furniture, camels, food, and sometimes even servants.

How did they do that?

Some early structures are still a mystery to us today, like Stonehenge – a circle of huge standing stones in England. No one knows for sure what it was for (perhaps an ancient calendar? perhaps a temple?) or even how it was built! It is guessed that the huge stones were moved to the site using rollers and pulleys, and geologists have proved that they were brought from 240 miles away!

Classical period

The architecture of Ancient Greece and Rome is called 'classical' and features different types of columns. Doric columns are the simplest, a plain 'shaft' (the long bit of the column) with a simple square 'capital' on top. Ionic columns have taller shafts with lines carved into them and the capital looks like a scroll. The third and most decorative type of column is called Corinthian. The shafts are carved like the Ionic columns and the capitals are decorated with a pattern of flowers and leaves below a small scroll. The classical style has been copied a lot throughout history and is admired for being ordered and symmetrical but also beautiful.

Medieval period

During the medieval period, kings built stone castles to defend their lands and rich lords built grand manor houses. The medieval Church was very rich. It built lots of

churches and cathedrals in the gothic style, with pointed arches above windows and doorways. Although these great churches and cathedrals were all built from stone, most buildings at the time were built from cheaper local materials. Earth and clay were made into bricks, forests were cut down for cheap wood, and roofs were thatched with reeds, straw or heather.

Although wooden houses were popular and cheap, they could also be dangerous too. Catching fire easily, the many timber buildings in London helped the rapid spread of the Great Fire of London that left 200,000 people homeless in 1666.

Renaissance architecture

Renaissance architecture came from Italy in the 14th century and was similar to the classical style with lots of symmetry and simple lines. Baroque followed this in the 17th century, with the classical elements becoming more complicated and decorated. In the 18th century a style from France called Rococo took over. This was even more highly decorated with lots of curves and elaborate details. Unsurprisingly, in the 18th and 19th centuries people started wanting the simpler lines of classical architecture again and Neoclassicism (or 'new classicism') became popular.

Brick buildings only began to be really popular after the Industrial Revolution. New factories began to make lots and lots of bricks that were cheap and easily transported along newly built canals to wherever buildings were needed.

Industrial Revolution

After the Industrial Revolution in the 19th century, two different architectural styles became fashionable. One was the Arts and Crafts movement, which looked back in time to craftsmanship and handmade, personal details. The other was a European style called Art Nouveau ('new art'). This was stylish and modern but, like the Arts and Crafts movement, it also took its inspiration from nature.

Modern day architecture

In the 20th century new technology meant that new materials like plastics, large panes of glass and huge steel girders could be used in architecture. Art Deco was popular, using lots of plastic and bright colours, and Modernist thinkers like the French architect Le Corbusier designed functional 'machines for living in' from concrete and glass.

Q&A?

Who was Le Corbusier?

Charles-Edouard Jeanneret, widely known as Le Corbusier, was an architect from Switzerland. He was famous for modernism and for his concern that his buildings should improve people's lifestyles.

What is Art Nouveau?

It is a style of decoration and architecture that was very popular in the early 20th century, characterised particularly by leaves and flowers in flowing, curved lines. Favourite motifs (patterns) in Art Nouveau design were shells, flowers and peacock feathers.

The Arctic

The Arctic is a very cold, windy, and often snowy area of land located around the North Pole. The area immediately around the North Pole is not a continent but is the Arctic Ocean, much of which is frozen. When we refer to the Arctic we usually mean the area of land within the Arctic Circle and which almost completely surrounds the Arctic Ocean.

The latitude line

The Arctic Circle is one of the major lines of latitude we see named on maps of the Earth. This is the latitude line that is 66° north of the equator. All land to the north of this circle is within the Arctic Circle, and has an arctic climate. The area immediately around the North Pole does not consist of land but frozen ice. Submarines can sail under this ice.

Melting ice

In recent years global warming has meant that the Arctic ice is not extending as far south as it once did and in the summer the ice is melting so much that ships may soon be able to sail around the northern coasts of Canada and Russia.

Tundra

The most northerly parts of North America, northern Europe and Asia are within the outer regions of the Arctic Circle. This frozen ground is above the tree line and is covered with hardy plants like moss and lichen. This land is called tundra and it supports less life than most other areas because of the cold temperatures, strong, dry winds, and the permanently frozen soil.

Are there really jellyfish in the Arctic Circle?
Yes. Jellyfish can be found wherever there is water, whether in the icy Arctic or the Mediterranean.
Can you use mobile phones at the North Pole?
No, it's too far away from the nearest base station.

During the summer the sun shines throughout the day and night, but the temperature rarely rises above 50°F (10°C).

Much of Siberia, Greenland, north Canada and Alaska are within the Arctic Circle. That is the part of the Northern Hemisphere where, once a year, the sun is continuously visible for at least 24 hours. This is known as the Land of the Midnight Sun.

People also live in these lands. The Inuit (formerly known as Eskimos) live here all year round, and the Sami (Lapps) bring their reindeer here during the summer months.

Animals of the Arctic

Many animals live within the Arctic Circle on the land, on the ice and in the sea, and they have adapted to extreme conditions. They may have coats that thicken in the coldest season or that change colour in order to provide protection from predators.

During the coldest periods some animals hibernate. This means that they go into a very deep sleep, usually in underground burrows.

The Arctic fox is well adapted for the cold harsh climate of the Arctic. If it can't find sufficient food it looks for the scraps left by other animals.

The collared lemming is one of the tiniest Arctic animals. It is a small rodent that burrows under the snow or ground.

Polar bears and seals are being threatened by the reduced amount of Arctic ice. As the ice shrinks these animals have fewer and fewer places to hunt and fish. There are many other animals, birds and sea creatures living in this harsh area, but penguins do not venture into this region. Some birds, such as the Arctic tern, spend the summer months in the Arctic, but when the weather turns very cold and food becomes scarce they fly away to warmer areas. This behaviour is called migrating. The Arctic tern is a fairly small bird but it migrates over 22,000 miles (35,000 km) each year. This is thought to be the longest migration distance of any bird.

Art

Throughout history, people have used art to decorate their homes, capture the places and people around them, and to express their feelings. There are as many different types of art as there are people, as every artist makes art only they can make, but the main types of art are drawing, painting and sculpture. The oldest artwork in existence is cave painting.

Cave paintings were painted by prehistoric man, using natural materials like charcoal, tree bark, coloured dyes made from berries, and sometimes even blood! The paintings usually show an animal being hunted, such as a bison. They were painted on the limestone walls of the caves by prehistoric man, and showed incredibly vivid images of bison, bears, mammoths and rhinoceroses.

The cave paintings are early versions of what are called frescoes. Fresco, meaning 'fresh' in Italian, is a form of painting in which paints are applied to wet plaster. By 1500 BC, the way people painted had changed from painting onto cave walls, to painting in the fresco style. They used frescoes to decorate the walls of their homes. The ancient Greeks and Romans painted frescoes. When the volcano Mount Vesuvius erupted in Italy in AD 79, it buried the towns of Pompeii and Herculaneum under scorching lava and ash. Although this was terrible for the people buried and killed, it meant that the wonderful frescoes in Pompeii were perfectly preserved. Today, we can see this amazing collection of frescoes. They tell us lots about the Roman way of life, because they show us people going about their work. We can see how people farmed, what they ate, what they dressed like, and even what their hairstyles were like!

Many centuries later, European kings and queens and their wealthy subjects wanted large paintings to hang in their castles and grand houses. These were painted with oil paints upon huge canvases, displayed in carved frames. Oil paintings were very expensive and so paintings several feet across showed their owners to be both cultured and wealthy. The paintings were often portraits of the noblemen themselves or of their family, or of their houses or horses. Other popular subjects were gods and goddesses from Greek or Roman mythology, etc. The famous painters of the day such as Leonardo da Vinci and Michelangelo made their names painting works like this, of subjects they were paid to paint.

Fascinating Facts

Some cave paintings, such as the ones in the Chauvet cave, France, are an amazing 30,000 years old!

Nowadays there are many art schools and colleges, but in the past to train to be an artist you had to be apprenticed to a successful painter or sculptor. A master painter would teach the apprentice things like how to use oil paints and different techniques for life drawing (drawings of people) and still life (drawing objects). Apprentices were encouraged to imitate the master's style – many successful artists produced so many works for rich clients that many are thought to have been finished or even painted entirely by their apprentices!

For the great artists of the past the artistic ideal was to be realistic and lifelike, making sculptures that looked like real people or paintings of fruit that looked like as if you could reach out and eat it. For modern artists, this has become less important. With the invention of the camera you could easily get a perfect portrait of a person or perfectly capture a scene. Many artists instead wanted to capture the impression you get from looking at a scene instead of recording exactly what it looks like. A famous group called the Impressionists were among the first artists to do this.

Surrealists like Salvador Dali painted strange paintings about his dreams. And cubists like Pablo Picasso painted portraits where the faces were made up of cubes and circles. Many modern artists are famous for breaking the old rules like this, and lots of 'movements' and changes in art happened when groups of people have started making art in a new and exciting way.

What is Leonardo da Vinci's most famous painting?

The Mona Lisa.

Which Australian artist painted a recent portrait of Queen Elizabeth II?

Rolf Harris.

Asia

Stretching from the frozen Arctic Ocean to the Equatorial islands of Indonesia, Asia is the world's largest continent. It contains the world's highest mountain – Mt Everest, on the border of Nepal and Tibet, 29,035 ft (8,850 m), as well as the world's deepest lake – Lake Baikal, which is located in Siberia, Russia, north of the Mongolian border, 5,369 ft (1,637 m) deep – that's more than one mile (1.6 km) straight down!

Oil and gas

Asia is rich in natural resources, with over 75% of the world's oil and gas reserves. Russia has plentiful supplies of oil and gas but they are difficult to source as they are under Siberia's frozen soil. Arabia has just 10% of the world's needs.

Forestry and agriculture

Forestry is extensive throughout northern and eastern Asia. Rice in grown in large quantities, and another main agricultural product is wheat.

Industry

The two most heavily populated countries in the world,

ARCTIC OCEAN

RUSS

KAZAKHSTAN

Black Sea — Tbilisi — Caspian Sea — Ulan B — MON

Ankara — GEORGIA — Baku — Bishkek — Alma Ata

ARMENIA — Yerivan — AZERBAIJAN — TURKMENISTA — Tashkent — KYRGYZSTAN

TURKEY — Ashkhabad — TAJIKISTAN — Dushanbe

Bierut — SYRIA — Baghdad — Tehran — Kabul — Islamabad — CHI

LEBANON — Damascus — IRAQ — IRAN — AFGHANISTAN

Tel Aviv — Amman — PAKISTAN

ISRAEL — Tirat Zevi — JORDAN — KUWAIT — Kuwait City — NEPAL — Thimphu

Doha — BAHRAIN — OMAN — New Dehli — Kathmandu — BHUTAN

Riyadh — QATAR — Abu Dhabi — Muscat — Dhaka — Cherrapunji

SAUDI ARABIA — UNITED ARAB EMIRATES — INDIA — MYANMAR (BURMA)

San á — YEMEN — OMAN — Veintiane — THAILA

BANGLADESH — Yangon (Rangoon) — Ban

Colombo — Kuala Lumpur

SRI LANKA

INDIAN OCEAN

Jak

| 0 | 300 | 600 | 900 | 600 miles |
| 0 | 500 | 1000 | 1500 | 2000 kilometres |

Why do some women in Asia wear brass rings around their necks?

These women are from the Padaung – part of the Karen tribe. There are many reasons given; some say it prevents them being bitten by tigers; others suggest it to makes the women unattractive so they are less likely to be captured by slave traders. But some believe that a long neck is very attractive.

Are all of the islands of Indonesia inhabited?

No. Approximately 7,000 of the islands are inhabited. They cover such an expanse of water that they spread over three time zones.

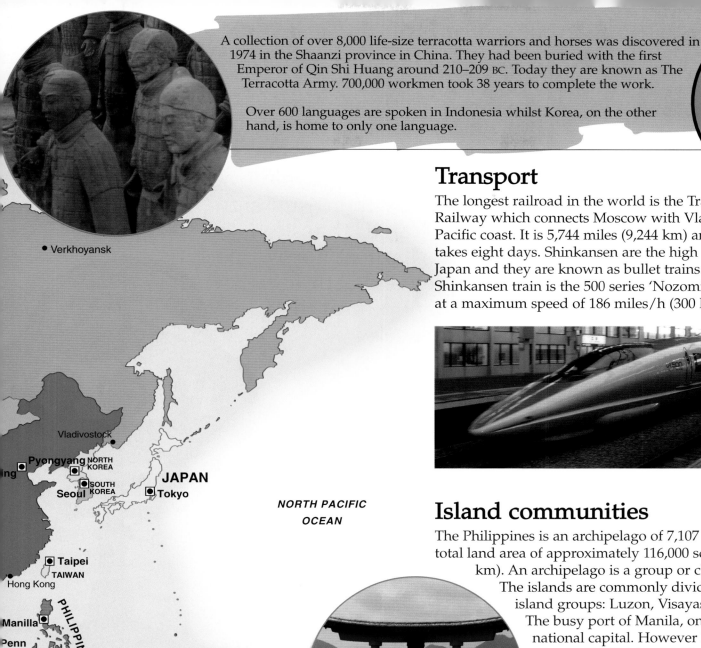

A collection of over 8,000 life-size terracotta warriors and horses was discovered in 1974 in the Shaanzi province in China. They had been buried with the first Emperor of Qin Shi Huang around 210–209 BC. Today they are known as The Terracotta Army. 700,000 workmen took 38 years to complete the work.

Over 600 languages are spoken in Indonesia whilst Korea, on the other hand, is home to only one language.

Fascinating **Facts**

• Verkhoyansk

Vladivostock

Pyongyang NORTH KOREA

JAPAN

Seoul SOUTH KOREA

Tokyo

NORTH PACIFIC OCEAN

Taipei
TAIWAN
Hong Kong

PHILIPPINES

Manilla

Penn

Seri

BRUNEI

INDONESIA

Transport

The longest railroad in the world is the Trans-Siberian Railway which connects Moscow with Vladivostok on the Pacific coast. It is 5,744 miles (9,244 km) and the journey takes eight days. Shinkansen are the high speed trains in Japan and they are known as bullet trains. The fastest Shinkansen train is the 500 series 'Nozomi' which operates at a maximum speed of 186 miles/h (300 km/h).

Island communities

The Philippines is an archipelago of 7,107 islands with a total land area of approximately 116,000 sq miles (300,000 sq km). An archipelago is a group or cluster of islands. The islands are commonly divided into three island groups: Luzon, Visayas and Mindanao. The busy port of Manila, on Luzon, is the national capital. However Indonesia has almost 18,000 islands! About 7,000 of these are inhabited, scattered around the equator, giving the country a tropical climate. The most populated island is Java (one of the most densely populated regions on Earth, where about half of the population of Indonesia lives).

Environment

The Chernobyl nuclear disaster in Belarus in 1986 caused widespread devastation over a large area and still the neighbouring towns are uninhabitable.

China and India, are in Asia; they are also the two fastest growing economies. These countries and the huge area of the Russian Steppes are losing their communities as people leave the land to find work in the booming new industrial areas. There is an enormous contrast between the lives of the rich and those of the poor in this continent.

Manufacturing has traditionally been strongest in east and southeast Asia, particularly in China, Taiwan, Japan, Singapore and South Korea. The industry varies from manufacturing cheap toys to high-tech products such as computers and cars.

On August 6, 1945 a nuclear bomb was dropped on Hiroshima killing an estimated 80,000 people and heavily damaging 80% of the city. In the following months, an estimated 60,000 more people died from injuries or radiation poisoning. Since 1945, several thousand have died of illnesses caused by the bomb. The Torii (gate) to the Shrine at Miyajima on Itsukushima Island is much photographed by visitors to Hiroshima. Itsukushima Island is considered to be sacred.

Astrology

Many newspapers and magazines today have a horoscope section, and most people know their 'star sign'. But astrology has been around for much longer than newspapers. Did you know that the earliest horoscope was made in 410 BC? Ancient people used astrology to make decisions of every kind – when to hunt, fish, plant, even when to make war or peace.

Astrology is the study of the movements of stars and planets. Astrologers believe these movements have an influence on what happens to people on Earth, and that by making certain calculations, they can use the positions of stars and planets to predict the future. Such a prediction is called a horoscope.

Astrology dates all the way back to an ancient people called the Babylonians, over four thousand years ago.

Although millions of people can now read their daily horoscopes, at first horoscopes were only for royalty. Eventually the study of astrology was spread from the Babylonians to the Greeks, then later to the Romans and throughout the world.

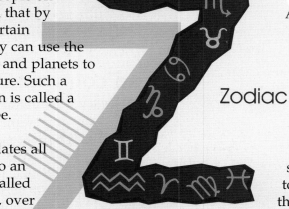

Zodiac

Signs of the Zodiac

Sign	Symbol	Dates
Aries	the Ram	March 21–April 19
Taurus	the Bull	April 20–May 20
Gemini	the Twins	May 21–June 20
Cancer	the Crab	June 21–July 22
Leo	the Lion	July 23–August 22
Virgo	the Virgin	August 23–September 22
Libra	the Scales	September 23–October 22
Scorpio	the Scorpion	October 23–November 21
Sagittarius	the Archer	November 22–December 21
Capricorn	the Goat	December 22–January 19
Aquarius	the Water carrier	January 20–February 18
Pisces	the Fish	February 19–March 20

Famous Astrologers: John Dee, Nostradamu, The Three Wise Men, Mystic Meg.

Astrology began to lose popularity as a science in the 17th century, when it became widely accepted that the Sun and not the Earth was the centre of the Universe.

fascinating **Facts**

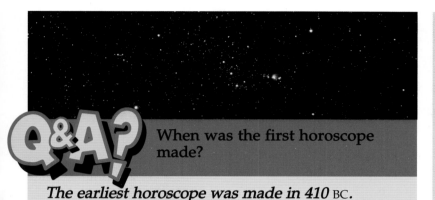

Q&A?

When was the first horoscope made?

The earliest horoscope was made in 410 BC.

How do I know what my zodiac sign is?

Your zodiac sign depends on the position of the sun in the sky when you were born.

Zodiac stones

Each zodiac sign has several 'birthstones' associated with it. Here are some of them:

Aries	amethyst, garnet, ruby, quartz
Taurus	peridot, jade, lapis lazuli, quartz
Gemini	agate, peridot, pearl, moonstone
Cancer	pearl, moonstone, sapphire, ruby, garnet
Leo	amber, diamond, topaz, ruby, garnet, peridot
Virgo	peridot, sapphire, aquamarine, blue topaz
Libra	blue topaz, aquamarine, rose quartz, opal, amethyst
Scorpio	rose quartz, opal, sapphire, topaz, smoky quartz
Sagittarius	amethyst, sapphire, topaz, smoky quartz, turquoise
Capricorn	onyx, garnet, turquoise, lapis lazuli
Aquarius	aquamarine, fossils, jet, garnet
Pisces	amethyst, aquamarine, bloodstone

Chinese astrology

The Chinese Zodiac is just as ancient as the Western one, and quite different. In traditional China, dating methods were cyclical – which means something that is repeated over and over again. The years on a Chinese calendar are grouped into sets of 12. Each year is assigned an animal name or 'sign' according to a repeating cycle. Therefore, every 12 years, the same animal sign would return.

Dog	1910, 1922, 1934, 1946, 1958, 1970, 1982, 1994, 2006
Boar	1911, 1923, 1935, 1947, 1959, 1971, 1983, 1995, 2007
Rat	1912, 1924, 1936, 1948, 1960, 1972, 1984, 1996
Ox	1913, 1925, 1937, 1949, 1961, 1973, 1985, 1997
Tiger	1914, 1926, 1938, 1950, 1962, 1974, 1986, 1998
Rabbit	1915, 1927, 1939, 1951, 1963, 1975, 1987, 1999
Dragon	1916, 1928, 1940, 1952, 1964, 1976, 1988, 2000
Snake	1917, 1929, 1941, 1953, 1965, 1977, 1989, 2001
Horse	1918, 1930, 1942, 1954, 1966, 1978, 1990, 2002
Goat	1919, 1931, 1943, 1955, 1967, 1979, 1991, 2003
Monkey	1920, 1932, 1944, 1956, 1968, 1980, 1992, 2004
Rooster	1921, 1933, 1945, 1957, 1969, 1981, 1993, 2005

Chinese astrologers believe you can tell what a person is like from the year they were born, as a person will have characteristics like those of the animal assigned to that year. For example, a person born in the Year of the Dragon is expected to be bold and successful. In the Chinese calendar, the beginning of the New Year falls somewhere between January and February, depending on the phases of the moon. At New Year, dancing and animal masks are used to welcome in the animal of the New Year.

Astronomy

Astronomy means to study the night sky and all of the stars, planets, moons, asteroids and meteors within it. It includes the whole universe, not just our own solar system. It's also about how the stars, moons and planets move around one another.

Galaxies

There are billions of galaxies in the Universe. Some galaxies are called 'spiral', because they look like giant pinwheels in the sky. The galaxy we live in, the Milky Way, is a spiral galaxy. Some galaxies are called 'elliptical', because they look like flat balls. A galaxy may be called 'irregular' if it doesn't really have a shape. A new type of galaxy was discovered recently, called a 'starburst' galaxy. In this type of galaxy, new stars just seem to 'burst out' very quickly.

What is the Universe?

It is a huge wide-open space that holds everything from particles (minute pieces of matter – electrons or protons) to galaxies (enormous collections of gas, dust or stars). No one really knows just how big the Universe is. Astronomers try to measure it with an instrument called a spectroscope to tell whether an object is moving closer to the Earth or further away from it.

The Milky Way

This is the galaxy that our solar system belongs to. It is over 100,000 light-years wide. A light-year is a unit of distance. It is the distance that light can travel in one year. One light-year is equal to 5,900,000,000,000 miles (9,500,000,000,000 km). It is a spiral galaxy because it has long arms which spin around like a giant pinwheel. Our Sun is a star in one of the arms. When you look up at the night sky, most of the stars you see are in one of the Milky Way arms. It is known as the Milky Way because the ancient Romans called it the Via Galactica, or 'road made of milk'.

Scientists believe that billions of years ago there was a powerful explosion called the Big Bang. This explosion set the Universe into motion and this motion continues today.

Stars twinkle because we see them through thick layers of turbulent (moving) air in the Earth's atmosphere. Stars would not appear to twinkle if we viewed them from outer space or from a planet/moon that didn't have an atmosphere!

Stars

Stars are held together by gravity. There may be millions, or even billions, of stars in one galaxy.

Stars use a lot of energy, which produces light. Small stars will shrink after they've used up their power and will become a 'white dwarf'. Eventually, the star will stop producing any light at all and become a 'black dwarf' and it will stay that way forever.

In large size stars, nuclear fusion (production of energy) will continue until iron is formed. The iron acts like an energy sponge and soaks up the star's energy. This energy is released in a big explosion called a supernova (a star explosion that causes the star to shine millions of times brighter than usual). A small star will then become neutron star (a tiny piece of matter), and a larger star will become a black hole.

Black holes

It's very hard to see a black hole. Black holes were once massive stars that used up all their power. As they died out their gravity made them collapse. Any object that gets too close to a black hole will be pulled inside it. We know they are there because of the effect they have on other objects that are near them. Any object (dust or a star) that gets too close to a black hole will be pulled inside it. As the objects fall toward the black hole, they heat up and get very hot. Scientists can use special instruments to measure the heat the objects give off.

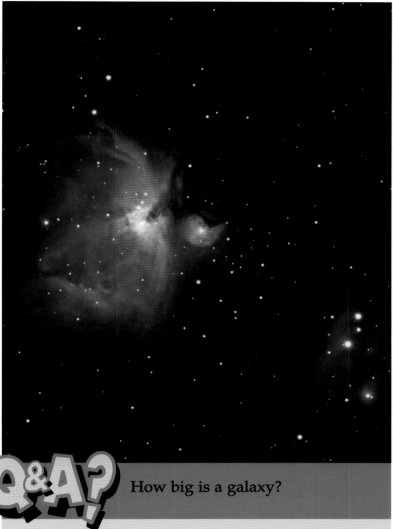

Q&A?

How big is a galaxy?

A typical galaxy has 100,000,000,000 stars in it. That is a lot of stars! They don't often bump against each other, though, because galaxies are so big.

What is an astronomer?

An astronomer is a person who studies the planets and stars. They use very sophisticated equipment, such as radio telescopes.

Australia

Australia is the largest island on the continent of Australia Oceania. Native Australians have inhabited it for over 42,000 years. European explorers and traders starting arriving in the 17th century and in the 18th century the British claimed part of the eastern half of the continent as a penal (prison) colony. This area became known as New South Wales. The population grew and eventually five more states were successively established over the course of the 19th century.

These were Victoria, Queensland, Northern Territory, Western Australia and South Australia. The island to the south of the mainland is Tasmania. On 1 January 1901, the six colonies became a federation and the Commonwealth of Australia was formed.

What is a flying doctor?

Australians living in the outback can be far from the nearest town. The Flying Doctor service started in 1928 to provide emergency health care.

Was Tasmania once joined to Australia?

Yes, it is believed that the island was joined to the mainland until the end of the most recent ice age, about 10,000 years ago.

After the Second World War the Australian government promoted an immigration programme: over half of the migrants were British; others were Greek, German, Dutch, Italian and Yugoslav. Today over 90% of the population are of European descent; others are from Asia and the Middle East. Over 150 nationalities are represented in the population.

Canberra is Australia's capital, but Sydney is its largest city and commercial centre, as well as having the world famous opera house and the 1,650 ft (503 m) long Sydney Harbour Bridge – which has eight lanes of roadway, two railway tracks, a cycle track and a walkway.

Native Australians

The native Australians, known as Aborigines, were the first inhabitants of Australia. The term Aborigine includes a number of native peoples throughout Australia Oceania. These native Australians were hunter-gathers; this means

The world's fussiest eater is the koala, which feeds exclusively on eucalyptus leaves. It eats only six of the 500 species, sifting through 20 lb (9 kg) of leaves daily to find 1 lb (0.5 kg) to eat.

Although hunters have used throwing sticks in many parts of the world, the most famous of all such weapons is the Aborigine's boomerang, which may be the world's only returning throwing stick.

Fascinating **facts**

Range, or Eastern Highlands. This is Australia's most substantial range of mountains, which stretch from northeastern Queensland into the central plain in western Victoria.

The Great Barrier Reef

The Great Barrier Reef, situated off the coast of Queensland, is the world's longest reef, stretching 1,243 miles (2,000 km). It is a breeding ground for green and loggerhead turtles and home to humpback whales and dolphins. Among the many fish that inhabit Australia's surrounding waters are sharks, rays and lungfish. The lungfish is unusual because it has lungs as well as a gill-breathing system.

The Reef is under threat from the crown-of-thorns starfish which eats the living coral, and also from rising sea levels and tourism, which damage the fragile coral ecosystem.

Isolated communities

The Alice Springs School of the Air provides an educational service for children living in settlements and covers over 386,000 sq miles (1 million sq km) of Central Australia. These children live in an isolated environment and their school classes were conducted via shortwave radio until very recently. Today most schools use wireless Internet links to receive their lessons.

that they moved from place to place in search of food. They had no permanent buildings.

When the Europeans arrived they brought disease with them, and many of the native people died from illnesses such as smallpox. Today, many have abandoned their traditional tribal way of life and live in towns and cities, making up 1.5% of the population.

Climate

While a large proportion of inland Australia is desert, 40% of the country enjoys a tropical climate. Snow falls in the Australian Alps at the south end of the Great Dividing

The Aztecs

The Aztecs were the last native American rulers of Mexico. Around the end of the 12th century, their wandering tribe left its home in the north and settled in the Valley of Mexico, which they called 'Anahuac'. Here they built their capital city, Tenochtítlan. Over the next 200 years, the Aztecs built a powerful empire of around 12 million people.

In Tenochtítlan the Aztecs built awe-inspiring temples and giant pyramids where they sacrificed captured prisoners to their gods by cutting out their hearts. They had a mighty army and grew rich by collecting tributes (payments) from all the tribes they conquered.

The fall of the Aztec Empire

The great Aztec Empire came to an end suddenly. In 1519, when Aztec civilisation was at its height, Spanish explorers ('conquistadors') arrived in Mexico led by a man named Hernán Cortés. The Spanish made war on the Aztecs and defeated them. The last independent Aztec Emperor, Montezuma II, was captured by the Spanish and killed. The Aztec Empire crumbled and the Spanish invaders took over.

The Aztec gods

As farmers, the Aztecs depended heavily on the forces of nature and worshipped many of them as gods. Their chief god was Huitzilopochtli, the sun god and god of war. Other gods worshipped were Tlaloc (the god of rain), Quetzalcoatl the Feathered Serpent (the god of wind and learning), and Tezcatlipoca the Smoking Mirror (god of the night sky).

The Aztecs believed they had to keep their 'good' gods strong by making human sacrifices to them – if they failed to do this, they believed other 'evil' gods would destroy the world.
The Aztec priests used stone-bladed knives to cut out the hearts of up to 1,000 people a week and offer them to the sun god. Most of the people sacrificed were captured war prisoners, though Aztec warriors would sometimes volunteer for the most important rituals – they believed it was a great honour to be chosen. According to legend, in 1487 Aztec priests sacrificed more than 80,000 prisoners of war at the dedication of the rebuilt temple of the sun god!

A sacrifice to Tzcatlipoca

Every year, during the fifth month, the Aztec priests would select a young and handsome war prisoner. For one year he lived in princely luxury, treated as though he were the god

Art and Writing

The Aztecs wrote in small pictures called 'pictographs'. This form of writing was very difficult to learn and was mainly done by priests or scribes.

The Aztecs made wonderful jewellery using gold, silver, copper, emerald, turquoise and jade (they prized jade above all other materials). They also fashioned vividly-dyed cloth, dramatic stone sculptures and elaborate garments made of the feathers of tropical birds.

himself. Four beautiful girls dressed as goddesses were chosen as his companions. On the appointed feast day he climbed the steps of a small temple and at the top he was sacrificed by the removal of his heart!

The story of Tenochtitlán

At first, the Aztecs were a poor, ragged people, driven from place to place. Then their leader, Tenoch, had a vision. The sun god Huitzilopochtli told him to lead his people to a swampy island in the middle of Lake Texcoco. There he should look for an eagle perched on a cactus, eating a serpent. On that spot, they were to build their city. The city they built in about

1325 was named Tenochtitlán ('the city of Tenoch') and was built on one natural and several artificial islands in the swampy lake. The Aztecs built bridges and causeways to connect the city to the mainland, and canals to enable people to move around easily. The city quickly grew from a collection of mud huts and small temples to the capital city of a mighty empire – by 1519 about 60,000 people lived or did business there. Today Mexico City stands in the same place.

Two calendars

The Aztecs had two calendars, a religious one and a solar one. The religious calendar told them when to consult their gods. The solar calendar was used to fix the best time for planting crops. A religious year had 260 days. A solar year had 365 days – 18 months of 20 days each and 5 'spare' days.

Q&A?

Did the Aztecs play musical instruments?

Yes, especially during religious ceremonies. The most common instruments were rattles, whistles, trumpets, flutes, copper bells, and shells.

What did the Aztecs eat?

Corn was their main crop. Women ground the corn into coarse flour to make flat corn cakes called tortillas, which were their principal food. Other crops included beans, chilli peppers, squash, avocadoes and tomatoes.

Butterflies *and* Moths

Butterflies are amongst the most colourful and beautiful types of insect on our planet. Both butterflies and moths belong to the Lepidoptera group of insects. We tend to see more butterflies as they are generally active during the day whereas moths tend to be seen more at night.

The life cycle of all butterflies and moths has four distinct stages: starting as an egg, then caterpillar (larva), pupa (chrysalis) to the final stage of imago (adult). The process of change from one stage to the next is called metamorphosis. The final three stages of the Monarch butterfly (caterpillar, pupa and butterfly) are shown above.

How do butterflies keep safe from their predators?

With their wings closed, butterflies face the sun so that their shadow is small and predators are less likely to notice them.

How do butterflies get their energy?

Butterflies spread their wings out in the sunshine to soak up the warmth which gives them energy to fly.

Most butterflies and moths live only a few weeks although some, such as Red Admirals, will find somewhere sheltered to hibernate (sleep) during the winter before emerging again in warmer weather in the spring. During their short lives they all have to find a mate and lay eggs ready to become the next generation before they die.

Female butterflies and moths lay their eggs on plants. Each type of caterpillar has a particular type of plant which it prefers so the eggs will be laid on these plants ready to provide it with food as it hatches. Caterpillars have very strong jaws which they use to cut themselves out of their egg and escape from their shell which they then eat

before going on to eat plant matter. The caterpillar's hard jaw contains a tough substance called chitin. As the caterpillar grows it sheds its skin (moults) as it outgrows it. When it reaches the stage of its final moult the caterpillar stops eating and finds a sheltered place to pupate which means that it changes into a pupa or chrysalis. Some caterpillars spin a cocoon around themselves whilst others wrap themselves in rolled-up leaves. As a pupa the caterpillar undergoes the transformation into a butterfly or moth. This process takes several weeks. Once the adult is ready to emerge it gradually spreads out its wings pumping blood into them as they expand and dry. The adult is then ready to fly and begin the life cycle all over again.

Many types of butterfly and moth are now extinct or in danger of extinction. This has happened because they have been caught, collected and displayed for their beauty or because their natural habitats (where they live) have been destroyed by farming or building.

Butterfly wings are covered with shiny, coloured scales which reflect the light, shimmering as they fly.

Peacock butterflies have circles on their wings which look like eyes and are designed to frighten their enemies and so protect them from danger.

The ragged edge and brown colouring of a Comma butterfly enables it to look like a dead leaf on the ground.

Fascinating Facts

Cameras *and Photography*

The word camera comes from the Latin camera obscura meaning 'dark chamber'. A camera obscura is a dark box with a hole in one side, so that light projects an upside-down image onto the opposite end of the box. In the past this was sometimes done with a whole dark room – people would stand inside it to view the image!

Pinhole cameras

The simplest type of camera is like a camera obscura and called a pinhole camera. It is a small, light-tight can or box with a black interior and a tiny hole in the centre of one end. The end opposite the pinhole is flat so that film or photographic paper can be held flat against it. The pinhole has a cover to stop light entering the camera when you are not taking a picture. It was used in the 16th century as an artist's tool. It did not use film but just projected the image onto a piece of paper.

How do cameras work?

Other cameras are more complicated versions of these earlier models and use a lens instead of a hole. Lenses (discovered in the late 13th century) are pieces of curved glass that magnify – make bigger – the image and concentrate the incoming light. Opposite the lens is a light-sensitive surface, either film or, in digital cameras, an imaging device. When you take a photograph, light reflects off the object being viewed, through the lens and onto the light-sensitive surface. White objects reflect the most light and black reflect the least, changing the material in different amounts and leaving an image. Photographic film is developed in a darkroom using chemicals that bring out and 'fix' the image.

Early photographic prints

Experiments were made in the 18th and early 19th centuries to try to make a lasting print from the image viewed. Several people discovered ways to do this. In 1826, Josephe Nicéphore Niépce recorded a negative on paper. (A negative is where the image is reversed, so that dark appears light and light appears dark.) In 1839 Louis Jacques Mandé Daguerre 1839 invented a method for making positive prints on a silver plate.

The wet-plate process

The popularity of photography exploded when a new wet-plate process was invented. It combined detail with the ability to make multiple prints. There was great demand for family portraits and all kinds

of other pictures. Photographers travelled to far-off lands, bringing back pictures of new animals and tribal peoples. Scientists used stop-action photography to show, for the very first time, how animals moved!

The dry-plate process

In 1871 the dry-plate process was invented. This was easier and faster than the wet-plate and meant pictures did not need to be developed on the spot in mobile darkrooms.

Q&A?

When was the camera obscura first used?

Although the first drawing we have of a camera obscura is by Leonardo Da Vinci in the 16th century, the ancient Greeks used this device to view solar eclipses safely!

What is the earliest surviving photograph?

The earliest known surviving photograph is an outdoor scene taken by Niépce in 1826 or 1827. Niépce called his process 'heliography', meaning 'sun writing'. It was a slow process which required about 8 hours of bright sunlight!

This new process and the invention of smaller cameras meant photojournalists were able to go to many new places, bringing back pictures for newspapers and magazines. Documentary photography became popular, recording how people lived and also wars. Photography began to be accepted as not just an aid to the painter but an art form in itself!

Modern cameras

Over the years cameras have become smaller, lighter and easier to use. Recently digital cameras have become popular, and many people even have cameras on their mobile phones! Digital photography allows people to make prints very easily and store their photographs on computers or send them to friends and family by email.

Photography today

Nowadays photography is available to us all and we are surrounded by images from all over the world. Photography has had a huge effect on business, education and journalism. The police use photographs to record crime scenes and even recognise criminals. Advanced cameras are also used in science, astronomy and medicine, allowing people to see the far-off stars and even the insides of living human beings!

Roll film

In 1888 George Eastman introduced roll film (replacing individual plates) and began to sell roll-film cameras. Now people could easily take pictures themselves. There were many developments like portable lights, colour film and Polaroid film, which created a finished print in seconds.

Fascinating Facts

The word photography comes from the Greek words for light and writing. The earliest surviving photograph dates from 1826. Daguerreotypes were made with toxic mercury!

Castles

When we use the word 'castle', we most often mean a self-contained fortress built to defend against enemies and control the area around it. Besides being used for protection, castles sometimes served as residences for the lord or monarch. During the Middle Ages, feudal lords who wanted to protect their people and expand their power built large numbers of castles all over Europe.

Early castles

The first castles were constructed of wood and so were easily destroyed by fire. Later castles were built of stone and therefore much more robust. Many early stone castles consisted of a single tower. As time went on, however, castles became bigger, more elaborate and better designed for defence. Many of these castles survive today.

Where castles were built

When possible, castles were built in places that were easy to defend, such as hills, mountain passes, peninsulas, and islands in lakes. They were often built to protect important strategic places such as ports and river crossings.

Castle design

Most castles had a keep, or central tower. The keep usually had several floors and included lodgings for the lord and perhaps his family and other important people. Castles usually had outer walls – sometimes several layers of them! – to provide the first line of defence when the castle was attacked. If the walls

Many English castles were destroyed or badly damaged during the Civil Wars of the 17th century because Oliver Cromwell wanted to remove all traces of royal power.

The word dungeon comes from the French word donjon, meaning tower or keep. Prisoners in medieval castles were more often held in the highest room of a tower than in what we would now call a 'dungeon'.

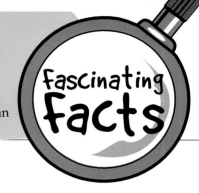

Fascinating Facts

were breached (broken through), the people in the castle could retreat into the keep. When many people needed protection, walls could be built around a whole city or town. In addition to the outer walls, castles had towers and battlements from which to watch for enemies. Castles with round towers were more difficult to attack because rocks bounced off the curved walls.

Castles under siege

When the castle was under attack it was said to be 'under siege'. Attackers would try many different ways to take over the castle. They would climb the walls or break them down by throwing heavy rocks at them, using machines such as catapults. Battering rams would be used to try to break down the gates. If a siege went on for a long time the attackers might try to starve out those who lived there by ensuring that no new supplies could get in.

Defending a castle

Inside the castle defenders would have a good view of their attackers from the high battlements and towers and would use bows and arrows to keep them away. There were often small slits so that archers could fire their arrows without being hit themselves. If attackers got close to the castle and put tall ladders up the walls those inside would pour boiling water and hot sand onto them from the tops of the walls to keep them away. After the invention of gunpowder in the 13th century, however, defending a castle became harder and harder.

Castles since the Middle Ages

By the late 1600s, gunpowder and artillery had become so effective that castles were no longer useful for defence. As life became more peaceful, many of the castles that still survived were used for other purposes. For example, in the Scottish highlands, castles were often used for courts presided over by the laird. Others, such as the Tower of London and the Bastille in Paris, were used as prisons. Today many castles survive as monuments to the past, and large numbers of people visit them every year.

What is the 'iron ring' of castles?

This is a series of strong stone castles built in Wales by King Edward I to control the Welsh population. They include the castles of Caernarfon, Harlech and Conwy.

Where does the word 'castle' come from?

It comes from the Latin word 'castellum', meaning fortress. The word castrum, used for the wooden forts built by Roman soldiers, means a fortified place.

China

China, the world's most heavily populated country, has a continuous culture stretching back nearly 4,000 years. Although its birthrate has slowed down, it is now the world's fastest-growing economy. The current industrial growth is concentrated in manufacturing household goods and clothing, resulting in China being the largest oil consumer after the USA, and the world's biggest producer and consumer of coal.

The rapid industrialisation has created vast differences between the wealth of urban workers and those remaining as peasant farmers. Pollution is a major issue, but in recent years the government has announced a wish to slow economic growth and to solve some of the problems it has caused.

Q&A?

Do the Chinese have an alphabet?

No. Each word has its own unique symbol or character. It is a system that goes back 3,600 years. It has helped the different groups of Chinese to understand each other because although they speak many types of language the written form can be understood by all. Traditionally the Chinese have written vertically in columns arranged from right to left.

Is rice the main food staple in China?

It is in the south but in the north the Chinese people eat more wheat-based products such as noodles or steamed buns.

Three Gorges Dam

There has been a massive investment in hydroelectric power, including the Three Gorges Dam project, which is to dam the Yangtze River. The dam is 607 ft (185 m) high, and 7,575 ft (2,309 m) long. Once running at full capacity, it will have a potential of more than 18,000 megawatts, making it the world's largest hydroelectric generating station. China also hopes that the dam will help control flooding on the Yangtze River, which in the past has claimed hundreds of thousands of lives.

Fishing – with cormorants!

On some of the rivers of China, fishermen catch fish without nets or hooks by using cormorants. The birds have a ring put round their neck to stop them swallowing the fish they catch

Ürümqi

C

Mount Evere
29,050ft
8,850m

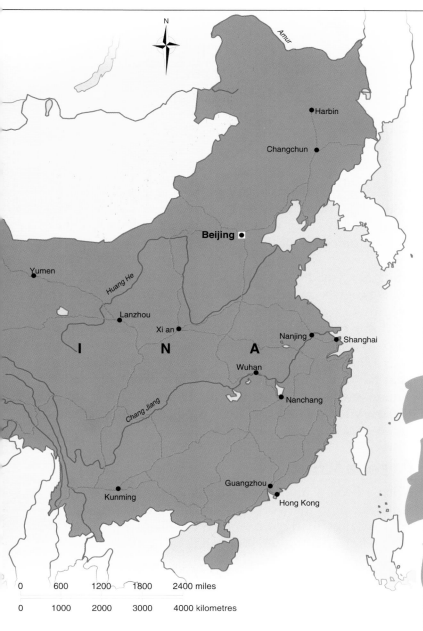

are: Dog, Boar, Rat, Ox, Tiger, Hare or rabbit, Dragon, Snake, Horse, Ram or sheep, Monkey, Rooster.

Legend suggests that in ancient times, Buddha asked all the animals to meet him on Chinese New Year. Only 12 animals came, and so Buddha named a year after each of the animals present. People born in the year of the dog are said to possess the best of human qualities as they have a deep sense of loyalty, are honest, and can keep a secret. But they can occasionally be a little selfish too.

At 2,150 miles (3,460 km) long, the Great Wall of China is the longest wall in the world, nearly three times the length of Britain. It also has 2,193 miles (3,530 km) of branches and spurs. It is said to be the only human-made structure that is visible to the naked eye from the moon.

In the 11th century the Chinese learned how to bake their pottery at temperatures high enough to produce porcelain (very fine, thin and hard). When this pottery came to Europe it was called china and that name continued when European potters learned how to make it themselves.

fascinating Facts

when they dive. After the cormorants return to the boat, the fisherman takes the fish from the bird's throat and sends it off again.

Chinese Calendar and New Year

Chinese New Year is a very important holiday in China. It is celebrated in late January to early February (depending on the year). Chinese New Year starts on a New Moon and ends with the lantern festival on the full moon 15 days later.

Unlike most calendars the Chinese calendar does not count the years in numbers but each year is given one of twelve animal names. The twelve animals of the Chinese calendar

Climate

W hen we talk about climate we generally mean the weather. Will it rain? Will it be hot or cold? How hot? How cold? But climate and weather are different.

Meteorology

Meteorology is the study of weather and weather conditions all around the world. Meteorologists can tell us about the temperature, rainfall and wind at any given place. They can tell us if there is likely to be a

thunderstorm, a hurricane or flash floods. All of these factors make up what we think of as weather. Weather is what is happening now or likely to happen tomorrow or the next day.

Climatology is the study of climates and climate change. Climatologists can tell us what climate conditions to expect around the world. They are more interested in statistics – did it rain more in March this year than it did in March last year? And the year before that – and even in the last 50 years! The world has nine clear climatic zones. Each of the areas has a name, so that when we talk about a temperate climate or tundra, we know what to expect. For example, in the winter, we expect it to be mild and wet in Athens, Greece and snowy in New York, USA.

Forecasting

When we know all of these details we can judge if the climate around the world is changing. Are there more hot, dry days now than there were in 1950? Or does it rain more now than in 1950? If we know that, farmers will know which types of crops to grow on their land. Water companies will know if they need to make provision for water shortages. Seaside towns will expect more people to

Are there any places that never have rain?

There are places with very little rain or even no rain at all. The driest place recorded is Calama in the Atacama Desert in Chile, The average rainfall is just 0.1 inches (3 mm) per year, but there was a period of time when no rain fell there for 40 years.

Where is the wettest place ever recorded?

The wettest place recorded is Cherrapunji, India, where 360 inches (9,300 mm) of rain fell in one month!

visit the beaches. Will the farmers be able to harvest their crops? Will there be more floods? Where will we go for our holidays?

Mountain Climate
Wetter than the lowlands and 2°F (1°C) cooler for every 490 ft (150 m) increase in altitude.

Temperate Grassland Climate
Cold winters and warm summers. Mainly dry.

Temperate Forest Climate
Mild winters and cool summers. Abundant rain falls all year.

Hot Desert Climate
Very hot and dry all year.

Tropical Rainforest Climate
Rainfall is heavy all year. The annual rainfall is often more than 100 inches (250 cm). It is also hot and humid.

Coniferous Forest Climate
Very cold winters are common, with cool and mainly dry summers.

Tropical Grassland Climate
Hot all year. Two seasons only – one dry and one wet.

Mediterranean Climate
Hot dry summers and mild, wet winters.

Polar and Tundra Climate
Polar: dry and frozen all year. Tundra: dry and frozen part of year.

The highest temperature ever recorded was 136.4°F (58°C) at Al Aziziyah in Libya. Libya is a hot desert area.

The lowest temperature ever recorded was –128.56°F (–89.2°C) at Vostok in Antarctica, which is in the southern polar region and so is very cold.

Clocks

Clocks are machines for measuring time. The earliest timekeeping devices were straight sticks or poles, stuck in the ground. As the sun moves from sunrise to sunset, the shadows it casts change. They change direction and also get shorter and or longer (the shortest shadows are cast at noon when the sun is directly overhead). This method of telling the time developed into shadow clocks called sundials. Sundials have a circular 'dial' or 'clock face' with the hours marked on it. We can sometimes see sundials in gardens today.

Some people also measured time by using candles that burned down very slowly and at a known rate. Others used large 'hourglasses' in which grains of sand ran slowly through a small hole from one 'glass' into another.

Early mechanical clocks

The earliest known mechanical clock was invented by a monk in the year 996, but it was nothing like the clocks we have today. Clocks similar to the ones we use, with a clock face and a moving 'hand', were invented in France in the 14th century. The French monks wanted accurate clocks to keep track of set times for prayer, and to 'sound' the hours on a bell or gong. Many churches have

How does a water clock work?

Water clocks (called 'clepsydra', water-stealers) were flower-pot shaped bowls marked with the hours on the inside. Water trickled out of a small hole at the bottom and the level left inside showed what time it was. Water clocks were used in China as early as 3,000 BC and were still in use in the 20th century in parts of Africa!

Why do we have to wind up some clocks?

Old clocks needed winding every day to keep them running! A new design, using coiled springs for power instead of pendulums and weights, meant clocks could become much smaller. Travel clocks became very popular and the rich began to carry pocket watches. These were not very accurate but were often made with expensive materials and very finely engraved. The richer someone was, the more elaborate their watch-case.

'sounding' clocks that ring out multiple hours (five rings for five o'clock, and so on). Perhaps the most famous sounding clock is the one that rings 'Big Ben' on the Houses of Parliament in London, England.

The pendulum

An Italian astronomer, Galileo Galilei (1564–1642), noticed an interesting fact about the swing of a weight on the end of a long piece of string (called a 'pendulum'). No matter how much force you use to swing the pendulum, it takes the same amount of time to swing back and forth. In 1657 a Dutch scientist, Christiaan Huygens, worked out what length the pendulum needed to be in order to use it to measure time. The first 'longcase' (or 'grandfather') clock was designed in 1670 by an English clockmaker who placed a clock in a tall wooden case to hide the mechanism.

Telling time on ships

The most accurate clocks were still pendulum clocks, but on board ships the movement of the sea disturbed the swing and made them useless. The problem was solved by an English clockmaker, John Harrison (1673–1776). His marine chronometer (timekeeper) was accurate enough to be used on long journeys.

Clocks today

Modern mechanical clocks are very accurate and do not need winding because they are powered by batteries. Electronic clocks have become very popular in the 20th century. Many modern electric clocks are 'digital', showing the time using numbers instead of moving hands. Scientists have now made atomic clocks which are accurate to a billionth of a second, and will not lose or gain a single second in 20 million years!

Clocks for the home

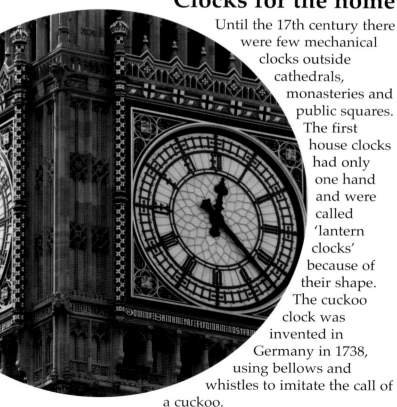

Until the 17th century there were few mechanical clocks outside cathedrals, monasteries and public squares. The first house clocks had only one hand and were called 'lantern clocks' because of their shape. The cuckoo clock was invented in Germany in 1738, using bellows and whistles to imitate the call of a cuckoo.

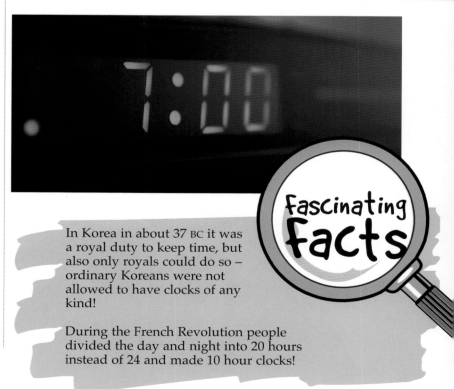

Fascinating Facts

In Korea in about 37 BC it was a royal duty to keep time, but also only royals could do so – ordinary Koreans were not allowed to have clocks of any kind!

During the French Revolution people divided the day and night into 20 hours instead of 24 and made 10 hour clocks!

Codes *and code-breaking*

Codes have been used throughout history to save time but also for secrecy. Codes and ciphers are not the same. A message in code has words, phrases, or messages replace by different words, letters, or symbols. Writing a message in code is called encoding. Ciphers, on the other hand, replace every single letter, number, or symbol with a different letter, number, or symbol. Writing a message using this method is called enciphering.

The two kinds of cipher

There are two main types of cipher. The first is called a 'transposition' cipher, when the letters of a message are scrambled up following a system that allows the message to be unscrambled by the receiver. For example, 'codesorciphers' (codes or ciphers) might become 'ocedoscrpiehsr'. Here each pair of letters has been reversed. So 'co' becomes 'oc', 'de' becomes 'ed' and so on. The second type is called a 'substitution' cipher. This is when letters are substituted for other letters or words for other words, for example, 'xe' being written for the letter 'j' or 'cabbage' being written for the word 'house'. This is what is most commonly meant when people say someone is talking 'in code',: 'did you buy some butter?' being the secret code for 'we attack at dawn'.

Ciphers in history

Ciphers are essential in times of war as a message written in normal language would be easily understood by the enemy and give away military secrets. People throughout history, including Julius Caesar and Mary Queen of Scots, have used codes and ciphers. Military messages are sent in code between camps of soldiers or from generals to their troops. Other groups of people in history have also used secret codes to communicate with each other. Early Christians would draw a fish to tell other Christians who they were, and tramps in the 19th century would chalk secret symbols onto houses to let other tramps know that the inhabitants would either give a good meal or were unfriendly.

Breaking enemy codes

The military often employs cryptographers to study enemy ciphers. A common way to 'break' a code is to look at what words, symbols or combinations of letters turn up most frequently in the message. In English, the most common letters are E, T, O, A, N (in that order) and the most common combinations are TH, HE, IN, AN. This is called 'frequency analysis' and was discovered as a

reliable method for breaking early transposition ciphers as early as the year 1000. Even complex codes are still vulnerable to this method as it is still possible to spot frequent letters and to use them to solve the puzzle.

How does Morse code work?

Morse code is made up of 'dots' and 'dashes'. A dot is a short tap of the telegraph key (or flash of the lamp) and a dash is 3 times longer.

What is 'Semaphore'?

Semaphore is a famous code that uses a pair of flags in different positions to spell out words.

'Code-talkers'

During World War One many Native American languages were used for the sending of secret messages because these languages were spoken by only a very few people. Following this, Navajo 'code-talkers' were used in important US missions in World War Two. This tribal language was an extremely complex and unwritten language with no alphabet. The code-talkers used the language itself but also a substitution cipher. Seemingly unrelated words stood for letters of the alphabet, for example the Navajo words for ant, abacus, alphabet, and apple would all stand for the letter 'a'. Other words and phrases were given special code-words, for example the word for 'hummingbird' meant 'fighter plane'. The code was never cracked.

Machines and cryptography

The most famous cipher machine was the German 'Enigma' machine used in World War Two. This machine encoded a message several times over instead of just once, and the parts which set the code, called the rotating discs, were changed daily, thus making the code even harder to solve

The British captured one of these machines and used mathematicians to break the codes. The very first

computers were invented and built to help solve the code. They were so large that they filled a whole room!

Computers have meant that much more complicated ciphers can be invented, but it is also possible to use computers to break codes.

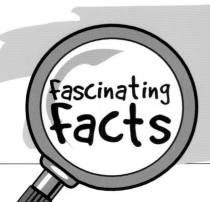

Fascinating Facts

International Morse Code was very useful in helping ships communicate quickly and for sending distress signals. The US Coastguard only stopped monitoring Morse code transmissions in 1995!

The International Code of Signals was compiled by the British Government in 1857 to be used by boats. This code uses different colours and shapes of flags to represent letters and numbers.

Darwin *and* Evolution

Charles Darwin (1809-82) was one of England's most famous scientists. His studies of plants and animals lead to his famous theories about a process called 'evolution'. Evolution is the idea that plants and animals have changed, developed or 'evolved' over time. Many nineteenth century scientists who studied living animals and the fossils of extinct ones were interested in evolution. A fossil is an animal or plant that has been preserved for millions of years. Darwin was one of the first people to suggest how evolution might happen and to make society take notice of these ideas.

Voyage around the World

As a young boy, Darwin was very interested in nature and the world around him. He went on long hikes and helped his older brother with his chemistry experiments. While at

Does everyone believe in evolution?

Although the scientific theory of evolution has been accepted by most people today, some still believe in the literal truth of the Bible.

Were Darwin and Wallace the first people to think about evolution?

No. An ancient Greek philosopher (thinker) called Aristotle believed that 'higher' forms of life had descended or 'evolved' from 'lower' forms.

Cambridge University he was introduced to the Rev. John Stevens Henslow who was a professor of botany (the science or study of plants). Henslow got Darwin an exciting job as a naturalist (somebody who is knowledgeable about natural history) on the HMS *Beagle* in 1831. The ship sailed on a five-year round-the-world voyage in order to study the coasts of South America, Australia, New Zealand and many smaller islands.

On the voyage, Darwin collected evidence of many new species (types) of plants and animals. He also began to think about evolution after he found lots of different species of tortoises on different islands. He had a theory that all the different tortoises had originated (come from) a single species of tortoise and had adapted to life in different ways, eventually becoming many different species.

Creation

In the Biblical account of creation, the earth was created by God in seven days and humans and all the animals were created in the forms we know today. Evolution argued that this was not the case, and that animals developed gradually over many millions of years.

On the Origin of Species by means of Natural Selection

In 1858 a young scientist called A. R. Wallace sent Darwin an essay he had written. Darwin was shocked to find Wallace had the same ideas as his own! The two men decided to publish their ideas at the same time, announcing them at a joint lecture. Darwin rushed to finish his book and published it in 1859. It was called 'On the Origin of Species by means of Natural Selection', normally shortened to On the Origin of Species.

Darwin's theory of Natural Selection was based on the idea that plants, animals and people are all reproduced slightly different. For example, you are not identical to either of your parents. Some of these differences give an advantage which mean a plant or animal is more likely to survive and reproduce, passing the differences on. Over many hundreds of generations this would result in a new species being created. These new species might be 'better' or more complex than the old ones, meaning that over millions of years very simple forms of life would evolve into complex ones. This is where we get the famous idea of man evolving from monkeys, or rather from the same ancestors as modern-day monkeys have – men and apes are like the different species of tortoise found by Darwin.

The way natural selection works can be seen in 'selective breeding'. This is when people breed plants and animals in order to encourage certain characteristics, making larger hens or brighter flowers. For example, the vegetables cabbage, kale, Brussel sprouts and cauliflower were all bred from the same wild plant!

Darwin continued to work on his theories until he died, The importance of all his work was recognised and he was given a state funeral. He was buried in Westminster Abbey, near other famous scientists like Isaac Newton.

Before Darwin, people thought that species had never changed throughout history.

The vegetables cabbage, kale and cauliflower were all bred from the same wild plant!

fascinaTing FacT

Desert life

Because deserts are so dry the people and animals which live there have to adapt their lives to the harsh conditions. Camels can survive for a week without water, whereas most animals need to have regular access to water for drinking or by consuming it in their food. People who live in deserts, like the Bedouin people, usually live in groups and move from place to place with their animals. Where people do settle and build homes in the desert the houses usually have flat roofs and small windows.

Deserts are generally rocky and bare and only partly covered in sand. Where there are large amounts of sand, the strong wind in sandstorms blows it into huge piles making sand dunes. It can then be very difficult for people to find their way as the landscape is constantly changing.

Plants which are found in deserts need very long roots to reach water underground, or thick stems which soak up water. Cacti can store water inside their stems and the whole plant swells up when it rains. In less severe conditions plants with leaves are often pale grey to reflect the light, and need very little water to grow. Seeds lie dormant during dry periods and grow and bloom and produce new seed very quickly when the rains come. In some places there are oases in deserts, where there is water. Palm trees often grow around an oasis.

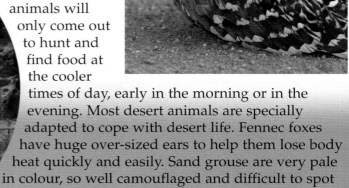

Many animals live in deserts, although they are rarely seen. As deserts are normally very hot during the day and very cold at night, most animals will only come out to hunt and find food at the cooler times of day, early in the morning or in the evening. Most desert animals are specially adapted to cope with desert life. Fennec foxes have huge over-sized ears to help them lose body heat quickly and easily. Sand grouse are very pale in colour, so well camouflaged and difficult to spot among the rocks.

How many sorts of camels are there?

There are two types of camel: dromedary and Bactrian. The majority of the world's camels – about 15 million worldwide – are dromedaries with one fatty hump on their back where they store fluid. The less numerous camel is the Bactrian or Asian camel, which has a shaggier coat and two humps.

There are deserts on every continent on Earth. They are the driest places in the world and sometimes there is no rain for many years.

Llamas, which come from South America, are closely related to camels. They are also traditionally used for carrying goods and for their meat. Llamas are smaller than camels, weighing about 150 kilos and measuring just over a metre in height.

How is sand made?

Because of the extremes of temperature in deserts the rocks are continually expanding and contracting in the heat of the day and cold of the night. This causes the surface of rocks to break off into tiny fragments, which become sand. As the sand is blown about, new rock surfaces are exposed and the process continues.

Camels

How can camels go so long without water when other animals cannot?

Although camels don't have to drink very often, perhaps only once a week, when they do drink they can consume as much as 100 litres at a time. That would be the same sort of quantity as half a tank of petrol in your family car.

Camels are often called 'ships of the desert' as they are used for carrying people and heavy loads of supplies across deserts. They are also used for the milk, meat and skin which they provide. Camels can grip very thorny food from plants with their tough lips and large teeth. In a sandstorm they protect themselves by pressing their ears flat, closing their eyes and sealing their mouths and nostrils almost completely. In this way they avoid breathing in sand or getting it in their eyes, which are protected by very long eyelashes.

Which is the world's largest desert?

The world's largest desert is the Sahara Desert in northern Africa. The Sahara covers nearly 10 million km² (square kilometres).

Dinosaurs

The word dinosaur comes from the Greek word dino (terrible) and the Latin word saurus (lizard). Although dinosaurs became extinct (died out) millions of years ago, we know that they existed because we have discovered dinosaur fossils. A fossil is an animal or plant that has been preserved for millions of years. A cast forms when mud and stones are deposited on animal or plant remains and, over millions of years, they turn to stone. Sometimes whole insects or plants are covered in amber or ice, so that they are perfectly preserved.

Early developments

The first dinosaur fossils were found a few hundred years ago. In 1822 an English couple, Mary Ann and Gideon Mantell, found what they thought to be the teeth of some huge, extinct iguana. Then, in 1841, the British scientist Sir Richard Owen realised that these bones were not those of any creature living at the time. In 1842 he gave these ancient creatures the name 'dinosaurs'.

The Bone Wars

Early palaeontology which is the study of fossils or extinct plants and animals was often based more on guesswork than true scientific evidence. This situation was improved when two rival and wealthy Americans, Othniel Marsh and Edward Cope, raced to excavate fossils in the Rocky Mountain region. In the late 1800s, their separate teams, armed against Native Americans and each other, dug up tons of bones from several sites. All in all, Marsh and Cope's rivalry (the 'Bone Wars') uncovered 136 new species. And their fossil displays created a huge interest in dinosaurs all around the world.

Discovering dinosaur species

The first dinosaur species to be discovered was Iguanadon, in 1822. Two years later, 1824, Megalosaurus was discovered. Dinosaurs have been discovered all over the world. For example, Ankylosaurus was discovered in Antarctica!

The earliest dinosaur known to have existed was the Eoraptor, a meat-eater that lived about 228 million years ago.

Micropachycephalosaurus (tiny thick-headed lizard) has the longest name of any dinosaur, but it is one of the smallest ever discovered – it was only about 1.5-3 ft (0.5-1 m) long!

Fascinating facts

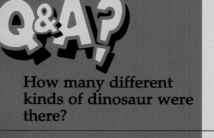

Q&A?

How many different kinds of dinosaur were there?	*There were more than 500 kinds that we know of, and more are still being discovered!*
What does the name 'Mesozoic' mean?	*It means 'middle animals'.*

Feathered dinosaurs have been found in China, making people think there might be a link between birds and dinosaurs. Tyrannosaurus Rex was discovered in 1902.

What were dinosaurs like?

Some dinosaurs walked on two legs, they were bipedal, and some walked on four legs, they were quadrupedal. William Parker Foulke discovered the dinosaur Hadrosaurus. This was an important find because it

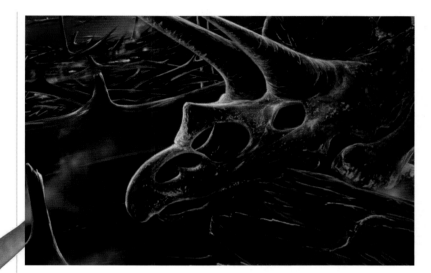

was the first nearly complete dinosaur skeleton ever discovered. It was also clearly bipedal, and until that time scientists had believed that all dinosaurs walked on all fours like modern lizards. We think that smaller dinosaurs like Velociraptor were speedy and that bigger ones like Ankylosaurus were slow. We also know that some dinosaurs were plant-eaters like Triceratops and some were meat-eaters like Tyrannosaurus Rex. Plant-eaters are sometimes called herbivores, and meat-eaters are sometimes called carnivores.

Studying dinosaurs today

Nowadays, rather than finding and studying new dinosaurs, scientists mainly look at how dinosaurs might have lived and what their habitats were like. But it is very difficult to learn everything about them, and some things we will probably never know. Because no human being has ever seen or heard a dinosaur, we will never be sure what they looked like, what colour they were, or what sounds they made. To guess these things, scientists study living

creatures they think might have behaved like dinosaurs. Dinosaurs lived during the Mesozoic period of Earth's history, sometimes known as the 'Age of Reptiles'. They lived on earth for more than 165 million years but suddenly became extinct 65 million years ago. There have been many suggestions for why they became extinct, but scientists think that the most likely cause was an asteroid hitting the earth, causing huge changes in Earth's weather and temperature to which the dinosaurs couldn't adapt.

Einstein

A lbert Einstein (1879–1955) is considered one of the most important scientists of the twentieth century. In 1921. His name has become another word for genius, so if you say that someone is another Einstein, you are saying that person is extremely intelligent.

Einstein's childhood

Einstein spent his childhood in Germany. His father showed him a compass when he was five, and he realised that some kind of force must have been moving the needle. This was one of the most important moments in Einstein's life. Although he was thought to be a slow learner, he was very good at mathematics at school, and also built models and mechanical toys for fun. Having studied his brain after death, scientists now think he learned differently from other people because of the way his brain was made up.

The Special Theory of Relativity

After he left school he got a job working in the Swiss patent office. He spent all of his spare time studying physics. Whilst there, he came up with his Special Theory of Relativity (1905) and studied the movement of atoms. Einstein assumed that everything in the universe was moving and so all motion and all measurements we take are relative. Time and space are normally thought of as different, separate things. Einstein thought of them as one thing, and that they acted together. Instead of talking about things having three co-ordinates (three dimensions in space), he gave them four co-ordinates (the fourth being time). It is from Einstein that science fiction gets the term 'space-time continuum'! Einstein's Special Theory abandoned the traditional laws of physics and geometry.

The General Theory of Relativity

Albert Einstein became Dr Albert Einstein and worked at many universities as a professor. Publishing his General Theory of Relativity (1915), he pointed out that light rays passing near the sun must be bent very slightly by the sun's gravitational pull. Eclipse observers in 1919 and 1922 proved that this was true, and he became world famous.

In his theory, Einstein argued that objects become heavier when they move faster, and so people can never travel at the speed of light because they would become vastly (perhaps even infinitely) heavy. Einstein's theories are most important in astronomy and when studying atomic particles that travel at vast speeds.

The Einstein Cross

In 1936 Einstein wrote about gravitational lensing, which means the light from a distant source appears to be spaced around another bright object which is not so distant. This

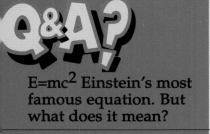

Q&A?

E=mc² Einstein's most famous equation. But what does it mean?

It means that the energy of a body at rest (E) equals its mass (m) times the speed of light (c) squared.

Why didn't Einstein wear socks?

He hated the way that the big toe makes a hole in a sock, so he stopped wearing them.

became known as the Einstein Cross. The central light spot is about 400 million light years away, while the outer light spots are 8 billion light years away!

Highest honours

Einstein was awarded the Nobel Prize for Physics in 1921 for general contributions to the study of physics. At this point, his work on relativity was still disputed.

Later work

In 1934, Einstein's possessions and his German citizenship were taken away from him by the German Nazi government because he was Jewish. He had already accepted a job in the United States, so he left Germany. In the United States he worked on a wider extension of his theories, publishing his Unified Field Theory in 1950. This theory expanded his earlier theories to include his ideas about electricity and magnetism, explaining both these forces. But Einstein never found a way to test it.

Fascinating facts

Einstein was very forgetful.

As a child, Einstein was given violin lessons. He hated them, and gave up the instrument, but later, he enjoyed listening to Mozart's violin works.

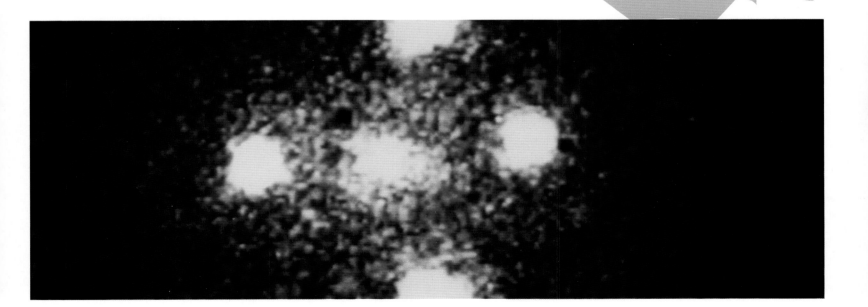

Electricity

Electricity usually means either an electric current, which is the flow of tiny electrically charged particles, or static electricity, a build-up of electrically charged particles in an object. We can easily convert electricity into other forms of energy such as heat and light.

Thomas Edison gave us one of the most familiar sights in our homes today when he perfected the light bulb in 1879, and since then we have developed hundreds of uses for electricity.

Electric current and circuits

Electric current is the flow of electric charge through a material. If electricity can flow easily through a material then

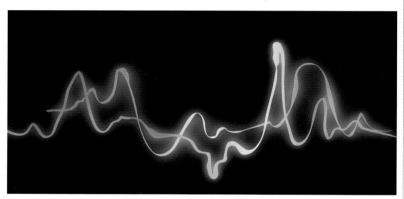

that material is called a conductor, if it is difficult for electrical charge to move through a material then it is called an insulator. Most metals are very good conductors, most non-metallic materials such as air and plastics are good insulators – this is why electrical plugs have plastic covers and wires are encased in rubber. Ceramics are also good insulators and are used in overhead pylons to separate the wires carrying the electrical current.

In order for electrical current to flow there must be a closed path of a conductive material between two areas of different electrical charge. In most man-made

Where does the name 'electricity' come from?

Both 'electricity' and 'electron' come from the Greek word for amber, which is electron.

Who was the first person to generate an electric current?

Michael Faraday, in 1831. He did this by moving a magnet in and out of a coil of wire, causing an electric current to travel through the wire.

electrical circuits it is electrons flowing through metal wire that make up the electric current.

The strength of an electrical current is measured in amps and depends on the resistance of the material the charge is flowing through (resistance is measured in ohms; conductors  have lower resistance than insulators and so allow larger currents to flow) and the charge difference or electrical potential difference across the circuit. This potential difference is measured in volts and can be thought of as the force 'pushing' the electrical charges around the circuit.

Whenever electric current flows it generates heat in the material it flows through. The amount of heat depends on the strength of the current and the resistance of the material. Michael Faraday was the first man to generate an electric current, which he achieved in 1831 by moving a magnet in and out of a coil of wire. This caused an electric current to travel through the wire.

Fascinating Facts

Putting the distribution lines for electricity underground protects not only the cables but also the beauty of the countryside.

Wind or water power can be used to turn a turbine and produce electricity. This cuts down on the use of fuels like coal and oil.

ELECTRICAL SAFETY TIPS

- Never play near, or touch, a transformer. The electricity from it could kill you.
- Never fly a kite near electrical lines.
- Never touch wires. Only an electrician is safe to work on wires.
- Water conducts electricity. Never put electrical devices in, or too close to, water.

Power station to home: the electrical journey

In a power station, fuel is burned to heat water and turn it into steam. The steam pushes an enormous wheel, called a turbine, round at very high speeds. The turbine turns a huge dynamo called a generator, which makes electricity.

To get to the people who use it, the electricity first goes through a transformer which boosts its voltage so that it can be transferred more easily over long distances. It is then carried along power lines to substations near houses, factories and businesses. From the substation, it goes to all the places where it will be used. At the end of the electricity's journey, other transformers change it back into lower voltage electricity so it can be used safely.

Electricity entering your home passes through a meter, which records how much electricity you use. After that you can use it to switch on lights, kettles and computers. How many ways do you think we use electricity in our homes? Probably well over a hundred.

Lightning: electricity from the sky

In a storm cloud, moving air makes ice particles and water droplets rub together and become charged with static electricity. The positively charged particles then rise to the top of the cloud while the negatively charged ones sink to the bottom. The negative charges in the cloud are attracted to the ground – but because the air is an insulator the charges cannot flow. Instead the strength of the electric field between the cloud and the ground grows until it is strong enough to ionize the air, forming a conductive plasma. Once this happens the electric charges can flow from the cloud to the ground and the current that flows is so great that the air around it becomes white hot and explodes outwards, resulting in the bright flash of light and the sound of thunder.

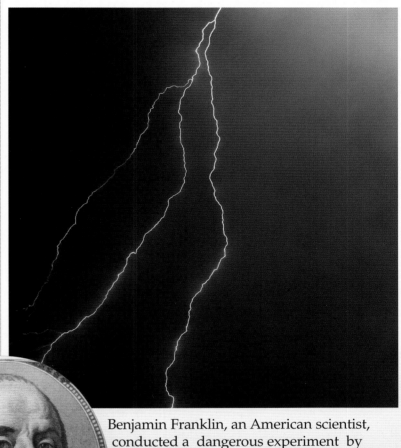

Benjamin Franklin, an American scientist, conducted a dangerous experiment by flying a large kite up on a long string into a storm cloud. An iron key was tied to the end of the string, and the electrical charge from the cloud ran down the wet string and made sparks when it hit the key. He was luckily unhurt, and his discoveries led him to invent lightning conductors.

Energy *natural and man-made*

Energy is what makes us grow and move. It is also heat, light and sound. Plants store energy and as they grow they obtain energy from the soil and light energy from the sun. This process is called photosynthesis.

Humans and animals get their energy from the nutrients and calories in food and drink. When you eat, your body uses food as fuel. Even when you think, you are using energy your body has gained from food you've eaten.

There are different kinds of energy. If you ride a bicycle, your body provides the energy to move the pedals and wheels. When a car moves, its energy comes from the fuel in its engine. We use energy to heat houses, power cars and buses, and for radios and factory machines. The technology we use in modern life requires a lot of energy.

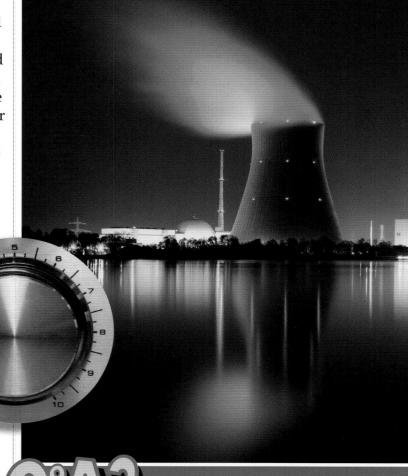

Q&A?

What happens if a television is left on standby?

A television or stereo left on standby will use between 10% and 60% of the energy it would use if it were switched on.

How can I save energy?

Turn off lights when you leave a room, use energy-saving light bulbs, and don't overfill the kettle.

Cut down car use. It is healthier to walk, and doesn't damage the environment.

A computer monitor left on overnight wastes the amount of energy it would take to print 800 pages.

fascinating
Facts

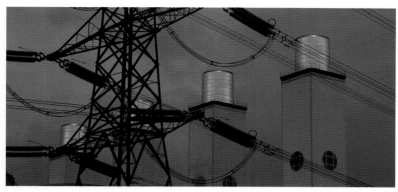

Most of the power we use every day is from electrical energy. Electricity is very convenient as it can be easily carried by wires to the electric sockets in our houses or stored in batteries. Most electricity is generated at power stations.

Power stations

Most power stations use fossil fuels such as coal, oil and gas. The fuel is burned to heat water which turns into steam, and the steam is used to move the parts of the generator, which produces electricity. Steam power was famously used to power trains in the early days of the railways.

Oil is also used to make the petrol that powers all our cars and buses. Fossil fuels are a finite resource: there is a limited supply of them, and we will eventually use them up. Many people ask what alternative energy sources we can use when the fossil fuels run out.

Hydroelectric power

Hydroelectric power is produced when the moving energy of falling water at river dams is used to power electric generators. The traditional version of this was the water wheel, used in small rivers and streams to power grain mills and early factories. Hydroelectric power can also be obtained from tidal energy using the twice-daily movement of the sea's tides.

Solar power

Solar power is produced when the energy from the sun is turned into electricity. Some people have solar panels on the roofs of their houses to

provide the power to heat the water for their baths or power their light bulbs. Solar power plants are possible in very sunny parts of the world, but a wide area of ground would have to be covered by solar panels to provide sufficient electricity.

Wind power

Wind power is produced when turbines harness the

power of the wind, especially in coastal areas where winds are strongest. Windmills have been used for hundreds of years as a source of power, but with modern technologies wind power can now be collected on a large scale from wind farms. Wind power is converted into electricity.

Nuclear power

Nuclear power is produced when a controlled nuclear explosion is used to power a large generator. Nuclear power stations create large amounts of energy, but the fuels they use are rare and expensive, and people worry that they are not safe and that they are harmful to the planet. There have been accidents at nuclear power stations in other countries, causing severe health problems from radioactivity. The waste from nuclear power stations is also radioactive and will remain so for thousands of years. So there is a problem of storing nuclear waste.

The European Union

The European Union (EU) is a group of democratic countries which have joined together. There are now 25 member states, and the EU has its own currency – the Euro. Not all of the countries use the Euro, preferring to keep their own currency.

Why a European Union?

Old frictions and rivalries between nations in the past led to instability or even war. Following World War I and World War II six European nations agreed to set up a group of countries within Europe who would work for permanent peace and also to encourage trade between each other. They called themselves the European Economic Community (or the EEC or the Common Market). These first six countries were France, West Germany, Italy, Belgium, the Netherlands and Luxembourg. The name European Union came later because the purpose of the EEC changed from being simply a trading partnershipinto an economic and political partnership.

What has the EU achieved?

Since it was founded, the EU has:
- achieved 50 years of peace in Europe
- helped to raise standards of living
- built a single Europe-wide market so that people, goods and money can move around as freely as if in one country
- launched the single EU currency, the Euro (€)
- strengthened Europe's position and voice in the world.

Which is the largest country in Europe?

By area France is the largest country, and Malta is the smallest. However Germany has the largest population and again Malta has the smallest.

Does the European Union have a president?

Yes. She or he is called the President of the Commission is selected by members of the European Council and is then approved by the European Parliament. The first president was Walter Hallstein from West Germany.

Euro notes are identical throughout the euro area, while coins have a common design on one face and designs representing symbols unique to each country on the other face.

London, England, has the largest population of any city in the European union, with over 7 million inhabitants. Berlin, in Germany, comes second with 3.5 million.

ARCTIC OCEAN

R U S S I A

• Moscow

Ust'Shchugor•

AND.	ANDORRA
BH.	BOSNIA HERZEGOVINA
CR.	CROATIA
CZ.R.	CZECH REPUBLIC
L.	LIECHTENSTEIN
LUX.	LUXEMBOURG
MC.	MACEDONIA
MN.	MONTENEGRO
MON.	MONACO
S.M.	SAN MARINO
SLA.	SLOVAKIA
SL.	SLOVENIA
SWITZ.	SWITZERLAND

What if we didn't have the EU?

Try imagining a world now without the EU: we would still need to get our passports stamped when visiting nearby countries. We'd have to change our currency when we crossed from France to Spain. European businesses would be involved in constant negotiations when working with one another, without being able to look at agreed guidance and rules. Some of the poorer countries in Europe might not have benefited from trade partnerships and grants. And although counties might argue, we still have peace.

The European Parliament

A lot of people are needed to do all of the work that is carried out by the EU.
The European Parliament represents around 450 million citizens. Its members are known as Members of the European Parliament (MEPs). Since the last European elections in 2004, there have been 732 MEPs.

The current 25 member states
Austria
Belgium
Cyprus
Czech Republic
Denmark
Estonia
Finland
France
Germany
Greece
Hungary
Ireland
Italy
Latvia
Lithuania
Luxembourg
Malta
Poland
Portugal
Slovakia
Slovenia
Spain
Sweden
The Netherlands
United Kingdom

Where is the European Parliament?

The parliament meets in two places – in Brussels and in Strasbourg – and the European Court of Justice is in Luxembourg. The European Bank is in Frankfurt.
For three weeks of the month the parliament meets in Belgium's capital city Brussels, where most committee and political group meetings take place, then for one week everyone goes to Strasbourg in France. The Strasbourg Parliament is on the border between Germany and France, which fought two world wars in the last century, it is also a symbol of Europe's peaceful new order.

Explorers

Human beings have always been explorers. Ever since cavemen set out to discover what lay beyond the horizon, we have been fascinated by the unknown and the undiscovered.

The promise of adventure

Nowadays we have complicated and detailed maps of the world. We learn all about geography and the peoples of other lands in school, and we can go to zoos or read in books about animals like lions and elephants. But imagine setting sail across an ocean not knowing what you would find, or being the first person from your country ever to see an elephant! Exciting adventures like these, and the promise of great treasure, have led people to become explorers, despite knowing they would face terrible dangers.

Early European explorers

As people learned to read and write they began to leave records of their travels. The medieval explorer Marco Polo (1254–1324) was the first man to cross the whole of Asia and to leave journals of what he had seen. Many great European explorers followed his example, returning from their travels with new maps and new treasures, and astonishing tales of the strange animals and plants and ways of life they had discovered.

The Age of Discovery

The 15th and 16th centuries are known as the Age of Discovery. At that time rival European countries, hungry for treasure and power, had powerful ships and navigational tools to help

them sail the oceans in search of new lands. The Spanish king Charles I gave the Portuguese sailor Ferdinand Magellan (1480–1521) five ships, and he set sail in 1519 on the first circumnavigation of (journey around) the globe. Many of his crew survived and the expedition was a success, but Magellan himself died during the voyage. The second successful circumnavigation was made by an English pirate called Francis Drake (1542–1596). Drake was supported by Queen Elizabeth, who provided him with ships and supplies in return for a large share of the treasures he promised to find. Although Drake sailed around the world, the treasures with which he presented Elizabeth were actually stolen from Spanish galleons!

Treasures from the East

Many explorers did return with treasures, although not the gold and silver they dreamed of finding but instead things like silks and spices from the Orient. Spices were at one time thought even more valuable than gold. They were highly prized by the wealthy for flavouring and preserving their food. For this reason we can see why the Portuguese explorer

Q&A?

Why do we sometimes refer to Native Americans as "Indians"?

That is what Christopher Columbus mistakenly called them, thinking he was in the Indies!

What is Il Milione?

That is the original name of Marco Polo's book about his travels to China. The name comes from Polo's family nickname, Emilione. We usually call the book 'The Travels of Marco Polo'.

The most famous of all these accidents is the discovery of the Americas by Christopher Columbus. Columbus set sail in 1492 thinking that, because the world was round, sailing west would get him to the rich East more quickly and safely. Not knowing that America existed, he sailed right into it!

Modern explorers

Since the Age of Discovery, exploration has continued. Explorers have discovered tribes in the heart of African rainforests, reached the North and South Poles and explored deep oceans in submarines. Modern-day explorers are often scientists, for example plant hunters looking for undiscovered species that might help cure diseases.

The journey continues

Perhaps the most exciting place we have yet to explore fully is the vastness of space, into which we send satellites and probes. One day astronauts may set out to travel to other planets just as Magellan and Columbus travelled to other lands!

Vasco da Gama (1460–1524) became famous for discovering a new and fast trading route to India.

New territories

When explorers went looking for gold they found other treasures and sometimes discovered places by accident. This was not surprising, because they didn't have good maps and believed the earth was much smaller than it is.

Fascinating
Facts

Christopher Columbus sailed over 5,000 miles of open seas.

The plant hunters of previous centuries brought us many of the plants we see in our gardens today. For example, tulips originally grew only in Turkey.

Film, Cinema *and* Theatre

For as long as people have told stories and acted them out, there has been some sort of theatre.

Greek theatre

Ancient Greek plays were not like those we see today. Firstly, a typical Greek theatre was huge – most seating around 15,000 people! These theatres were built into hillsides, with a semi-circular performance area for acting and dancing, and row upon row of tiered seating rising above it. With such a large space costumes had to be very bold, masks were wore to show emotions clearly. Gestures were made large and exaggerated so that everyone in the audience could see what was going on.

Ancient Greek plays had strict rules about characters, actors and plots. Every play had a chorus, a group of people who acted as narrator (storyteller) and portrayed the reactions of the public to events in the play, for example something the king had done or news about the Trojan War. With such a large space costumes had to be very bold, so masks were worn to show emotions clearly. Gestures were made large and exaggerated so that everyone in the audience could see what was going on.

New directions in theatre

Many theatre companies travelled around the country, performing in courtyards to local people, but in large towns and cities there were often several playhouses, though some early ones were little more than a raised wooden stage in an inn-yard. Later ones such as the famous Globe Theatre in London were purpose-built buildings with standing room for some and even elaborate covered seating for the higher paying customers. Theatres like the Globe often had devices such as trapdoors built into the stage for actors playing ghosts or goblins to appear from or disappear into!

The growth of modern theatre

The introduction of the proscenium arch during the 17th century established the traditional theatre form that still exists today. The proscenium theatre is one with a raised stage. It has a curtain that can be lowered or drawn closed. The space where the curtain falls is the proscenium arch. It was around this time that women began to join theatre companies.

The Hollywood sign in Los Angeles originally said 'Hollywoodland'.

Director Alfred Hitchcock appeared briefly in all of his films. These appearances are known as cameos.

During the 18th century the popular opera buffa (comic opera) introduced opera as a fashionable form of performance. An opera is a play with music. Mozart's The Marriage of Figaro is a very famous opera.

Alongside drama and opera, dance has played an important role in the theatre. Any form of organised movement (choreography) is called dance. Ballet, a very specific dance form, probably began in the 13th century, and eventually became very disciplined and is now loved by audiences around the world. The most well known ballets are Swan Lake and The Nutcracker.

The beginnings of film

As scientists experimented with different ways of capturing 'moving pictures' on film, it soon became possible to see actors on a screen instead of a stage. The Lumière brothers showed the first motion pictures to paying customers in Paris on December 28th 1895. These first films were very short, and included the first comedy, 'The Sprinkler

Sprinkled', which was about a gardener with a watering hose. The first real cinema was built in Paris in 1897 and movies became increasingly popular.

Early films

The first films were in black-and-white and were silent. Any words spoken by the characters appeared on the screen written on cards. Movie theatres often employed pianists to play music to match the action on screen. Full colour films were introduced in 1932. This added to the popularity of the cinema, and the 1930s became the 'Golden Age of Hollywood'. The cinema organ became extremely popular – sometimes the audience would sing along to the tunes.

What was the name of the first full-length 'talkie' (film with recorded sound)?

The first full-length 'talkie' was 'The Jazz Singer', released in 1927.

Who were Aeschylus, Sophocles, and Euripides?

They were the playwrights who wrote the only Greek tragedies that have survived and so are the most famous'

Fish *and* aquatic life

The world's oceans cover two-thirds of the Earth, and a huge variety of creatures live in the water. Fish constitute more than half the total number of known modern vertebrates (animals with backbones).

Crustaceans

There are approximately 39,000 species of crustaceans worldwide, including crabs, lobsters, shrimps, barnacles and woodlice. Most are aquatic (live in water) and the majority are marine (live in the sea).

Eels

Eels are fish that have evolved over time to lose their fins and scales. Some developed the ability to move over land, which is useful when they are stranded by receding floods. They are found in the sea and in fresh water. You may have seen puffins with lots of sand eels in their beaks.

Cnidaria

Cnidaria (with a silent c) are a group of animals including sea anemones, jellyfish and corals. Jellyfish are feared for their sting, which in some species can be deadly. The stings are caused by cells called nematocysts, which shoot out like miniature harpoons into their prey. The most dangerous species of jellyfish is the Chironex fleckeri, a box jellyfish from Australia. It is thought to have caused the death of more than 70 people during the last century in Australia alone!

Sea cucumbers

Despite their name, sea cucumbers are animals from the same family as sea urchins and starfish. In fact, they're more like giant leathery slugs than something to put in a salad. They come in all colours – from black to red-and-yellow-striped – and in all sizes. The largest is 6 ft (2 m) long.

Turtles

Some populations of green turtle migrate all the way from Ascension Island to the Brazilian coast to feed. During the breeding season they make the return journey to the island to mate and lay their eggs. What makes this journey so amazing is that the island is only 7 miles (11 km) wide, and the turtles travel 1,430 miles (2,300 km) each way.

Seahorses

The head of the seahorse resembles a horse's head, and its body has an elongated tail covered by about 50 rectangular bony plates. They can change colour so that they match their surroundings. This camouflage protects them from predators such as crabs, although with their bony armour there are very few animals that can eat them anyway. Seahorses are unique in that the male gives birth to the young and takes all responsibility for parental care.

Sharks

The whale shark is the largest fish in the world. It was probably named 'whale' because of its enormous size and the fact that, like most whales, it feeds by filtering water to take in small crustaceans and fish. But cold-blooded and with gills, these huge animals are a species of shark and harmless to humans. The basking shark is the second largest fish. It can be found off the shores of Britain. But if you swim in the sea, don't worry, this gaping giant feeds on plankton!

Shark attack

Great whites are top of the list of man-eaters, and are responsible for five to ten attacks a year. Their powerful teeth are triangular and serrated, and a great white can have as many as 3,000! These fearsome predators hunt fish, sea lions, seals, turtles, porpoises, and other sharks. They usually attack from below, taking a large bite of their prey and waiting for the victim to weaken from loss of blood. They can reach speeds of 25 miles/h (40 km/h) when in pursuit of prey, and have been known to leap out of the water. It is thought that shark attacks on humans are due to mistaken identity, as the silhouette of a swimmer viewed from below is similar to that of a seal or sea lion.

How many types of fish are there?

Scientists have recognised an estimated 22,000 living species, and new species are being discovered all the time.

Are woodlice insects?

Woodlice may look like insects, but in fact they're crustaceans and are related to crabs and lobsters. Most woodlice are found on land, but their ancestors used to live in water and woodlice still breathe with gills.

fascinating facts

The electric eel isn't a true eel; it's actually the most powerful electric fish. It builds up electricity in specially modified muscles and gives off a shock that's enough to kill its prey. It can produce a lethal charge of up to 500 volts!

The yellow-bellied sea snake's venom is more poisonous than a cobra's. These snakes have been known to bite humans, but if treated with respect they are not usually aggressive.

Flight

Since the earliest days, people have looked up at the sky and imagined flying like birds. In the legend, Icarus and his father made wings from feathers and wax, but Icarus flew too close to the sun, the wax melted, and he fell into the sea and drowned. In the real world, of course, they would not have been able to fly at all, because our arms are not strong enough for flight. In the natural world only birds, insects and some animals can fly. Birds use their wings to coast on warm, rising air currents. There are many different sizes and shapes of wings, and birds fly at different speeds.

Balloon flight

The first recorded manned balloon flight in history was made in a hot air balloon built by the Montgolfier brothers on November 21, 1783. The pilots, Jean-François Pilâtre de Rozier and Francois Laurent (the Marquis of d'Arlanders) flew for about 22 minutes.

Only a few days later Jacques Alexander Charles and Nicholas Louis Robert launched the first manned gas balloon. Again starting in Paris, the flight lasted over 2 hours and covered a distance of 25 miles (56 km).

Ballooning became fashionable and popular in the 18th century, and Ferdinand von Zeppelin made the first flight in a zeppelin (a type of airship) in 1900.

Early attempts at flight

Inventors first attempted, around 400 BC, to copy the birds by making wings and strapping them to their arms. None of these attempts worked, however, so people started to build machines to fly. They built gliders in the 9th century, which meant they could coast like birds on currents of air.

When was the first commercial passenger service?

In 1914, between St Petersburg (Russia) and Tampa, Florida (USA)

Who was the first woman to fly solo across the Atlantic?

Amelia Earhart made a transatlantic solo flight in 1932.

Aircraft

Aircraft are heavier than air but use thrust (forward motion created by the engine) to stay aloft. It was not until the start of the 20th century that heavier-than-air machines achieved flight. In 1903, the Wright brothers (Wilbur and Orville) built the first manned, power-driven, heavier-than-air flying machine. Their first flight was only twelve seconds long.

Acrobatic flying became popular, and newspapers offered large cash prizes for daredevil stunts. Long-distance flying also developed and an English newspaper sponsored a contest for the first flight across the English Channel. Louis Bleriot won this contest, flying from France to England in 1909 in a single wing plane. The first woman to gain a pilot's licence was Baroness Raymonde de la Roche, and the first aircraft to take off from water was flown by Henri Fabre.

Aircraft in wartime

The First World War was instrumental in the development of planes, from experiments to fully working machines. It was soon discovered that, to win the war, air control was vital. Aerial information, bombing and support provided valuable support to ground troops. World War I saw the birth of the fighter aircraft, or 'scouts', which still play a crucial role in modern history. The war also advanced bomber planes, so that they went from carrying only small bombs to deadly cargoes on purpose-built racks and housing.

In the 1930s both military and civil aircraft underwent a period of development. Commercial air travel was an accepted form of transport. The first airliners were born, and they began crossing larger distances. More

and more record-breaking flights were also being achieved. In 1927 Charles Lindbergh flew the first solo non-stop flight across the North Atlantic in his Ryan NYP monoplane, Spirit of St Louis.

Concorde

The Anglo-French machine Concorde was one of the world's greatest challenges in the history of aviation (flying). It cruised at more than twice the speed of sound at an altitude of 60,000 feet – eleven miles high. A typical flight from London to New York took fewer than four hours. Production of the plane ended in 1979, and all Concordes were withdrawn from service in 2000 after a crash near the Charles de Gaulle airport, Paris.

Helicopters

Helicopters were developed in the 20th century. The early designs were very unsuccessful, although some designs go back as far as the artist and inventor Leonardo da Vinci's sketchbooks. Helicopters are used in war, to transport troops quickly, evacuate injured soldiers, and also to fight. In the civilian world, helicopters can be used as 'air ambulances' to reach injured people quickly, and get them to hospital.

Helicopters can land in quite remote and restricted places as they don't need a runway for landing or taking off as most aeroplanes do.

Fascinating Facts

Captain Hans-Ulruch Rudel of Germany flew 2,530 combat missions during World War Two, and survived.

Human-powered and solar-powered aircraft have made successful flights across the English Channel.

The first air transport company was launched in 1843, but it failed because its prices were too high.

Food and farming

W e all know the importance of healthy eating to help keep us free from illness, and keep our bodies in good working condition. But do we know which foods to eat, and where they come from? Farming is an efficient way of growing the types of food people want to eat.

Healthy food

As a general rule, a balanced diet includes fruit and vegetables, bread, cereals or potatoes, milk and dairy foods, meat or fish, and in limited amounts of foods containing fat and sugar.

Five a day

To be strong and healthy, you need to eat lots of fruit and vegetables. This is important for good health, and can protect against illness. There are lots of fruit and vegetables which provide vital vitamins and fibre. Some of these can be grown in our own back gardens, such as carrots, broad beans, cucumbers, apples, gooseberries and rhubarb. Growing your own food helps to keep you active, and it's fun to do.

Dairy foods

As well as being one of the best sources of calcium, dairy products also provide protein, vitamins and minerals, and they're important for healthy bones and teeth. Milk and cheese are examples of dairy products. In Britain these foods come mainly from cows, sheep and goats.

Sustainable farming

Until early last century, all British farmers used sustainable methods, because they had little choice. Sustainable farming means growing food in ways that enable farmers to continue doing it. For example, traditional farmers depend on fossil fuels like oil for running their farm machines, on fertilisers to make plants grow better, and on pesticides to kill the insects that eat plants. When there's no oil left, how will farmers manage without tractors? What will they use instead of oil-based fertilisers?

Q&A?

Are there risks with GM food?

Many people are suspicious of GM ingredients in food, as we don't know the risks that may be involved with eating these regularly. It will probably be a while before we know of any possible side effects with GM foods.

Could GM farming be one solution to the problem of world hunger?

GM methods can increase production and lower the cost of food. They can be grown faster and cheaper, especially in areas suffering from drought.

Industrial farming

Industrial farming, also known as intensive agriculture, uses factory-type methods to produce large quantities of food. But in the long term, these methods may damage the land and pollute the air. Intensive farming depends on cheap and plentiful oil. It is not sustainable and people won't be able to keep on doing it because the oil under the ground will eventually run out. Also, the excessive use of oil is damaging the planet by causing climate change.

Organic farming

Organic farming is sustainable farming. It needs more workers and fewer machines, so more people will have farm jobs. And organic farming is said to be kinder to the land. But food produced by organic farming is more expensive than food produced by intensive farming.

Genetic engineering

Genetically modified (GM) crops are foods that have had a gene extracted from one plant, which has been placed into a different plant. GM crops are designed for many purposes, for example to produce a crop that stays fresh longer and to produce food with improved taste and quality.

GM plants could be kinder to the environment if they need fewer pesticides, fertilisers and water. Some people see GM technology as a way to help people in poor countries grow food.

Lack of calcium (found in dairy products and leafy green vegetables) can prevent healthy bones forming.

A deficiency of vitamin A (from carrots and other highly coloured fruit and vegetables) can harm your eyesight.

Kiwi fruits contain nearly twice as much vitamin C as oranges.

Oily fish is essential for the development of the brain and nervous system, whilst eggs contain many nutrients which are crucial for healthy growth.

Fascinating facts

Food *and Healthy Eating*

Healthy eating means having a healthy, balanced diet. Eating a range of foods every day is just as important to maintaining good health as taking regular exercise. Nutritional needs vary according to an individual's age and lifestyle. Eating too many foods which are not good for us can lead to being overweight and can also cause illness.

What is a balanced diet?

Generally having a good balance of grain foods, vegetables, fresh fruit, meat or fish and dairy products is considered to be healthy. It's better for our health if we don't eat too many sugary or fatty foods such as sweets and chips. Vegetarians, people who don't eat meat, should take care that they get enough protein from their food by eating nuts or pulses (peas and beans).

The elements essential to a balanced diet are:

- Grain foods: bread, rice, cereals and pasta – 6–11 servings each day.
- Vegetables: especially green leafy vegetables like broccoli – 3–5 servings each day.
- Fresh fruit: 2–4 servings each day.
- Protein: meat, fish, eggs, nuts, beans – 2–3 servings each day.

- Dairy products: cheese and yogurt – 2-3 servings every other day.

What's wrong with fast food?

Fast foods like burgers and deep fried foods are often very high in calories (units of energy) but low in nutrients. This means that it is very easy to gain weight by eating these foods, unless we take a great deal of exercise, but also need other foods to provide essential nutrients.

What about salt and sugar?

Salt helps to flavour food and to keep it fresh longer, but can lead to health problems such as high blood pressure if we have too much. Sugar is found naturally in fruit but high consumption of processed sugar, which is made from sugar cane or sugar beet,

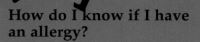

How do I know if I have an allergy?	*People with allergies may suffer from skin rashes, sickness or breathing difficulties if they eat the wrong food.*
Why should I exercise?	*Exercise, as well as eating sensible food, helps to keep our body healthy and active.*

Sugar on our teeth turns into acid within 5 minutes! The acid begins to dissolve the tooth surface and very soon dental decay occurs.

Did you know that more than half of your weight is just water? So as well as giving your body all the food it needs each day to keep healthy, you need at least 5 glasses of liquid each day.

can lead to weight problems and to diabetes. Because salt and sugar are contained in many ready-made foods which we buy it is often difficult to know how much we are consuming so adding as little as possible to foods is a good way to keep our consumption down.

What are allergies?

Some people are allergic to certain foods or ingredients. If you have an allergy it is important to check your food otherwise you may become ill. Some common allergies, which many people suffer from, are peanuts, shellfish, artificial dyes and colours. The labels on foods we buy usually have detailed nutritional information to help us to avoid foods which may make us ill.

Why is exercise important?

Exercise is important for many reasons – the best being because it keeps your body Healthy. Daily exercise helps prevent diseases, improves stamina, controls weight and will improve your quality of life. Like food, exercise should be balanced – building up a daily routine that mirrors the lifestyle that you lead.

France

France is the third largest country in Europe, and has the fourth highest population. Despite having a rural landscape, over 70% of the population live in the cities, with more than 16% in the greater Paris area.

Wines

France is known the world over for its fine wines, and its income from wine is higher than that of any other nation, though the Italians produce more quantity and the Spanish have more land under vineyards.

The different types of wine are grown in different areas of France according to the soil type and climate. Some of the well-known names are Champagne, Bordeaux and Burgundy. France did not export wine until after 1830, but it was in the last 50 years when transport links really improved that the French themselves started appreciating wines made outside their own locale. Before that they only drank their local wine.

Is it true that France is the world's most visited tourist destination with 75 million visitors a year?

Film stars flock to Cannes each spring; millions go skiing in the winter to places like Chamonix, and take beach holidays in summer. The great cities, monuments and scenery attract visitors all the year around.

Has France always been one of the world's most powerful and wealthy countries?

Yes for over the last 1,000 years. The Romans built roads, cities and aqueducts, such as Pont Du Gard and in the Middle Ages rich landowners and aristocrats built many grand chateaux.

Famous landmarks

In the 20th century many modern landmarks were built in Paris, the most famous being the glass pyramid at the entrance to the Louvre, the main art gallery which is home to Leonardo da Vinci's famous painting of the Mona Lisa, and the Pompidou Centre, which houses the Musée

Every July more than 100 professional cyclists race in the Tour de France. The race last three weeks and is approximately 2,485 miles (4,000 km) long.

A total of 270 million trees were destroyed by a storm that hit France in December 1999. The storm lasted 30 hours, and caused 87 deaths.

Fascinating **Facts**

National d'Art Moderne (The National Museum of Modern Art).

La Tour Eiffel

The Eiffel Tower (La Tour Eiffel) is the most famous landmark and tourist attraction in Paris. It was built in 1889 for the Great Exhibition and was originally only meant to be a temporary structure. It is named after its architect, Gustave Eiffel. It is by far the highest structure in Paris at 986 ft (300 m) excluding the radio antenna, which was added later.

It has been repainted 17 times since it was built, to protect it from rust. That is an average of once every seven years. It has changed colour several times, from reddish brown to yellow ochre, then to chestnut brown and finally to the bronze it is today.

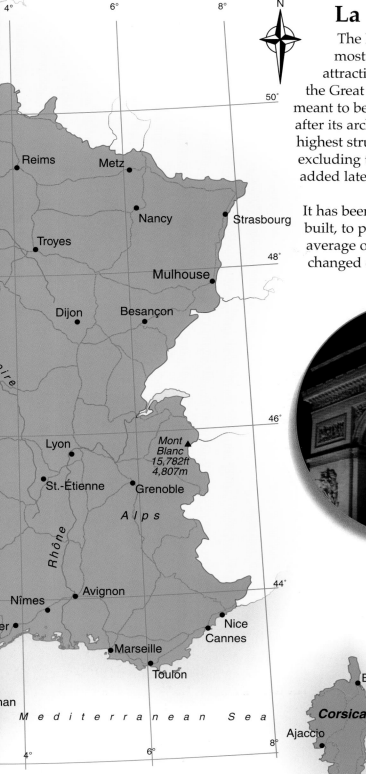

L'Arc de Triomphe

The Arc de Triomphe is another of the very distinctive landmarks in Paris. It copies the style that the Romans used to commemorate their military conquests, but is larger than anything that the Romans built. It was planned in 1806 to celebrate Napolean Bonaparte's victory at Austerlitz, but was not completed until 1836. In the early days of flying a dare devil flew his aeroplane through it!

Transport

France invests much money in excellent motorways and railways. Rail travel is cheap and the 186 miles/h (300 km/h) Train Grande Vitesse (TGV) connects all the major cities. There are also rail links to London and many other countries.

Power

Almost 80% of France's electricity is generated by nuclear power, and so the French people are less worried about high oil costs than almost any other European country. In mountainous areas, electricity is generated by hydro electric power stations.

Reims
Metz
Nancy
Strasbourg
Troyes
Mulhouse
Dijon   Besançon
Lyon   Mont Blanc 15,782ft 4,807m
St.-Étienne   Grenoble
Alps
Rhône
Avignon
Nîmes   Nice   Cannes
Marseille
Toulon
Bastia
Corsica
Ajaccio
Bonifacio
Mediterranean Sea
oire

Gandhi

Mohandas Karamchand Gandhi was born in Porbandar, Gujarat, India in 1869. He is more commonly known as Mahatma Gandhi ('Mahatma' means 'Great Soul' in Sanskrit), or Bapu, which in many Indian languages means 'father'. He became a great spiritual and political leader, and led the successful campaign for India's independence from Britain. He inspired the civil rights movement in America, and the movement to end racism and division in South Africa.

His family was Hindu, and so from an early age he followed that religion's teachings. These included being vegetarian (not eating meat), not harming living creatures, respecting others, and fasting (not eating or drinking for a long time) to cleanse the body. He did badly at school, and only just got in to Bombay University. He had heard that England was 'the very centre of civilisation', and he came to London in 1888, to study Law. However, he could not stomach the English food, and of course refused to eat meat, so he became a very active vegetarian, joining societies and writing articles about vegetarianism.

South Africa

As a young man, Gandhi was quiet, and not very interested in how the world was run. He often got very nervous in court. He started to change after he went to work in South Africa, in 1893. Several events made him start to stand up for himself and the rights of his countrymen. One of these was when a court judge asked him to remove his turban. Gandhi refused and stormed out of the court. Another time, a train conductor tried to make Gandhi move from First Class to Third, even though he had a First Class ticket. Gandhi used his lawyer's training to sue the company, and he won!

After learning of the racism, oppression and injustices towards Indians in South Africa, he started to become an active protester. He organised petitions to stop the government taking away the Indians' right to vote in elections and he founded the Natal Indian Congress in 1894.

Return to India

After twenty years helping his fellow Indians in South Africa, Gandhi returned to India to help people in his homeland. In the Champaran district, he helped poor farmers to get a better deal, and to raise standards of living in the poor, country villages. Then, in the Punjab, British Indian Army soldiers massacred 379 Indian men, women and children at Amritsar in 1919. This caused deep anger in India, and there was an increase in protesting, rioting and violence.

But Gandhi did not believe in violence. Gandhi had

developed the idea of peaceful non-cooperation in South Africa. It was known as the 'satyagraha', or 'devotion to truth'.

The Indian National Congress, a political party, accepted Gandhi's idea of non-violence, and made him leader of their party. From then on, Gandhi started leading towards independence.

Satyagrahas

By 1920, Gandhi was a leading figure in Indian politics. He organised satyagrahas against the government. They were always peaceful. For example, the Indians would boycott (stop buying) British goods to harm the British economy.

Unfortunately, Gandhi was arrested in 1922, and imprisoned for six years. He was released after only two years, but by this time the Indian National Congress had broken apart. Gandhi did not achieve much for several years, until the Calcutta Congress in 1928, where he demanded full independence from the British for India.

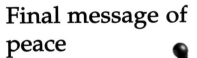

Final message of peace

Gandhi continued to negotiate with the British government for many years, and in 1945 he started negotiations with the new Labour government. In 1947, a plan was formed to create the separate, independent nations of India and Pakistan. India would be a Hindu country, and Pakistan a Muslim country. The old nation of India was divided, though, and there was rioting. Gandhi appealed for calm, and went on a fast, which

stopped the rioting. Sadly, Gandhi was shot dead by a young Hindu fanatic before he could see India become fully independent.

Gandhi is remembered as a man of peace and great wisdom. His message of peace and love will live on. As he said himself:

'When I despair, I remember that all through history the way of truth and love has won. There have been tyrants and murderers and for a time they seem invincible, but in the end, they always fall.'

He was assassinated in 1948.

Gandhi's birthday, October 2nd, is commemorated each year in India as Gandhi Jayanti, and it is a public holiday. There is also a Gandhi series of currency (money) in India.

Gandhi was nominated for the Nobel Peace Price five times, but did not win it once.

Genetics

Every human has similar characteristics, such as hair, legs and eyes. But because of our unique DNA, we all have different characteristics such as hair colour and eye colour. We inherit chromosomes from our parents, which carry all the genetic information needed to make each of us individual.

Each paired chromosome is composed of two tightly coiled strands of DNA (Deoxyribonucleic acid) that join in the middle to form an X shape. These strands of DNA have sections called genes, which contain the information that makes us unique. Unless you have an identical twin, your DNA is different from the DNA of every other person in the world, though it is the same in every cell in your body,

The vast majority of people have two copies of each gene, as we get one copy from each of our parents.

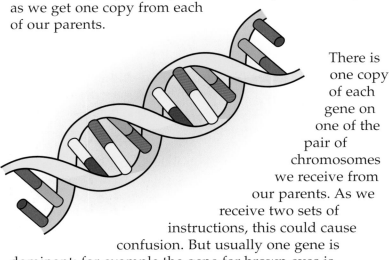

There is one copy of each gene on one of the pair of chromosomes we receive from our parents. As we receive two sets of instructions, this could cause confusion. But usually one gene is dominant: for example the gene for brown eyes is dominant over the gene for blue eyes (the gene for blue eyes is said to be recessive).

A momentous discovery

In 1953 two scientists, James D. Watson and Francis Crick, celebrated the fact that they had unravelled the structure of DNA. DNA is the material that makes up genes which pass hereditary characteristics from one parent to another. That momentous discovery was the culmination of research by scientists Maurice Wilkins and Rosalind Franklin. Powerful and controversial technologies are now available, including genetic engineering, stem cell research and DNA fingerprinting.

DNA fingerprinting

Each person's DNA is as unique as a fingerprint. Normal fingerprints occur only on the fingertips and can be altered by surgery. DNA 'fingerprints', however, can be taken even from bloodstained clothing and cannot be altered by any known treatment. Everyone has the same DNA chemical structure, but the order of the base pairs in each person's DNA is different. There are so many millions of base pairs in a set of DNA that everyone has a different sequence. By identifying repeated patterns of

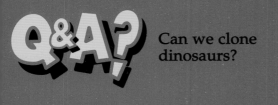

Can we clone dinosaurs?

Cloning DNA from prehistoric dinosaur DNA is impossible now. Dinosaurs have billions of base pairs in their DNA, while the most pairs we found are only up to pair 250. Although it is impossible now, it may someday happen in the future.

What is DNA fingerprinting used for?

DNA fingerprinting can be used for anything from determining a biological mother or father to identifying the suspect of a crime.

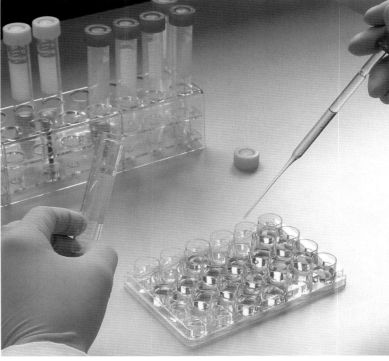

DNA, scientists can identify whether DNA samples are from the same person, related people or people who are not related.

Genetic engineering

Scientists have the power to manipulate genes using genetic engineering. For years humans have been breeding animals and plants to get the characteristics they desire, for example, species that produce a lot of babies or new plants. Two techniques used to do this are selective breeding (breeding animals and plants by controlling the environment) and cross breeding (breeding species with the same ancestors). A clone is any organism whose genetic information is identical to that of a 'mother organism'

from which it was created. Some clones exist in nature; others are created by scientists. Dolly the sheep was the first mammal cloned from an adult cell.

James Watson, Francis Crick and Maurice Wilkins were awarded the Nobel Prize for their work in 1962. Rosalind Franklin died of cancer in April 1958, aged just 37, so never received a Nobel Prize for her crucial work in the discovery of DNA.

A giant model of a section of DNA, built from laboratory clamps and pieces of metal, is now in the Science Museum in London.

fascinating Facts

Geology

Geology is the study of materials in the Earth, and their history. Geologists can find out which minerals a rock contains, and where rocks were formed. They look for signs of past geological events such as volcanoes, landslides, earthquakes, acid rain and tsunamis, and study rocks for signs of climate change.

Gemstones

Many gemstones come from inside the earth, and are dug out to make the stones used in jewellery. Sapphires are one of the most popular gemstones, with their lovely blue colour. Diamonds are one of the best-known gemstones. They are made of carbon which is almost pure, crystallised (formed into crystals) under extremes of heat and pressure. Diamonds may be colourless, or yellow, brown, orange, blue, green, pink or black. Brightly coloured diamonds are rarer and more expensive. The rarest and most highly prized colour is a deep pink-red. The deep blue Hope diamond and blue Eugenie diamond, both in America's Smithsonian collection, are among the world's most famous diamonds.

Pearls

Throughout history, pearls have been one of the most expensive and sought-after gems. Early man probably discovered the first pearls many thousands of years ago, while searching the seashore for food. Countless references to the pearl can be found in the religions and myths of many cultures. A natural or Oriental pearl forms when an irritant works its way into a particular species of mollusc. A mollusc is a water creature with a shell, such as an oyster, mussel or clam. As a defence mechanism, the mollusc produces a fluid to coat the irritant. Layer upon layer of this coating is deposited on the irritant, for protection, until a lustrous pearl is formed. A cultured

What are minerals?

Materials that can be mined (dug out) are called minerals.

Are there minerals in the sea?

Seawater contains many minerals, including up to half a ton of gold in every cubic kilometre (0.2399 cubic miles). But the cost of extracting the gold is greater than the gold itself.

(man-made) pearl undergoes the same process, but the irritant is a surgically implanted bead or piece of shell.

Sand

Sand is shell and rock that has been worn down by wind and rain into tiny grains.

Sand, gravel, silt and clay are collectively known as sediment, and are produced by the physical and chemical breakdown of rocks. The composition of sand depends on the source material. For example, the sand around volcanic islands is often made up of rock fragments and other minerals from volcanoes – it can even sometimes be black! In contrast, sediment found on the beaches of southern California is largely composed of quartz, one of the most long-lasting minerals.

In areas where there is no good source of sedimentary material from mountains or volcanoes, sand may consist of shell fragments, coral and the skeletons of small creatures.

Fascinating Facts

Only 20% of mined diamonds are used in jewellery, because most are unsuitable. A flawless diamond (without a flaw or fault) is vary rare.

A ham sandwich eaten on the beach may contain over 7,000 grains of sand.

Certain beaches and sand dunes create mysterious sounds that scientists can't explain. The sand may sing, whistle, boom, bark, and even croak like a frog.

Germany

A major industrialised nation, Germany is home to the world's third largest economy, after the United States and Japan. It is a leading producer of products such as iron and steel, machinery and machine tools and automobiles. The famous and luxurious cars of BMW, Mercedes and Porsche are all German makes.

Autobahn

The world's first motorway was built in Berlin between 1913 and 1921. By the end of World War II, the Autobahn network totalled 1,322 miles (2,128 km). There are now over 7,456 miles (12,000 km) of motorway, making the Autobahn network the world's second largest superhighway system after the United States Interstate system.

Why do German children go to school on Saturday mornings?

Their normal school day starts at about 8:00 a.m., and ends around 2:00 p.m. so Saturday morning school makes up for the shorter days.

Where do Germans go for beach holidays?

The German coast generally means heading for the North Sea or Baltic Sea coasts. Most Germans prefer to go south to France or Spain for warmer, sunnier beaches and swimming.

In Germany you can buy more than 300 sorts of bread and more than 1,500 types of sausages and cold meats.

Germans are the world champions in paper recycling, reusing over 75% of all paper consumed.

Berlin

Berlin, Europe's second largest city, is the capital of Germany. It is situated on the banks of the River Spree in the northeast of the country. The city attracts visitors of all

ages with its world-class museums, its new art scene and music clubs. Children especially like the city's beautiful parks and its two famous zoos. Each year since the early 1990s, the Love Parade, the world's biggest techno rave, has streamed through Berlin, bringing more than one million young people from all over the globe to each gathering.

Berlin Wall

After World War II Germany was split into West Germany and East Germany. Many East Germans moved to the West where life was freer and richer. In 1961 the East surrounded West Berlin with a concrete wall, 13 ft (4 m) high and 103 miles (166 km) long. At least 170 people died trying to cross the border. East Germany reunited with West Germany in 1990 and the wall was removed.

The Berlin Wall is now commemorated by a few remaining sections and by a museum and shop near the site of the most famous crossing point, Checkpoint Charlie.

Glass

Throughout the ages, glass has used by both artists and scientists. Glass was 'blown' by hand until the invention of a glass casting process around 1688 which made it possible to produce far greater amounts. In the early 19th century a glass-pressing machine was invented, and cheap, mass-produced glass articles were manufactured for the first time.

Coloured glass

Glass is normally green. Adding colorants can make it more transparent by 'cancelling out' the green colour or by changing its colour altogether. Some of the colorants used are light blue, dark blue, and red. Coloured glass has been used since ancient times for decorative purposes – it has been found by archaeologists in Roman mosaics, Viking beads and Egyptian enamels.

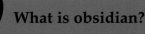

What is obsidian?

Obsidian is a shiny, black, translucent substance formed when volcanic lava comes into contact with water and is cooled quickly. It is glass produced naturally

Was early glass used only for decoration?

No. The Romans also used it for windows, mirrors and magnifying glasses.

Stained glass

The art of stained glass window making began in Eastern Asia among Muslim designers. Stained glass windows reached the height of their popularity in the late Middle Ages, when they were an essential feature of every church. Stained glass windows are made by cutting coloured glass into different shapes, then assembling the pieces to make a picture or design, using strips of lead or copper foil to hold the pieces together.

The pieces are soldered together and placed in a frame to create a finished window.

Fibre-optics

Optical fibres conduct light. They are made of very pure glass which allows light to be transmitted. This means that data such as telephone conversations, television pictures and computer transmissions can be sent in large volumes and over long distances without losing quality.

An optical fibre is thinner than just one human hair, yet stronger than a steel fibre of the same diameter. It can carry thousands of times more information than a copper wire, making optical fibre cables much lighter and more space efficient.

Glass in space

Space shuttles have triple-paned glass windows. The two outer panes are designed to withstand hot temperatures at re-entry to the atmosphere and the super-strong inner pane is designed to maintain the shuttle's cabin pressure. A special glass ceramic is used for the Shuttle's heat resistant tile retainers, protecting the Shuttle and its crew from the incredible heat of re-entry.

Recycled glass

It is much better to recycle used glass than to throw it away! New uses for recycled glass are being discovered all the time. For example, powdered glass can be used during brick and tile manufacture and 'processed sand' can be used to produce sports turf. Processed sand is artificial sand made from 100% recycled glass!

The world's largest...

Glass Sculpture

The largest glass sculpture ever made is a ceiling chandelier called Fiori di Como in the Bellagio Hotel in Las Vegas, USA. It measures 66 ft x 30 ft (20 m x 9 m) and was created by the American Dale Chihuly. It consists of 10,000 lb (4,535 kg) of steel and 40,000 lb (18,143 kg) of hand-blown glass in about 40 colours.

Windows

The largest windows in the world are those in the Palace of Industry and Technology at Rondpoint de la Défense, Paris. The three matching windows, made up of a large number of panes of glass, have an extreme width of 715 ft (218 m) and a maximum height of 164 ft (50 m). That means each window is bigger than a house!

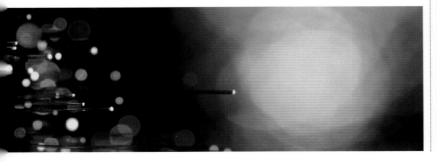

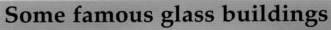

fascinating Facts

The oldest known specimens of man-made glass were discovered in ancient Egypt. The Egyptians considered glass as valuable as gold!

From the 14th century the most famous glass-blowing centre in Europe was in Venice (Italy). Venetian glass-blowers developed many new techniques and became famous for luxury items such as dinner ware and mirrors.

Some famous glass buildings

We are used to seeing glass as part of buildings, but some buildings are built almost entirely of glass.
• The Crystal Palace was built in London to house the Great Exhibition of 1851. Over 13,000 exhibits were displayed and viewed by over 6,200,000 visitors. After the Exhibition was over, the whole palace was moved to a new location in London in what is now called Crystal Palace Park. Sadly, most of this extraordinary building was destroyed by a fire in 1936.
• The Louvre Glass Pyramid is a large steel and glass pyramid at the front of the Louvre Museum in Paris, built as part of a new entrance to the museum.

Global Warming

Many scientists believe that gases in the air are causing Earth's climate to gradually become hotter. This is called global warming.

What is the greenhouse effect?

In Earth's atmosphere are tiny amounts of gases called 'greenhouse gases'. These gases let the sun's rays pass through to Earth but hold in the heat that comes up from the sun-warmed Earth. This is called the 'greenhouse effect' – a natural process by which the Earth's atmosphere traps some of the sun's energy. It is this warmth that allows the Earth to support life – just as a greenhouse in your garden traps heat to keep growing plants warm enough.

Temperature and climate change

Measurements from the past 100 years show that Earth's temperature has increased by 1°F (0.6°C). But scientists expect that over the next 100 years it will increase by an extra 2–6°F (1–3°C). This may not sound like much, but it could make the difference between life and death for some species on Earth, and dramatic changes to our climate!

A natural process gone wrong

Most scientists believe humans are now creating too many greenhouse gases, unnaturally increasing the greenhouse effect. When too many greenhouse gases are added to the atmosphere, the 'walls' of our greenhouse (the 'thermal blanket') get thicker. More heat gets trapped in the atmosphere and the temperature of the Earth goes up. A process that has been beneficial to life on earth becomes potentially harmful.

Q&A?

Where are glaciers found?

There is some kind of glacier found on every continent!

How long have we known about the greenhouse effect?

The French scientist Joseph Fourier first wrote about this in 1824, though he didn't call it the greenhouse effect.

Fascinating Facts

The last Ice Age was a mere 7°F colder than today. That's a little less than 4°C!

The six hottest recorded years in history were all in the 1990s.

What is causing global warming?

- Burning fossils fuels such as coal releases carbon dioxide, one of the greenhouse gases that contributes to global warming.
- Deforestation – cutting or burning down huge areas of the world's forests which increases the carbon dioxide in the atmosphere. This is because trees and other plants 'breathe in' carbon dioxide and 'breathe out' oxygen, thus helping to lower the amounts of carbon dioxide in our air.
- As rubbish decays, another harmful greenhouse gas called methane is released into the atmosphere.

Possible consequences of global warming

Melting ice – Ice covers 3% of the Earth's surface and is the world's largest supply of fresh water. Warmer weather causes glaciers (huge, slow-moving sheets of ice) – and even the polar ice caps – to melt. Many of our glaciers are already melting.

Rising seas – Melting glaciers add water to the ocean. Rising sea levels would mean coastal flooding and could cause salt water to flow into areas where salt would harm plants and animals.

Droughts and diseases – Cold places on Earth may become warmer, and this could mean a chance to plant crops in places formerly too cold. However, areas that already have hot climates might become too hot, bringing drought and leaving people without enough to eat. Tropical diseases like malaria might become more common in newly warmed areas.

Extreme weather – A warmer world is expected to experience more extreme weather – more rain during wet times, more powerful storms and longer periods of drought.

What can we do?

There are many things people can do to help stop global warming. These are just some of them:

- **Save electricity** – Use low-energy light bulbs and switch things off when they are not needed.
- **Reduce car use** – Walk, cycle or take the bus.

- **Recycle** – Plastic bags, cans, newspapers and many other items can be recycled, so that less rubbish goes to landfill sites. Buy recyclable products instead of non-recyclable ones.
- **Reuse** – Even better than recycling is using things again. Buy things that have less packaging and create less waste.
- **Choose items carefully** – Some cars are better for the environment than others because they can travel longer on a smaller amount of fuel.
- **Plant trees** – Trees absorb carbon dioxide from the air.

Gravity

Force is the pressure used when something is pushed or pulled. Forces are all round us. Gravity is a natural force that pulls objects on or near the Earth's surface towards its centre. In other words, it keeps us all fixed to the surface of the earth.

Gravity keeps the moon going round the Earth, the Earth going round the sun, and the sun going round the centre of the Milky Way. It's the weakest of the four fundamental forces of nature (electromagnetic, weak nuclear, and strong nuclear are the other three), but gravity is the force that governs motion in the universe.

Objects with mass (a measure of weight) attract each other, no matter how small or large they are. The strength of attraction depends on the weight of the objects and the distance between them.

Every object has a centre of gravity, the point at which the weight of the object is equally distributed. Objects with more mass have more gravitational pull, those closer together have less gravitational pull.

Q&A?

Are clouds affected by gravity?

No, because clouds are made of very small particles of ice and water and are too light, and so they just float. However they can combine together and form rain drops The rain drops are much bigger and so gravity pulls them down.

Is gravity the same everywhere?

Gravity at the equator is slightly less than at the North Pole, because the earth bulges at the equator and you are further from the centre of the earth.

In orbit

What keeps an object in orbit? What keeps the moon from falling to earth, or the earth from falling into the sun? An object remains in orbit around a mass, such as a planet, due to that planet's gravity. For instance, the earth is surrounded by it's own gravitational field, and so objects in orbit around the earth are attracted to the earth and therefore maintain their orbit. The force of the gravitational field depends upon the mass of the mass. The attractive force (the force which attracts the moving object) changes the motion of the object from a straight line to a closed curve, as it begins orbiting the massive body. In effect, the object is 'falling' around the massive body.

If you could turn off gravity, mathematicians predict that space and time would also vanish.

Astronauts discovered many changes in their bodies by living in a 'weightless' environment. Their bones lost calcium, their kidneys worked harder, there was excess fluid in their faces and chests, their muscles and hearts shrank.

Isaac Newton

He was the first person to study gravity seriously, and he had the insight to realise that the force that holds us to the Earth is the same one that keeps the planets in their orbits around the sun. He worked out the mathematical nature of the mutual (two-way) force, and he correctly argued that gravity acts across the entire universe.

Newton had read Galileo and Johannes Kepler's work on how planets circle the sun and how things fell to the Earth. He wondered whether the force that kept the moon from being thrown away from the Earth could explain gravity on the Earth's surface. Newton made this link in 1666, and called his findings the Law of Universal Gravitation. There is a famous story that Newton made the connection between the two ideas because of an apple falling in an orchard. However, it is more likely that the idea did not come to him in a flash of inspiration, but was developed over time.

Albert Einstein

Newton's description remained unchanged until Albert Einstein published his General Theory of Relativity in 1915. Einstein modified Newton's view of gravity by arguing that the gravitational force is a sign of the curvature of space-time. Although Einstein's idea is necessary for describing the evolution of the universe as a whole, Newton's theory works well enough when gravitational forces are not very strong.

You can read more about Albert Einstein on Pages 60-61

The Greeks

The ancient Greeks (mainly the Athenians, people from the city of Athens) believed that individuals should be free as long as they acted within the laws of Greece. To strive for excellence, no matter what the challenge, was the method by which they achieved such phenomenal accomplishments. Although many people became soldiers and athletes, others ventured into philosophy, drama, pottery and the arts.

Culture

The artistic talents of the Athenians can be viewed through many different forms which have survived for centuries, such as architectural designs, sculptures, pottery and fine jewellery.

At the Theatre of Dionysia, named after the god of wine, a religious festival was held in honour of the gods. For ten days Athenians filled the theatre to see plays performed by their favourite poets and playwrights. Women were not allowed to take part. The men wore elaborate masks and costumes while performing both male and female roles.

The Olympics

The Olympic Games were the greatest national festival for the Athenians. Held every four years, athletes came from all regions of Greece to compete in the great Stadium of Olympia and honour their supreme god, Zeus. At the conclusion of The Games, the winners were presented with garlands and crowned with olive wreaths.

Ancient Greece was not a single nation, but made up of a number of city-states called polis which were dotted across the mainland, the islands of the Aegean and Ionian seas, and along the coast of what is now Turkey.

Athens, named after Athena, the goddess of wisdom and the city's patron, was the intellectual centre of Greece, and one of the first city-states.

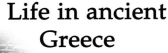

Life in ancient Greece

Athenian soldiers were required to serve two years in the military. After the first year, they were given a sword and a shield with the state's emblem on it. Although they

Why did the actors play male and female roles?

Women were not allowed to participate in drama activities.

What was the most important event at the Olympic Games?

The pentathlon, where an athlete competed in five different events.

served only two years, they could be called at any moment up to the age of sixty. Most wars between city-states were due to problems concerning harvests or

livestock, and lasted only a day or so. Heralds were government officials who travelled throughout Greece carrying important messages for their city-states. They held a special stick as a sign of their authority and were under the protection of the messenger god Hermes – people were not allowed to attack them, even during war, as this was seen as breaking international law. Farmers herded goats and sheep for their milk, meat and wool, as well as keeping pigs and chickens. The three most important crops were barley and other grains for grinding into flour, grapes, which were mainly used to make wine, and olives, which were crushed for their oil. Gods were usually served by priests in ancient Greece, and goddesses were served by priestesses. Often the job was for life, but some priests and priestesses were ordinary citizens who served for two to four years, or just during religious festivals. Their duties ranged from supervising rituals and taking part in festivals, to conducting weddings and funerals.

Mythology

This is a collection of stories that explain how the world began and described the lives of the gods and goddesses as well as of the ordinary people. The stories are passed down to us through oral and written traditions as well as from vase paintings.

The Cyclops were giants who were thrown into the underworld by their brother Cronus. But Zeus, son of Cronus, released the giants and in gratitude they gave him the gifts of thunder and lightning. So he became ruler of the Olympian gods.

Pegasus was the winged horse who was the son of Poseidon (god of the sea) and the Gorgon Medusa. Pegasus was entrusted by Zeus to bring him his lightning and thunderbolts.

Fascinating Facts

Heat *and* fire

Without the sun we wouldn't be here and there would be no life on earth. Humans have been using heat from the sun (solar energy) for thousands of years. In more recent times people used simple magnifying glasses to concentrate the light of the sun into beams so hot they made wood catch fire.

The Greeks were the first to use solar architecture, over 2,000 years ago. They built their houses so that the sun's rays entered during the winter, but couldn't enter during the summer. The Romans had the idea of putting glass in windows, which allowed the sun's light to pass through but trapped its heat. They even built glass greenhouses so that they could enjoy fruit and vegetables all winter.

In the 1700s people discovered that you could make water boil by collecting the sun's heat behind a few panes of glass – a solar hot water heater. From the early 1920s to the 1930s, people were heating their water with solar hot water heaters. But using solar panels to turn the sun's light into electricity is new. That technology was invented only 50 years ago.

Fire

Our ancestors created fire and used it to stay alive. They rubbed sticks against one another or hit pieces of stone called flint together, which created sparks that they made into fire. It provides warmth and comfort, it can cook and preserve food, purify water, sterilise bandages, be used to produce tools and weapons, as a signal for rescue, and provide protection from animals.

Fire needs three things: fuel, oxygen, and heat. The fuel can be a solid, a liquid or a gas. Oxygen is in ample supply all around us, in the air we breathe, and heat must be hot enough to cause ignition, for example a spark. If one of these three factors is missing, in what is known as the 'fire triangle', fire cannot burn. Fire-fighters extinguish fires by removing one or more of the sides of the fire triangle.

Big fires

Fires can be caused by carelessness, or by the forces of nature. Earthquakes can cause fires which will spread if there is no available water to put out the blaze. In 1923, a Tokyo earthquake caused a fire because tens of thousands of charcoal braziers had overturned.

Forest fires

Oxygen is all around us in the air, so a forest is always at risk of fire as it only needs heat to complete the 'fire triangle'. As well as being at risk from fire s being accidentally started by humans, wood can also set itself alight! When wood reaches 572°F (3000°C), it gives off a

Q&A?

Do you know which is the hottest place in the world?

Al 'Aziziyah in Libya is the hottest place in the world. It reaches temperatures of 58 degrees C (136.4 degrees F).

What should you do in the event of a fire?

- *Plan escape routes from your home, and practice using them.*
- *Install smoke alarms and maintain them by cleaning and testing them monthly.*
- *Learn fire prevention and safety procedures so you know what to do if a fire breaks out.*

The sun gives off more energy in one second than people have used since the beginning of time.

Ohio's Cuyahoga River caught fire in June 1969, due to the amount of oil and chemicals in it. The fire attracted national media attention, as people couldn't believe a river could become so polluted as to catch on fire.

Dragons are frequently presented as being large and powerful serpents which have magical qualities and which breath fire. Mythological (folk tale) creatures which have the characteristics usually associated with dragons are common throughout the world's cultures. Although there are creatures of the lizard family which resemble dragons there is no evidence that any ever existed which breathed fire.

fire reaches this area, it runs out of fuel and starves to death. If the fire is too large, however, planes and helicopters fly overhead, dropping water or special chemicals that smother the flames.

gas which reacts with oxygen to make a flame. The flame will heat the remaining wood, making the fire grow stronger. This will happen even on cold days.

Putting fires out

You may have fire extinguishers in your home. And the emergency services are at hand to deal with house fires and save lives.

In a forest, however, it is more difficult to put out a fire because of the lack of roads. Fire fighters use special tools to clear a large path in a circle around the fire so that the blaze is contained in a ring of earth. This is known as a fire line, a strip of land intended to rob a forest fire of its fuel. When the

House fires

Almost 70% of fatal house fires occur at night. Smoke is the most frequent cause of death, since it displaces the oxygen we breathe and fills the air with poisonous toxins.

Fire can be very dangerous, and children should never play with it.

The Human body *and* health

The human body is made up of bones, muscles, internal organs and skin. The bones act like a frame. Muscles are attached to bones and make it possible to move. Internal organs are responsible for the functions that keep us alive and allow us to be aware of what is happening around us. Skin is a special organ that covers the whole of the body, protecting it, and preventing it from drying out.

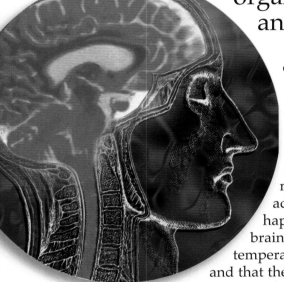

The brain

The brain works like a central computer monitoring what is happening outside and continually monitoring and adjusting what is happening inside. The brain ensures that body temperature is kept constant and that there is enough oxygen and glucose in the blood.

The digestive and respiratory systems

All parts of the body need a mixture of oxygen and glucose (energy). The digestive and respiratory systems provide these. The digestive system is made up of the mouth, the gullet, the stomach, and the small and large intestines. Food taken in through the mouth is broken down and the energy that it contains is absorbed. The waste products remaining eventually form faeces in the bowel. The respiratory system is made up of the nose and lungs. As we breathe oxygen is taken in and carbon dioxide is exhaled.

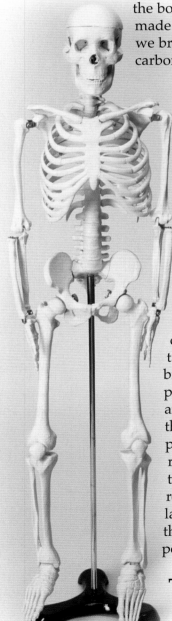

Oxygen and energy

Oxygen and energy are moved round the body by the circulatory system, which is made up of the heart and blood vessels. Blood is kept flowing through the circulatory system by the pumping action of the heart. Oxygen and energy are taken to muscles and carbon dioxide and other waste products are carried away. Carbon dioxide is taken to the lungs where it is breathed out. Other waste products are taken to the liver and kidneys. These organs filter the blood, removing waste products. Waste products removed by the kidneys go into the urine and some of those removed by the liver go into the large intestine. Urine collects in the bladder, which is emptied periodically.

The senses

The senses are the way in which we know about the

What is the largest organ in the body?
The skin.

How many times will the human heart beat in an average lifetime?
Your heart beats about 100,000 times in one day and about 35 million times in a year. That's 2,800,000,000 times in an average lifetime!

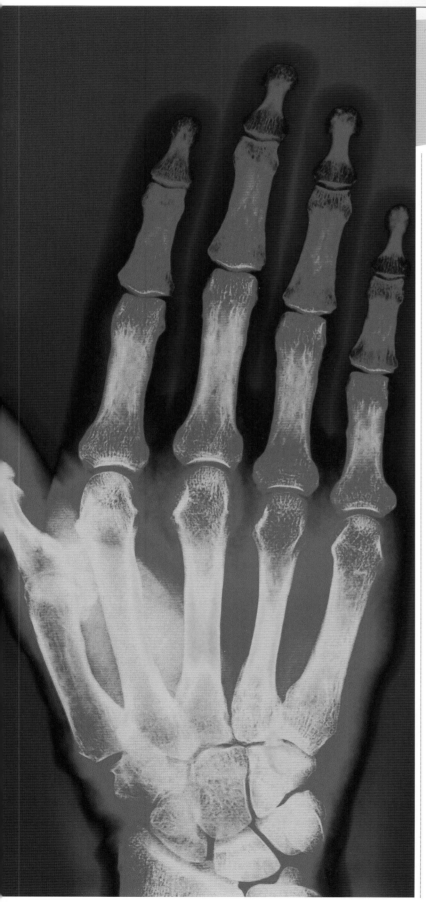

Fascinating **Facts**

Every 30 days we have a completely new skin.

There are more than 200 different bones in the human body.

The small intestine is 5 metres long.

world around us – they are sight, hearing, smell, taste and touch.

Eyes are designed much like a camera. Light enters through the pupil, and is focused by the lens on the retina – the light-sensitive surface at the back of the eye. This information goes to the brain.

There are two parts to the ear: the outer ear (the part we can see) and the ear canal – a tube that goes into the head. In the middle ear is the eardrum, sound waves make the eardrum vibrate and the vibrations are passed along three tiny bones to the inner ear (cochlea) which converts the movements into information that the brain interprets as sound.

The sense of smell depends on a collection of cells at the back of the nose, that are sensitive to minute quantities of chemicals, for example those given off by freshly baked bread.

The 'taste' of something is really a combination of smell and taste. When we eat or drink the tongue detects the basic tastes – sweet, sour, bitter and salty, and we also smell it. The brain puts both together and comes up with the overall taste.

Touch is different from the other senses because we have a sense of touch all over the body. Nerve endings in the skin can detect cold, heat, pain and pressure. Together these make up the sense of touch.

Keeping the body healthy

Keeping the body healthy involves:
- Eating a balanced diet to ensure that you have enough energy for activity and enough nutrients to grow and repair.
- Taking regular exercise to keep the muscles strong and the lungs clear.
- Getting enough sleep.
- Not smoking cigarettes because they contain chemicals that do long term damage to the lungs, heart and blood vessels.

Industry *and the industrial revolution*

Major changes in the way many people lived and worked took place in the late 18th century and early 19th century. This period of history is known as the industrial revolution. At this time there was very rapid development of technology and communication which had a very significant impact on peoples' lives in many parts of the world, especially in the USA and Europe.

Life before the industrial revolution

Up to the time of the industrial revolution most people lived and worked at home or nearby, mostly in villages or small towns. People worked on the land as farmers, or spun yarn and wove cloth on looms in their homes for making clothes selling their produce at markets to make a living and support their families.

Machinery before the industrial revolution

Until the invention of the steam engine most small machinery was

or wind power, such as the windmills for producing flour. Water wheels harnessed the power of water to grind wheat into flour. However, these mills were dependant on the natural resources of wind and water which could not be depended on to flow at a constant rate.

driven by water

THE PALATINE

Technological developments

Steam power

Steam power was first used to pump water from coal mines at the end of the 17th century but it was not until late in the 18th century that James Watt invented an improved and reliable steam engine with a separate condenser chamber. This steam engine, which was powered by burning coal, could be used to drive machinery in a mill or factory.

Spinning jenny

Spinning yarn from wool, cotton or flax

Where did the American industrial revolution begin?

The American industrial revolution began in Lowell, Massachusetts. Lowell was America's first planned industrial city

When did coal mining first begin?

Possibly in China in about 50 BC, and certainly the Romans used coal when they were in England. In America the Aztecs were using coal for heating and for making ornaments. By the Medieval period in Britain coal was being extracted from small-scale pits, but it was not until the industrial revolution that the mines employed lots of people

was speeded up by the invention of the spinning jenny by James Hargreaves in the 18th century. The process was much quicker by machine – previously people had worked on individual spinning wheels.

The first factories

As inventions were developed some industrialists saw the potential for bringing processes together into one place and so factories were created. Richard Arkwright was an inventor who also was also an entrepreneur and saw the benefits of this and built some of the first mill factories manufacturing yarn and weaving it into cloth.

The development of towns and cities

As the factory system developed people moved away from the countryside and large towns and cities were built to house the workers and the factories. Children would work from a very young age, often in dangerous jobs cleaning underneath large machines such as looms. The factories were usually very noisy places where people worked long hours.

Transport

Canals

Alongside the development of industry into large factories methods of transport were developed to transport raw materials in and finished goods out. In the late 18th century canals allowed bulky raw materials, such as china clay and fragile goods, such as pottery to be transported safely. Horses were used to pull the barges.

Railways

From the middle of the 19th century the development of the steam engine for steam locomotives meant that railway development progressed very rapidly in many parts of the world. Many railways were built close to the canals following the same routes between towns and cities and to and from the coast for speed and efficiency in trading. In addition to the metal tracks which were required for the trains to run on many bridges across rivers had to be built.

Fascinating Facts

One of the first safety lamps for coal miners, known as the Davy lamp, was named after its inventor Sir Humphrey Davy. Before the invention of safety lamps miners carried canaries with them. The canaries were extremely sensitive to the presence of poisonous gas in the mines and would die very quickly thus alerting the miners to the danger. Despite the use of safety lamps canaries were still taken into coal mines in Britain until late in the 20th century.

The first cast iron bridge in the world was built across the river Severn at the town which became known as Ironbridge near Shrewsbury, England. This area is often called the birthplace of the industrial revolution, being near to Coalbrookdale where iron was first smelted with coke. Ironbridge became part of a World Heritage Site in 1986.

Insects

Insects make up the largest group of animals on the planet. They first appeared on Earth more than 500 million years ago and exist in almost every part of the world. There are at least a million species of insect ranging from ants, beetles and butterflies to bees and wasps. They can vary in size, from the very smallest which are almost invisible to humans to some very large beetles.

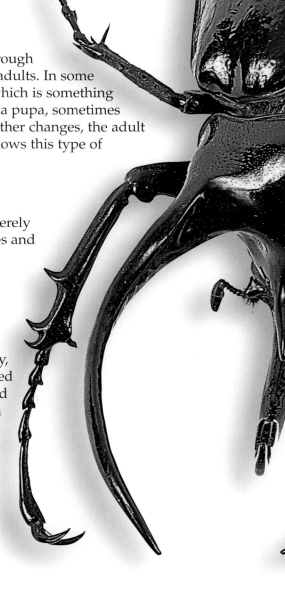

Development

Most insects hatch from eggs, and all go through different stages of development to become adults. In some species an egg hatches to become a larva, which is something like a worm. The larva grows and becomes a pupa, sometimes sealed up in a cocoon or chrysalis. After further changes, the adult emerges. The butterfly is one insect that follows this type of development.

How do insects affect human life?

Some insects are considered pests, for example termites, lice and flies. Some are merely nuisances, although others can cause many problems by spreading disease to crops and humans. Many insects, however, are very beneficial to both people and the environment. Some insects are very important because they pollinate flowers to produce seed and fruit. We have always relied on honeybees for honey, and the silk produced by silkworms played an important role in opening up trade with China many years ago.

What is the most dangerous insect?

The mosquito is probably the most dangerous insect because it carries deadly diseases such as malaria.

How many species of insect are there?

There are probably at least a million different species of insect ranging from ants and butterflies to bees and wasps. Not all species have been identified, so there could be as many as 30 million!

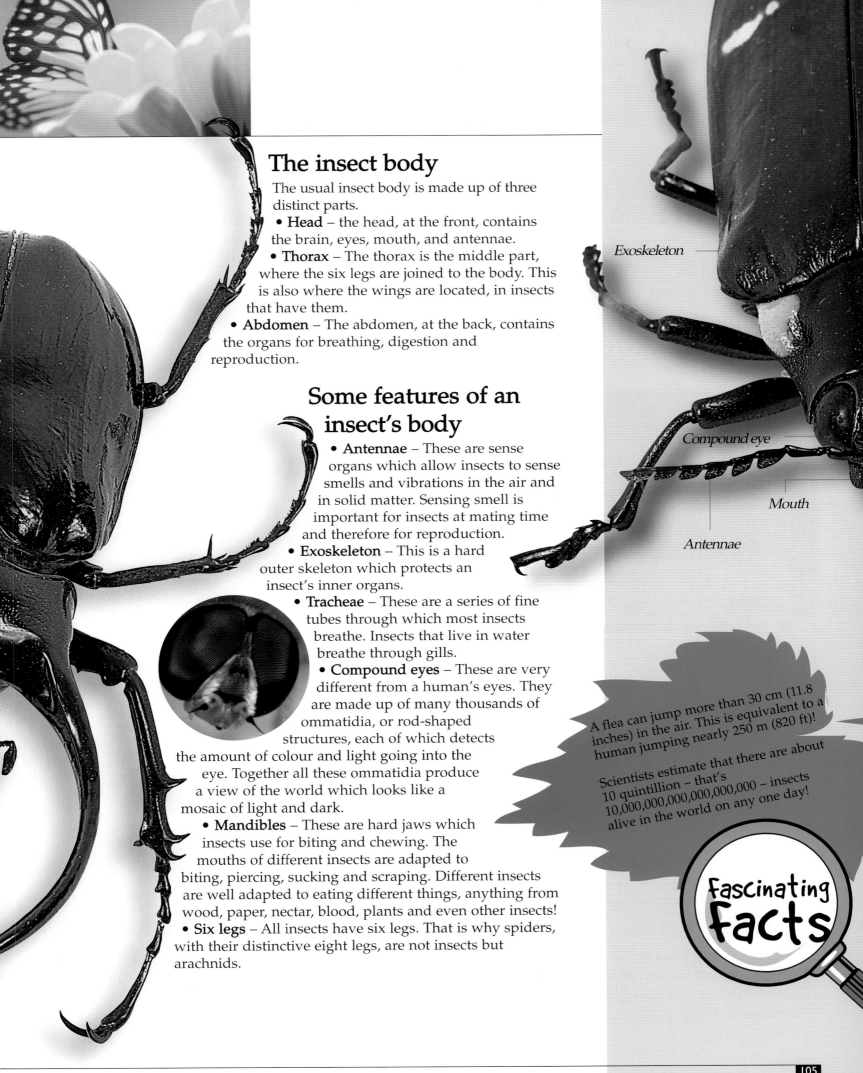

The insect body

The usual insect body is made up of three distinct parts.

- **Head** – the head, at the front, contains the brain, eyes, mouth, and antennae.
- **Thorax** – The thorax is the middle part, where the six legs are joined to the body. This is also where the wings are located, in insects that have them.
- **Abdomen** – The abdomen, at the back, contains the organs for breathing, digestion and reproduction.

Some features of an insect's body

- **Antennae** – These are sense organs which allow insects to sense smells and vibrations in the air and in solid matter. Sensing smell is important for insects at mating time and therefore for reproduction.
- **Exoskeleton** – This is a hard outer skeleton which protects an insect's inner organs.
- **Tracheae** – These are a series of fine tubes through which most insects breathe. Insects that live in water breathe through gills.
- **Compound eyes** – These are very different from a human's eyes. They are made up of many thousands of ommatidia, or rod-shaped structures, each of which detects the amount of colour and light going into the eye. Together all these ommatidia produce a view of the world which looks like a mosaic of light and dark.
- **Mandibles** – These are hard jaws which insects use for biting and chewing. The mouths of different insects are adapted to biting, piercing, sucking and scraping. Different insects are well adapted to eating different things, anything from wood, paper, nectar, blood, plants and even other insects!
- **Six legs** – All insects have six legs. That is why spiders, with their distinctive eight legs, are not insects but arachnids.

Exoskeleton

Compound eye

Mouth

Antennae

A flea can jump more than 30 cm (11.8 inches) in the air. This is equivalent to a human jumping nearly 250 m (820 ft)!

Scientists estimate that there are about 10 quintillion – that's 10,000,000,000,000,000,000 – insects alive in the world on any one day!

fascinating **Facts**

Japan

Japan consists of four main islands – Kyushu, Hokkaido, Honshu and Shikoku. About 70% of the land is covered with forested volcanic mountains such as Mount Fuji. Towns and cities are squeezed into the flat lands along the coast, with very high levels of population density. Earth tremors and earthquakes are frequent.

Climate

Summers are warm and humid, while winters are mild, although snow can be heavy in the mountains and the north – Sapporo hosted the Winter Olympics in 2002. Each year in February Sapporo is host to the ice festival. Around two million people come to see the hundreds of beautiful snow statues and ice sculptures which turn Sapporo into a winter dreamland of crystal-like ice and white snow.

Why are so few Japanese people overweight?

Their diet is mainly fish, rice and vegetables with very little deep-fried food.

Why are there so many earthquakes in Japan?

Japan is part of the Pacific ring of fire, an arc of islands and volcanoes caused by the junction between the Pacific and Eurasian plates of the Earth's crust.

The 34 mile (55 km) long Seikan Tunnel, which runs under the sea and connects the islands of Honshu and Hokkaido, is the longest in the world.

Japan has an efficient transport system linking the major cities and islands. Transport within cities is very effective, with speedy commuter trains and underground systems. The major cities are linked by the famous bullet train or shinkansen – probably the world's fastest regular train services. On busy days the service carries over a million passengers.

Fascinating Facts

Origami

Origami is a traditional Japanese pastime where a single square of paper is folded in different ways to create shapes such as animals and plants. The best-known origami shape, which many children learn from their parents or grandparents, is the crane. Other shapes include flowers, butterflies, crabs and even difficult creations like Christmas trees.

According to Japanese tradition, one way to pray for good health is by folding a thousand origami cranes. 'Sadako and the Thousand Paper Cranes' is the story of a girl who died of leukemia. In August 1945, when the atomic bomb was dropped on Hiroshima, Sadako was just two years old. Though the bomb did not kill her she developed leukemia when she was 11 years old. She had heard that a person could make her wish come true by folding a 1,000 paper cranes. Wishing for good health, Sadako began folding a 1,000 paper cranes. But she died at age 12, before her project was completed, and her classmates finished folding her cranes for her after she died.

Food

Japanese food relies heavily on simplicity and freshness, with many dishes eaten raw. A variety of different foods, mainly in small portions served with rice, forms the most important part of a meal. Fish is very popular. Japan is famous for sushi (vinegary rice eaten with seafood or vegetables) and sukiyaki (thin slices of meat served with vegetables, tofu and vermicelli).

Language *and* Communication

Communication means passing on information from one person to another, or to many people at the same time. When we say or write something to another person, or even just wave at them to say 'hello', we are communicating with them.

We do not have to use words to communicate – we can use other methods:

- Sound – like a fire-engine siren or a school bell.
- Signs – road signs can tell us how fast we are allowed to drive.
- Lights – an ambulance's flashing blue light means 'Get out of the way!'

Languages

To understand what someone else is saying to us, we need to know the same language as they do. Some languages are spoken by millions of people, others by less than a dozen.

Sign languages

Deaf people use 'manual language', making signs with their hands and fingers. A system of raised dots called Braille allows blind people to read by running their fingers over a page. You will also see bumps on pavements which warn blind people when they are approaching a hazard.

If you have ever used smileys in your text messages or emails, you have used sign language.

The spoken word

Spoken language was around for centuries before writing came into use. Memorising words was the only way to record anything. Many early societies did not write down their histories and tales, but people learned them by heart, and passed them on using speech. We call this oral history. Oral means 'by mouth' or 'spoken'.

The written word

People are believed to have started using writing around 6,000 BC. Ancient writing used pictures to represent words.

About 3,500 years ago, writing underwent its most important change. A people called the Phoenicians developed an alphabet. In an alphabet, symbols represent sounds rather than ideas or pictures. Combinations of these 'sound letters' can be used to make up words in more than one language.

The picture language of the Ancient Egyptians was called hieroglyphic.

The most common alphabet we use in the West today is called the Roman alphabet.

The printed word

The first books were hand-written, and very few people could read them. This all changed in the West with the development of the printing press by Johann Gutenberg in 1450. Large numbers of books could now be printed quickly and cheaply. A statue to commemorate his contribution to printing can be seen in Mainz, Germany.

Today between 5,000 and 7,000 languages are spoken in the world.

A six-month-old baby could learn any language easily.

Many people learn extra languages: someone who learns to speak other languages fluently is called bilingual (2 languages) or multi-lingual (3 or more languages).

In 1803 the first paper-making machine was invented, and in 1810 a printing press was first driven by steam power. Books do not have to be words printed on paper: we can now listen to books recorded on audio tapes and CDs, and we can download books from the Internet to read on our computer screens.

The transmitted word – and moving pictures

In 1844, the building of the first telegraph system enabled near-instant written communication over distance.

In 1876, the telephone was invented, and in 1877, sound was first recorded. People could listen to music played on phonographs (early sound systems) in their homes. In 1895, the first radio message was sent.

In the 1830s, photography allowed images to be captured, and in the 1890s moving pictures (the movies) arrived. One of the most familiar objects in our homes today is the television. This became popular in the late 1940s.

In 1962, the first communications satellite was launched into space. It made the first ever 'live' television broadcast to the United States, Europe, Japan and South America.

World Wide Web

The Internet and the World Wide Web were developed in the late 1960s. These are now popular ways to communicate and find information – like having a library in your own home.

Data (information) can be transmitted between computers. This allows people to send each other messages via email (electronic mail), or 'chat' by typing on-screen.

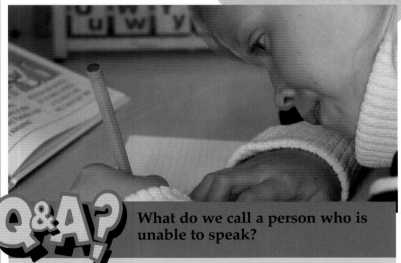

Q&A?

What do we call a person who is unable to speak?

The medical term is aphonia, and we would say that a person is aphonic. But these aren't commonly used words. Today we would say that a person 'lacked the power of speech', or that they were 'voiceless'

What is the most common sentence that is used to test typewriters and computer keyboards

'The quick brown fox jumps over the lazy dog'. This sentence contains all of the letters of the alphabet. It is called a pangram. There are other pangrams but this is the shortest and most memorable

Magic

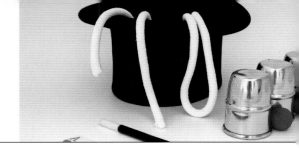

The magic done by magicians is an illusion, it is not real. Magicians use special props or mirrors to do seemingly impossible and 'magical' things. They often trick you into concentrating on something unimportant (this is called 'misdirection') while they quickly move the important prop or use a hidden mechanism. Because what we call magic is really trickery, we call the things that magicians do magic tricks.

Early magicians

Lots of people used to believe in real magic, that there were real living sorcerers and witches. Most magicians today wear evening clothes (a smart black suit with 'tails' and a white shirt), but before the 1800s magicians usually dressed like sorcerers, with long robes covered with stars and strange symbols. Magicians performing on street corners were sometimes accused of being witches. In 1584 a book called 'The Discoverie of Witchcraft' was published to explain how simple illusions were performed, to show that magicians were normal people and to make it easier to hunt out 'real' witches!

The growth of modern magic

Magic became more and more popular as time went on, especially among the rich. This meant that many magicians could stop performing at fairs and instead perform in large theatres or successful travelling shows. During the 1700s people were interested in all the new scientific discoveries that were being made, so magicians began to use pretend science. One magician, Katterfelto, used to lecture on science before his

Q&A?

Who was Harry Houdini?

Houdini (1874–1926) was one of the most famous magicians who ever lived. He did lots of different kinds of magic but he was most famous for being an escapologist. He escaped from lots of strange things, including a straitjacket (which is buckled up at the back and designed so the person wearing it cannot take it off), a locked chest thrown into a river, and a giant paper bag (without tearing it!)

What is a mentalist?

A mentalist is a magician who seems to be able to read your mind.

Magicians' assistants are often acrobats or contortionists – able to twist their bodies into strange shapes so they can fit into small boxes.

Magicians have to take a solemn oath not to reveal the secrets of their art. When they die, other magicians perform a ceremony where they break the dead magician's wand to make sure nobody else uses it!

Fascinating facts

magic shows! Science can be very helpful to magicians – for example, in the 'light & heavy box trick', a box seems light and easy to lift, but when a hidden magnet is turned on the box (which has a secret metal bottom) is attracted to it and becomes heavy and impossible to lift.

Familiar tricks

Levitation (floating in the air), sawing a woman in half, producing a rabbit from a hat, escaping from locked chests… these are all famous magic tricks, but many were only invented in the last century. The first woman was 'cut in half' in 1912. This was first done by a magician called P. T. Selbit, and then copied by many others.

Magicians often copy each other's tricks and improve upon them, giving them surprising endings when audiences become too familiar with an old trick. Magicians also use lots of different 'magic' words such as 'abracadabra' and 'alakazam'.

Television magic

After the arrival of movie theatres, magic acts became less popular as audiences went to see films instead. But the invention of television gave magicians new opportunities and led to lots of new tricks. For instance, a magician called Channing Pollock made doves seem to appear from nowhere in the 1950s. 'Close up' magic is magic which is only performed to a few people, like card tricks and tricks where balls disappear under cups. Television meant that small tricks could be shown to all the viewers at home, giving close up magic larger audiences than ever before.

Lots of magicians perform on television nowadays. They all follow three rules written by magician Mark Wilson in the 1960s: 1) Always have a live audience 2) Never have the camera cut away from (stop looking at) a trick as it is being performed, and 3) Let viewers know that they are seeing just what the studio audience sees. These three rules help people at home know that the television process is not tricking them.

Famous magicians today

There are lots of modern magicians who make their magic into huge shows though each do it in their own way. Siegfried and Roy, for example, use comedy and drama in their show and make a cheetah appear instead of a rabbit. David Copperfield mixes rock music into his show, whereas Penn and Teller show you how some old tricks were done just to make their own tricks look more amazing and magical.

Magnetism

All magnetism is caused by movement of electrical charges; whenever an electrically charged particle moves it creates a magnetic field, or area in which a magnetic force can be felt. This may seem strange at first, after all magnets aren't electrically charged but they clearly are magnetic.

Q&A?

How do magnets attract iron and other magnetic materials?

When the magnet is brought close to the magnetic material, the fields in the material align with the magnet and 'pull' the material towards it.

What are the Northern Lights?

The Aurora Borealis or Northern Lights are produced when charged particles trapped in the Earth's magnetic field are released into the atmosphere causing some gases to give off light in 'curtains' and 'ribbons'.

If you take a magnet and repeatedly rub it from the top to the bottom of an iron nail you will find that the nail becomes magnetised.

Take an ordinary magnet, put it under a piece of paper, sprinkle iron filings over the paper. See the way the filings align themselves to the field of the magnet!

All materials contain tiny particles called electrons. These electrons have an electrical charge and spin around, so generating tiny magnetic fields. In most materials these tiny magnetic fields all point in different directions so overall they cancel out – but in some materials these tiny fields tend to align so that they point in the same direction and so add together to make a larger magnetic field. These materials are said to be magnetic – iron is an example of a magnetic material.

Even in a magnetic material like iron not all the little magnetic fields are pointing in the same direction, instead you get lots of regions – within each region the magnetic fields are all aligned but the different regions are still pointing in different directions. This means the material's overall magnetic field is still pretty small. However if a magnetic material like this is placed in another magnetic field all the regions will tend to align to point in the same direction as this field – so they all end up pointing in the same direction and the material then gets its own net magnetic field too!

The Earth is a magnet!

Electrical currents in the liquid iron at the core of the Earth create their own magnetic field, closely aligned to the axis around which the Earth rotates. This magnetic field is how compasses work and how we navigate. Take a magnet and suspend it so it's free to rotate, then the magnet will settle so that it's aligned with the Earth's magnetic field. This means it will be pointing almost North–South. The magnetic north is nearly but not quite at the same place as the geographic North Pole.

Navigating by magnetism

Humans are not the only creatures to use the Earth's magnetic field to find their way about. Recent studies have shown that many creatures, from bacteria to whales, can sense the Earth's magnetic field and use this information to navigate by. Loggerhead sea turtles for instance can sense the intensity and direction of the Earth's magnetic field and use this to navigate their 8,078 miles (13,000 km) migration around the Atlantic Ocean.

Dynamos and motors

A changing or moving electrical charge generates a magnetic field; similarly if an electrical conductor such as a length of wire is moved through a magnetic field then an electrical current is created in it. This effect was first discovered by Michael Faraday in 1831 and is at the core of almost every electrical generator to this day – a loop or coil of wire is rotated inside a permanent magnet, and as the coil moves through the magnetic field an electrical current is created inside the wire. Devices like this are called dynamos.

This same relationship between magnetic field, current and motion is used in the electric motor. As with a dynamo a coil or loop of wire is positioned within a permanent magnet. However, rather than moving the coil to generate electrical current an electrical current is passed through the coil and generates motion – the coil rotates!

Media

Since humans first learned to talk, they have tried to communicate with one another. Ancient civilisations wrote on wood or materials such as papyrus (an early kind of paper made from reeds). Later, pages of writing began to be gathered together in books. The Church was active in spreading the word of God, and monks would copy out religious works by hand.

What do we mean by media?

Today the word media can be anything from books, newspapers and magazines to CDs, DVDs, the Internet and email, and from films, television, computer games and adverts to radio, the postal service and the telephone.

Who was William Caxton?

Caxton was the first person to use a printing press to print books in English. The very first English book was a story about the Trojan War which appeared in about 1475.

What are scriptoria?

These were the writing halls where medieval monks used to spend long hours copying out books. These books were often beautifully illustrated with illuminations (hand-painted pictures).

The growth of modern media

The 20th century saw a big rise in the use of different kinds of media. Factories used machinery to produce things like newspapers, books and vinyl records quickly and cheaply.

Criticisms of the media

These days, we are surrounded by media. Not everyone thinks this is good, however. For example, some governments do not like their citizens to criticise them in the newspapers or on television. These countries do not have what we call 'freedom of the press', which grants citizens free speech and allows them to speak their minds. Some people think that in countries which do have free

speech and freedom of the press, people are being swamped by the media. This can cause people to become stressed and sometimes even unwell. Also, people worry that they do not have enough privacy in the modern world. Satellites can track people's mobile phones, and personal information can be stolen over the Internet.

information to sell things to us. Knowledge will become available even more quickly, and humans might become even more clever!

Ways the media help us

But most people agree that an increase in the use of media is a good thing. The media can be used to educate us,

through books, magazines and newspapers, or through films that make us think (such as documentaries). The media can also entertain us, through films, music or computer games.

Media and the future

What will the future hold for humans and the media? As computers and microchips become capable of more and more exciting things, we will see the Internet get faster and faster. Ways of storing music, such as our CDs, will become even smaller, and music will be stored digitally as computer files. Computers will help shops and businesses to know more about what we like to buy, and they will use this

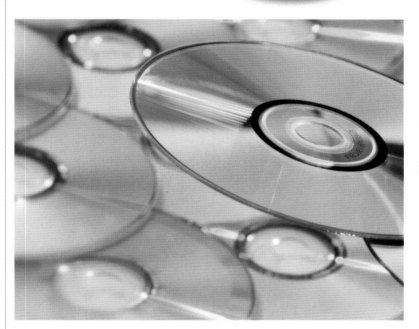

Timeline of invention

1443 Guttenberg invents the printing press and prints the Bible.
1876 Alexander Graham Bell invents the telephone.
1890 Telephone wires are put up in New York.
1913 Portable record player invented.
1916 Radio invented.
1922 The BBC (British Broadcasting Corporation) is formed.
1927 'The Jazz Singer' is the first film with sound.
1936 The BBC starts the world's first regular television service.
1957 Sputnik I, the first satellite, is launched.
1962 Telstar satellite sends an image across the earth.
1965 Vietnam War is shown on television.
1970 Early version of the Internet is developed.
1971 Computer microprocessor is pioneered.
1981 Laptop computer invented.
1983 Early mobile phones.
1995 Introduction of Windows 95 makes computers and the Internet popular.

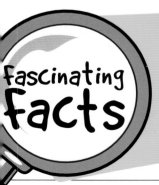

fascinating facts

John Logie Baird, inventor of television, transmitted the first long distance TV pictures from a room in the Central Hotel, Glasgow.

The Herald is one of the oldest English language newspapers. It was first published in 1783 and was then called the Glasgow Advertiser.

Medicine *and* disease

A ncient peoples used plants and herbs for healing. The earliest record of this is a series of cave paintings in Lascaux, south-west France, before 13,000 BC. Later, in Ancient Egypt about 3,000 BC, the first surgery was being practised and the details of it written on papyrus (paper made from a grass-like plant called sedge).

Herbalism

Herbalism means the use of plants for healing. Apothecaries, the first pharmacists, made their own medicines and ointments. Plants are still widely used today, for medicines and in traditional remedies. Morphine and codeine (from the opium poppy) and aspirin (from the willow tree) are used as painkillers. Digitalis from the foxglove is used to treat heart conditions, while quinine from the bark of the cinchona tree has long been used to combat malaria.

However, even though plants are natural they must be used very carefully. Wrongly administered, they can make people ill rather than cure them.

Modern medicine

Many discoveries and inventions in the 19th century have created great advances in medicine which are still important today. The death rate of new mothers was dramatically cut after 1847, when Ignaz Semmelweis experimented with doctors using soap to wash their hands. This was followed by Joseph Lister's experiments leading to the invention of antiseptics in 1865. Meanwhile Louis Pasteur linked micro-organisms with disease, making a great advance in medical thinking. In preventive health care, Pasteur also made the first anti-rabies vaccine in 1885 and invented pasteurisation of milk, helping to limit the spread of disease. In the late 1880s Robert Koch made the first important discoveries in bacteriology.

Q&A?

Why is children's medicine called paediatrics?

The word paediatrics is derived from two Greek words, paidi which means 'boy' and 'iatros' which means 'doctor'.

Who invented the sticking plaster?

The adhesive plaster was invented in 1920 by Earle Dickson, who was a cotton buyer for a company that made bandages. He invented the sticking plaster because it was easy to use – his wife had lots of kitchen accidents!

The combination of 19th century medical discoveries and inventions and improved living conditions led to higher life expectancy, and a significant reduction in disease, for

people in many parts of the world. Further developments in the 20th century have led to vastly improved levels of health around the world, and higher expectations of health.

Specialist areas of modern medicine:

Dermatology	treatment of skin conditions
Neurology	dealing with the brain and nervous system
Oncology	treatment of cancer
Ophthalmology	treating eyes
Orthopaedics	treatment of the spine and other bones
Paediatrics	children's medicine
Psychiatry	dealing with mental illness
Surgery	invasive treatments, which 'enter' the body

Timeline of medical inventions

1280	spectacles (glasses)
1540	artificial limbs
1714	the mercury thermometer
1792	the ambulance
1796	vaccination
1816	the stethoscope
1846	anaesthesia
1853	the syringe
1865	antiseptic treatments
1885	anti-rabies vaccination
1887	contact lenses
1895	X-rays
1928	antibiotics
1967	heart transplant
1979	ultrasound

Garlic was given to Roman legionnaires at Hadrian's Wall to help them fight off colds and flu in the bitter English winter.

The earliest known doctor was Hesyre, physician to King Djoser in 27th century BC Egypt, where the earliest woman doctor was also known to have practised medicine.

The Middle Ages

The Middle Ages in Europe are commonly dated from the end of the Roman Empire in the 5th century until the early 16th century. They are often called the medieval period (sometimes spelled 'mediaeval' or 'mediæval').

Medieval scientists believed that all things were made up of four basic elements: earth, air, fire and water. They thought that if they were combined in the right amounts, any substance could be made. They even thought they could turn lead into gold! This science was called alchemy. During the Middle Ages, nearly a third of every year was given over to religious holidays.

The Feudal System

People in the Middle Ages lived under a way of life known as the Feudal System. In this system, the King gave land to his knights and nobles in return for them lending him troops and fighting for him themselves in time of war. The nobles (lords) let peasants live on and farm their land. In return for this, the peasants farmed the land and paid rent to the landlord. This rent was not paid in money but by giving the landlord some of their crops.

Strip farming

Life for ordinary people was very hard. Unlike today, where farmers farm large fields of crops, in the Middle Ages the land was divided into small strips, which each peasant family would farm. Farming methods were very basic, and often the crops would fail, meaning the people would not have enough to eat. The fields were ploughed with a team of oxen pulling a plough. Peasants hoed and harvested their own strips, but worked together on big jobs such as ploughing or haymaking. Working together was essential, as a failed harvest could mean starvation for the whole village. Life for the rich was much more pleasant. They lived in big castles and manor houses. They wore bright clothing made of expensive material, and went hunting. They would have big feasts where there was lots to eat and drink.

Religion

Religion was very important during the Middle Ages. There was one predominant religion in Europe: Catholic Christianity. Church services were conducted in Latin, the scholarly and diplomatic language of the day. The Church controlled most aspects of everyday life. The Church grew very powerful during this time, partly because people would give land and money to the Church when they died. Many churches and cathedrals were built across Europe, such as the Cathedral of St. Michael and St. Gudula, Brussels (Belgium). Also, many people became monks or nuns, and lots of monasteries were built.

The Crusades

Religion was also the reason for one of the longest wars in history, the Crusades. These were a religious war, to try to free Jerusalem and the Holy Land from the Muslims. When the Christian soldiers returned from the Crusades, they brought back many ideas, goods and inventions from the Arab world. Westerners adopted the Arabic system of counting, which is the one we still use today. Previously, people had used Roman numerals, which you can sometimes still see today on clock or watch faces. Some clocks were designed showing both systems.

Gunpowder

Gunpowder was also introduced into Europe during the 14th century as a weapon of war. It had been invented in China, and used for both weapons and fireworks. At first, early guns were dangerous. In fact, they were more likely to kill the person firing them than the intended target, because they were so unreliable. Later, though, as the guns became more reliable, gunpowder changed warfare greatly.

The written word

The printing press, which was also a Chinese invention, became popular in Europe at the end of the 14th century. It meant that books could be produced more quickly, cheaply and reliably. People were able to buy books for themselves, meaning that knowledge could spread throughout the world more quickly. You can read more about printing and the written word on the Media page (p114).

Medieval scientists believed that all things were made up of four basic elements: earth, air, fire and water. They thought that if they were combined in the right amounts, any substance could be made. They even thought they could turn lead into gold! This science was called Alchemy.

During the Middle Ages, nearly a third of every year was given over to religious holidays.

Q&A?

What other inventions were brought to Europe during the Middle Ages?

The abacus (a machine for counting), buttons and paper money.

Why were church services read in Latin?

Latin was the ancient language of the Roman Empire, where the Christian Church began.

Fascinating Facts

Moss

Mosses are small plants, classified as bryopsida, which usually grow matted together in small groups in damp and shady places. They rarely grow more than 5cm tall. Mosses have thin wiry stems covered in tiny leaves.

How is moss different from a plant?

Mosses do not have flowers and their leaves tend to be much simpler than those of many plants.

Where do you find moss?

Mosses are commonly found in damp places where light levels are very low. They are often found in wooded areas growing on rocks near streams or on fallen logs and tree stumps. Some mosses have adapted to city living and grow between cracks between paving.

Sphagnum mosses form large acidic bogs in peat swamps. Large dead cells within the leaves are able to store significant amounts of water keeping the area very damp or even water-logged. As the moss slowly rots it turns gradually into peat which has traditionally been used by gardeners as a soil improver.

What is it used for?

Moss can be cultivated, and in Japanese gardens moss growth is encouraged to create a sense of calm and tranquillity.

In the late 19th century there was fashion for collecting moss into mosseries in many British and American gardens. Samples of different mosses were collected and grown in carefully controlled conditions to mimic the way they would be seen growing in the wild.

Some birds, such as long-tailed tits, collect moss with which to line their nests, valuing it for its softness as it dries out.

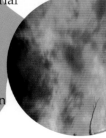

Fascinating Facts

Sphagnum mosses were used to bind soldiers' wounds during World War II as they were found to be highly absorbent and possessed some antibacterial qualities.

In some areas of the countryside in Britain mosses were used to put out fires because not only were the mosses available in large quantities in nearby streams but also because of their ability to absorb large amounts of water.

Lichen

Like plants, lichens take energy for growth from the sun through the process of photosynthesis. However, as they are small and slower growing than plants and have no roots so they can grow and flourish in more extreme conditions.

Adapted to life in harsh and extreme condition lichens are found living anywhere from frozen soil in the Arctic to baking rock in desert areas.

What's interesting about lichen?

Lichen is eaten by reindeer in Arctic regions and used as a nesting material by some squirrels. Lichens are very sensitive to air pollutants and lack of lichen growth in some places in the world can indicate high levels of pollution particularly in industrial areas.

Q&A?

Where do you find lichens?

Lichens live on a variety of surfaces including soil, trees, rock and stone.

Lichens can survive in space. In an experiment conducted in 2005 two species of lichen were sealed in a capsule and launched on a Russian Soyuz rocket. Despite being subjected to temperatures ranging from −20°C to 20°C (−4°F to 68°F) in the vacuum and radiation of space for 15 days the lichens were found to be completely unchanged.

Fascinating facts

Mountains

A mountain is a landform that extends above the surrounding terrain in a limited area. This usually refers to landforms over 2,000 ft (610 m) in height. Mountains cover 20% of the world's land surface and more than half the world's fresh water originates in mountains. There are mountains on every continent, under the sea and even on Mars!

Mountains are formed over millions of years by volcanoes, erosion and disturbances in the Earth's crust. The Earth's crust is made up of six massive plates. When two of these plates collide, the land can be pushed upward forming mountains.

There are five basic kinds of mountain:

Dome mountains are formed when a great amount of melted rock pushes its way up under the Earth without folding or faulting; the result is a rounded dome. The dome is eroded as it is raised above its surroundings, forming peaks and valleys.

Fold mountains form when two plates smack into each other and their edges crumple. The Himalayas, Alps and Andes were created in this way.

Fault-block mountains are formed when faults in the Earth's surface force some blocks of rock up and others down. Instead of folding, the earth fractures and the blocks are stacked. This is how the mountains of the Sierra Nevada in North America were formed.

Volcanic mountains form when molten rock ('magma') erupts from deep inside the earth and piles up on the surface. Mount St Helens in North America is an example of a volcanic mountain.

Plateau mountains are plateaux that have been worn down by erosion, and most have large areas of high-level flat land.

Mountain ranges

It is unusual for a mountain to stand alone – usually they exist as part of mountain ranges. A mountain range is a chain or group of mountains that are

Q&A?

How are glaciers formed?

On the very coldest parts of some mountains, snow may build up and turn into rivers of ice that move incredibly slowly downhill.

Which is the tallest mountain in the solar system?

The tallest mountain in the solar system is Olympus Mons – on Mars!

close together. The longest mountain range in the world is formed by the Andes Mountains, which are more than 4,474 miles (7,200 km) long and stretch through seven South American countries. The highest mountain range in the world is the Himalayas (whose name means 'Land of Snow'). This range contains the highest peaks in the world, and runs through Pakistan, India, Tibet, Nepal, Sikkim and Bhutan.

Mountain climate

Mountains tend to be much wetter places than lowlands. They also tend to be colder – the higher you climb up a mountain, the colder it gets. This is why many mountains have snow on the top all year round, above what is called the snowline. Climate zones change quickly on mountains, so that one can climb from tropical jungle to the ice of a glacier in just a few kilometres. The higher you climb, the lighter and thinner the air becomes.

Mountains can also affect local climates – in some areas,

What's in a name?

Mt Everest has three different names. In the Nepali language it is called Sagarmatha (Head of the Sky), and in Tibetan it is called Chomolangma (short for Jomo Miyolangsangma, the name of a Tibetan goddess who is one of the Five Sisters of Long Life). The mountain was given its English name by Andrew Waugh, the British surveyor-general of India, who named it after Sir George Everest (the first person to record the height and location of the mountain).

for example, they block rain, so that one side of the mountain may get plenty of rain but the other side is dry desert.

Mountain people

About 10% of the world's 6 billion people live on mountains. Eleven million people live in the Alps, making them the most densely populated mountain area. Not only animals but humans as well have adapted to living in mountain environments – for example, the South American Uru tribe have larger hearts and lungs to help them breathe the thinner air at high altitudes.

Mountain animals

Mountains are a bleak habitat for animals; and the higher you get, the more bleak it becomes. Most mountain mammals have evolved thick woolly fur (like the yak), and mountain sheep and goats (like the ibex) are very sure-footed to help them on the rough terrain. Some of the highest mountain ranges are home to a variety of endangered species. For example, musk deer, Bengal tigers and snow leopards live in the Himalayas.

Mountain plants

The lower slopes of mountains are often covered with forest, while the tops of mountains are usually treeless. The place above which trees will not grow is called the treeline. Nevertheless, there are some plants that survive at very high altitudes where the terrain is mostly bare rock – mostly alpines, mosses and lichens.

Mountains and tourism

Over 50 million tourists head for the mountains each year. They are attracted by the clean air and beautiful scenery, and activities such as hiking, climbing, canoeing, skiing and snowboarding. Although tourism brings in money and creates jobs for mountain populations, there is also the risk that too much can do harm to the environment and local economy – through erosion, pollution from traffic, leaving litter, and raising the price of land and food.

fascinating Facts

Facts about Mountains

- The world's highest mountain peak on land is Mount Everest at around 29,035 ft (8,850 m) above sea level.
- Some islands are really the top of giant mountains poking out of the sea!

Music

Spanning the centuries, music has always played a part in mankind. Music is an expressive form of language and can be used in a variety of ways to tell stories, convey emotions and play a part in entertainment and enjoyment. In eastern Europe there still exists the same style of music as was present many centuries ago, passed down through the generations as ballads and religious musical prayers.

Meanwhile, in mainland western Europe, groups of 'troubadours' performed courtly poetry as well as music and dance in southern France. They travelled widely, and their music led to similar groups of poet-musicians, called 'trouveres' continuing this style in northern France.

Greek tragedy

The Ancient Greeks used music in their tragedies. The plays were interspersed with songs sung both by actors and chorus and there would also be dancing by the chorus. There would also have been instrumental music, perhaps on a stringed instrument called a kithara, or on pipes. Some of the Greek gods were associated with music. In Greek mythology Orpheus could use music to bring objects to life.

Church music

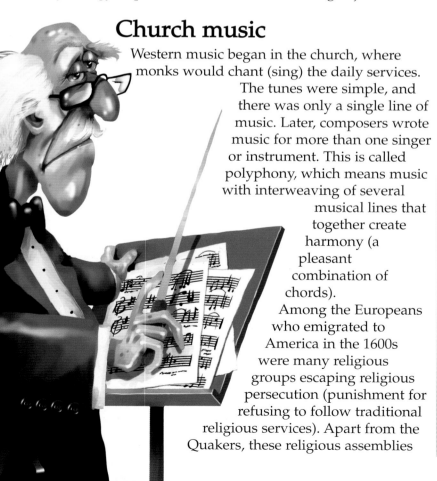

Western music began in the church, where monks would chant (sing) the daily services. The tunes were simple, and there was only a single line of music. Later, composers wrote music for more than one singer or instrument. This is called polyphony, which means music with interweaving of several musical lines that together create harmony (a pleasant combination of chords).

Among the Europeans who emigrated to America in the 1600s were many religious groups escaping religious persecution (punishment for refusing to follow traditional religious services). Apart from the Quakers, these religious assemblies

all used music in their worship, and so European religious music became the recognised music of the early American churches.

Classical music

Wolfgang Amadeus Mozart was a musical genius, who could write music by the age of five, and was performing for kings by the age of six. Ludwig van Beethoven wrote nine wonderful symphonies, and many other works.

What is perfect pitch?

Perfect pitch, or absolute pitch, means the ability to identify a single note just by hearing it, or to be able to sing a note without the benefit of a musical instrument as a guide.

What are the Proms, and why are they called the Proms?

The Proms are a series of daily orchestral concerts, taking place over eight weeks at the Royal Albert Hall in London, UK. The name refers to the original practice of audience members promenading, or strolling, in some areas of the concert hall during the concert. Promenading now refers to the use of the standing areas inside the hall.

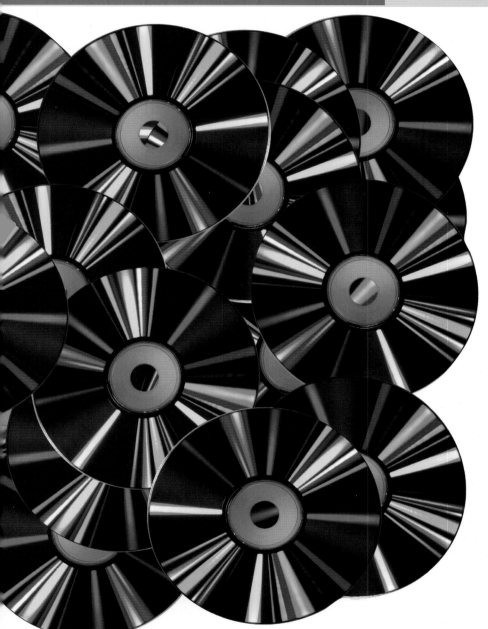

Music in the home

In the last century, music became more widely available with the arrival of radio. People could listen to radio programmes in their own homes. Also, with the invention of the gramophone (an early type of record player), people could buy vinyl records and listen to their favourite pieces again and again. Before these new kinds of technology, the only way to hear music was in person, in the concert hall.

Rock and Pop

In the 1950s and 1960s, Rock 'n Roll arrived. A pop group called The Beatles changed the face of music forever in the 1960s, selling millions of records and taking popular music in new directions. Today, we have CDs instead of records and can download from the internet too!

Music in the Theatre

Music has been used in the theatre for thousands of years. From the Ancient Greeks, to the Elizabethan theatre, to the modern musical, music forms a part of the theatre experience. Opera is a special kind of play, where the actors are also singers, and where the words are sung. Operas often have well known stories as their plots, such as plays by William Shakespeare.

He went deaf towards the end of his life, but continued to compose music.

Different styles of music have developed over the centuries. A symphony is a long piece of music written for an orchestra. The orchestra has grown over the years, to include more instruments and also newer instruments like the clarinet and saxophone.

fascinating facts

Mozart wrote his first symphony at the age of eight!

A concerto is where a single instrument plays 'with' an orchestra (concerto means 'concert' in Italian).

Napoleon Bonaparte

Napoleon Bonaparte is one of the most famous rulers France has ever had. This brilliant military leader, nicknamed 'the little Corporal', was born in Corsica in 1769. By 1804, he had risen from the lowly position of Second Artillery Lieutenant to become Emperor of the French nation.

Napoleon was educated in French military schools and soon came to public attention as a rising star. He led the troops that put down a Royalist uprising in Paris in 1795. and as a reward he was made leader of the Army of the interior and soon after, the Commander in Chief of the Army in Italy.

In 1799 he took over the government, making himself First Consul. French government had been in a fragile and confused state since the French Revolution of 1789. Napoleon strengthened and centralised it, introducing many social and legal reforms. Amongst other things, he created the bank of France and reinstated Roman Catholicism as the state religion.

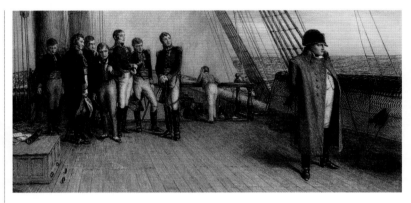

The Battle of Trafalgar

In 1805, Napoleon was planning to invade Britain. This plan was cancelled after his joint French and Spanish fleet suffered defeat at the naval Battle of Trafalgar. The French and Spanish lost 22 ships out of 33; the British lost none. However, the British did lose one of their greatest naval commanders – Admiral Lord Nelson, who was wounded and died late in the battle.

Q&A?

What did Napoleon say an army marches on?

Its stomach.

What did Napoleon crown himself in 1804?

Emperor Napoleon the First.

The Russian Campaign of 1812

In 1812, Napoleon invaded Russia with his Grande Armée ('Great Army'). The Russians retreated before him, devastating the land as they went and drawing Napoleon further into Russia. Although he captured the capital city of Moscow, Napoleon could not supply his army from the ruined countryside and was forced to begin a retreat. Illness, starvation and the bitter Russian winter killed large numbers of his troops during the long retreat.

He went on to greatly expand the borders of the French Empire, but Britain, Prussia, Russia and Sweden allied against him, and in 1814 they captured Paris. Napoleon was forced to abdicate and was exiled to the island of Elba near Italy.

The 100 Days

Napoleon escaped from Elba in early 1815 and returned to France with only 600 guardsmen. When French soldiers of the 5th Regiment were sent to arrest him, Napoleon walked towards them alone saying 'Soldiers of the 5th, you recognise me. You can shoot your Emperor if you dare.' Shouting 'Long live the Emperor!' the whole regiment joined him instead. Thousands of old soldiers and regular troops flocked to join him as he advanced on Paris. In March, the Bourbon King fled and Napoleon resumed power.

Thus began the '100 Days' of Napoleon's second reign.

The Battle of Waterloo

This battle was fought between the French (commanded by Napoleon) and the Allied armies (commanded by the Duke of Wellington from Britain and General Blücher from Prussia). It was Napoleon's final defeat, and brought to an end 23 years of war in Europe. Waterloo cost Wellington 15,000 dead and injured and Blücher around 7,000. It cost Napoleon 25,000 dead and wounded, 8,000 prisoners and the crown of France.

The '100 Days' of Napoleon's second reign ended at the Battle of Waterloo, when his army was defeated by those of Britain and Prussia. Napoleon was exiled again, this time to the tiny British-owned island of St Helena in the South Atlantic Ocean. He died there on 5th May 1821. In 1840, his remains were returned to France and interred with much ceremony under the Dome des Invalides in Paris.

'Able was I ere I saw Elba' This sentence, supposedly uttered by Napoleon, is something called a palindrome. That means the sentence reads exactly the same backwards as it does forwards. Try it!

Napoleon's Grande Armée of over 500,000 troops is the biggest army ever seen in Europe.

fascinating Facts

Native American Peoples

The Native American Peoples are the tribes of people who were living in America before Europeans went to live there. Christopher Columbus, sailing from Spain, thought he had found a new route to the Indies but found the Americas instead. Because he did not know America existed, he called the tribes he met 'Indians', so for a long time they were known as 'American Indians'.

Native American tribes

Native Americans are thought to have migrated (moved to live) from Siberia over 11,000 years ago. They were able to do this because during the Ice Age there was a 'land bridge' joining these two continents. They settled into many largely peaceful tribes all across America, forming small hunting and farming communities. America is a very large country and the land and weather vary considerably. Many hundred Native American tribes lived across America living in ways that suited their territory. Each tribe had different traditions, art and religious beliefs, and also different languages

Northwest

In the Northwest it was warm with lots of rain and woodland. The Haida, the Tsimshian and the Nootka lived on a diet of salmon, wild fruits and berries. They lived in wooden houses, sailed wooden canoes, ate from wooden bowls and even wore tightly woven wooden hats to keep out the heavy rains! Some tribes had totem poles, large wooden poles carved with symbolic animals, telling the history and legends of the tribe.

Central Plains

On the dry, grassy Central Plains some Native American tribes were farmers, living in dome-shaped earthen houses and farming corn and beans. Other tribes were nomads, living in movable 'tepees' (houses made from animal skins stretched over a wooden frame) and hunting bison. The huge bison supplied almost everything the nomadic tribes needed to stay alive – meat for food, bone for tools and skins for housing and clothing.

Central Plateau

The Spokan, the Paiute and the Shoshone lived in the hard Central Plateau area. They gathered food like roots and fruit and also hunted small animals. They made acorn bread by pounding acorns and mixing them with hot water. They often lived in shelters like the tepees of the plains tribes, but instead of animal skins the

lived in caribou-skin tents, and made nets and bags for hunting and laces for their snowshoes from caribou leather thongs.

Southwest

In the Southwest the Hopi lived in towns built into cliffs and canyons called 'pueblos'. They were farmers, growing corn and beans. They also grew cotton which they wove into fabric for their own clothes and blankets and to trade with other tribes for things like buffalo meat. The men wove cloth and worked the farms. Women made pottery, decorated in many colours.

The Europeans

The arrival of the Europeans had a huge effect on Native Americans and their way of life. The European presence introduced at least a dozen strange diseases during this era that American Indians had no natural immunity against. It is believed that more native people died due to foreign diseases than were lost in wars fighting for their homelands.

Q&A?

What did Christopher Columbus call the Native American people?

Indians.

What is a powwow?

A Native American get-together, for making tribal decisions or for celebration, often involving ceremonial dancing and drumming.

pole frame was covered with woven mats of plants and reeds. These were called 'wickiups'.

Eastern Woodlands

In the Eastern Woodlands lived deer-hunters, the Natchez, the Choctaw and the Cherokee. They lived in dome-shaped 'wigwams' or in long wooden houses and wore deerskin clothing. The men were hunters and the women farmed small gardens of corn and beans.

Northern areas

The Northern areas were hard places to live. The Chipewyan hunted caribou (native American moose), caught fish and gathered berries and edible roots. They

Fascinating Facts

Wampum are strings of knots and beads used by the Iroquois to record tribal tales. They are also used as a unit of measure (for counting).

Some words in English have Native American origins:
• Kayak, from the Yupik word 'quayq'
• Igloo, from the Inuit word 'iglu', meaning 'house'
• Moose, from the Abenaki word 'mos'
• Pecan, from the Illinois word 'pakani'
• Toboggan, from the Micmac word 'topaghan'

Natural disasters

Throughout history there have been many natural disasters, the most deadly recorded as being droughts and famines. Floods are the next most deadly, followed by earthquakes. Transportation accidents are next, then wind storms. Other deadly disaster types include extreme temperatures, wind storms, transportation accidents, landslides, industrial accidents, volcanoes and forest fires.

Hurricanes

One of the most damaging events is the hurricane, a fierce rotating storm with an intense centre of low pressure (the eye of the storm) that only happens in the tropics.

They are formed when large areas of the ocean become heated, and the air pressure drops. This causes thunderstorms and strong surface winds. As they travel long distances, gathering energy from the ocean, they are likely to be classified as strong tropical cyclones. A tropical storm can only be classified as a hurricane if it sustains wind speeds above force 12 on the Beaufort Scale.

Tornadoes

Tornadoes are caused by a collision of warm and cool air streams. A rotating area of low-pressure storm clouds form, and air within a low-pressure front rises, creating a strong upward draught like a vacuum cleaner. Surrounding warm air is drawn in from ground level, causing it to spin faster and faster. These strong air currents can create a spiralling funnel of wind that can reach speeds of 300 mph (483 km/h).
Heavy objects, such as cars or even cows, can be sucked up and flung around like confetti. Many people have been killed in cars while they were trying to outrun a tornado, and although it is sometimes possible to escape, it is generally not a good idea.

Earthquakes

An earthquake is a tremor (shaking) of the earth's surface. It is usually caused by the release of underground stress along fault lines. Fault lines, or simply faults are rock fractures which show signs of movement. In spite of extensive research and sophisticated equipment, it is impossible to predict an earthquake, although experts can estimate the likelihood of an earthquake occurring in a particular region.

The point where the seismic activity occurs is the epicentre, where the earthquake is strongest. But it doesn't always end there, seismic waves travel out from the epicentre, sometimes creating widespread destruction as they pass.

Volcanoes

A volcano is formed when molten rock, called magma, explodes through the earth's crust. Volcanoes vary in their structure – some are splits in the earth's crust, some are domes, shields, or craters. When the magma bursts through the earth's surface it is called lava. Sometimes ash and cinders comes from the volcano, and also pumice, which is very light rock that is full of air bubbles and which can float on water.

Is a tsunami always caused by an earthquake?

A tsunami is caused by earthquakes, landslides, volcanoes or a massive impact, such as if a meteor crashed into the sea. Sometimes tsunamis have calmed down by the time they reach the shore; on other occasions they can be devastating.

What was the biggest known tornado?

In May 2004 in Nebraska, USA, the Hallam tornado became the record-holder for width, at nearly 2.5 miles (4 km). This is probably close to the maximum size for a tornado.

Tsunami

A tsunami is a chain of fast-moving waves caused by sudden trauma in the ocean. They can be generated by earthquakes, or volcanic eruptions. Tsunamis are also incorrectly known as tidal waves, but unlike tidal waves they are not caused by changes in the tides.

As a tsunami leaves the deep water of the open ocean and travels into the shallower water near the coast, it is slowed down by the shallow water and its height grows. Tsunamis batter the coast with tremendous amounts of energy.

They are most common around the edge of the Pacific, where more than half the world's volcanoes are found. Over the deep Pacific Ocean, a tsunami travels at about 800 kph (500 mph). If an earthquake happened in Los Angeles, a tsunami could hit Tokyo quicker than you could fly between the cities by jet.

Asian Tsunami

On Boxing Day 2004 the world witnessed the terrible power of one of the deadliest disasters in modern history. An undersea earthquake occurred about 8 a.m. local time. This triggered a series of lethal tsunamis that spread throughout the Indian Ocean. Waves up to 30 m devastated the shores of Indonesia, Sri Lanka, South India, Thailand and other countries.

10% of the world's population lives under threat from active volcanoes.

Often when an unusually destructive hurricane hits, that hurricane's name is retired and never used again. Since 1954, forty names have been retired.

Hurricane Katrina was the costliest and one of the deadliest hurricanes in the history of the United States. It was the sixth-strongest Atlantic hurricane ever recorded.

fascinating **Facts**

Natural fibres

Natural fibres are made from plants and animals. They have a wide variety of uses, including fabrics for clothing and furnishing, and paper for newspapers and books.

Wool

Wool is made from the fur of animals of the caprinae family (chamois, goats, sheep, and their relatives). Wool is mainly from sheep, but cashmere comes from goats, angora from rabbits and alpaca from llamas. Wool is mainly from sheep, but cashmere comes from goats, angora from rabbits and alpaca from llamas.

The processing of wool starts when a sheep is sheared (clipped), which usually happens once a year in the spring. At this stage the fleece is very greasy: it contains a lot of lanolin which protects the sheep from wind and rain. Most wool is creamy white although some breeds of sheep produce grey, black or brown wool.

Today most of the world's wool is produced in Australia, China and New Zealand, although it is also produced in many other countries.

Most wool is used for clothing: it is spun into yarn for knitted garments or woven into cloth. Some wool, from breeds of sheep with coarser wool, is also used for furnishings such as rugs and carpets.

fascinating Facts

Sheep's wool does not burn, so is used for insulation and also to cover the hammers inside a piano.

When silk culture was first introduced into the UK, many people planted mulberry trees. Unfortunately most of these were black mulberry trees. Their fruit tastes better to humans, but silk worms prefer the leaves of white mulberry trees.

Cotton

Cotton comes from the cotton plant gossypium, which grows in tropical parts of the world. The cotton itself is

the fibre around the seeds of the plant, which looks like a fluffy cotton-wool ball when it is growing.

Once processed, the cotton fibre produced is very strong. Spun into fine yarn, it has many uses. The invention of machines like the Spinning Jenny in 1764, and Arkwright's spinning frame in 1769, enabled cotton fibres to be processed quickly and cheaply. This led to a big cotton industry in many northern English towns. Even today there is evidence of this industry in many former cotton mill towns in Lancashire.

The Ancient Egyptians had cotton cloth as early as 12,000 BC, and in Mexico the weaving of cotton cloth with feathers and fur dates back to 7,000 BC. In India and Pakistan cotton has been grown, and processed for making into clothes, for more than 6,000 years.

Today cotton is produced on every continent. Most cotton is now mechanically harvested and then processed into yarn for making a wide variety of textiles. Cotton yarn can be woven or knitted to make fabric and is used to make clothing, towels and bed linen. The cotton seed which remains can be turned into vegetable oil for cooking.

Linen

Linen is produced from the flax plant (linum). In the past linen was produced in many European countries with the right climate: Scotland, Ireland, Northern France, Belgium and the Netherlands. Today, most linen is produced in China.

When flax is processed into linen, it makes a cloth strong enough to be used for tents and ships' sails. It is especially strong when wet, and can be washed at very high temperatures.

Linen fabric is used for clothing and household linen. It can also be made into very strong paper, suitable for bank notes. It can even be used to make books.

Silk

Silk is made from the cocoons of the silk worm – protective cases for the larvae or young. Cultivated silkworms live on the leaves of the white mulberry tree (Morus alba) which is native to eastern Asia. During the harvesting process the larvae inside the cocoon dies, which some people think is unacceptable even when the resulting fabric is so beautiful.

Silk fabric has a natural sheen to it created by the fibre's triangular structure which reflects light at different angles, causing it to shine and sparkle.

Silk fabric was developed in China, probably as long ago as 6,000 BC.

Why did Roman legionnaires used wool to line the breastplates of their armour?

To cushion themselves against the harsh metal.

Do you know what linseed oil is made from?

Linseed oil, traditionally used by artists in oil painting, is made from flax seed.

Natural Resources

Many countries use coal, oil and gas for their energy. These are called 'fossil fuels' because they have been formed from the remains of prehistoric plants and animals. However, they are 'non-renewable', meaning they cannot be renewed or replaced. Coal and oil will eventually run out, or become too expensive to get from the ground. But some energy sources are renewable – they never run out. The sun provides renewable energy, because it shines every day. Wind energy is also renewable: the wind stops blowing – but it always starts again!

Fossil fuels like coal and oil provide about two-thirds of the world's electricity and 95% of the world's total energy, including heating and transport. Coal is used in power stations to generate (produce) a lot of electricity, quite cheaply. Also, transporting the coal to the power stations is easy. So, power stations (which make electricity) use coal, oil or gas because they are very efficient fuels.

Pollution

The main disadvantage of fossil fuels is pollution. Burning coal or oil produces carbon dioxide, which contributes to the 'greenhouse effect', warming the Earth. Secondly, burning fossil fuels produces sulphur dioxide, a gas that causes acid rain which damages plants. Thirdly, mining (digging up) coal can ruin and destroy large areas of the landscape, and spoil the beauty of the countryside.

Non-renewable resources

Once we've burned all the coal, oil and gas, there isn't any more. Our consumption of fossil fuels has nearly doubled every 20 years since 1900. This is a particular problem for oil, because we use it to make plastic and many other products.

Renewable energy

In addition to the sun and the wind, there are several sources of renewable energy: plants, the Earth and the oceans.

Q&A?

How can waves be used to make electricity?

The tides and the winds drive the oceans waves. The oceans move forward and back, following a regular pattern. The energy of the oceans tides can be captured by special machines.

What is geothermal energy?

The inside of the Earth is very hot. Geothermal energy uses the Earth's internal heat for various uses. This energy from the Earth can be used to heat buildings or make electricity.

Sun and wind

Sunlight, or solar energy, can be used directly for heating and lighting homes and offices, for generating electricity, and for heating water. Solar power can also be used in factories.

Hydropower

Falling water can be used to drive a turbine – a spinning machine which makes electricity. This is called hydro power (hydro and water). Waterfalls can be used to make hydropower. Perhaps the waterfall was there already, or a dam can be built on a river to make a new waterfall.

Biomass

The living material in plants is called biomass. Biomass can be used to produce electricity, chemicals or fuel for cars. For example, the oil in some plants can be used to make a kind of petrol.

Fascinating Facts

The average household throws away almost 19 lb (8.5 kg) of paper each week. Most types of paper can be recycled; the more paper we recycle the fewer trees need to be cut down – because paper is made from pulped trees!

Hydrogen is the most abundant element on earth. It can be burned as a fuel, or converted into electricity.

New Zealand

New Zealand lies halfway between the Equator and the South Pole. It is over 1,200 miles (1,931 km) from Australia and comprises two main islands plus smaller ones. The South Island is the largest land mass, and is divided along its length by the Southern Alps, the highest peak of which is Aoraki/Mount Cook, 12,316 ft (3,754 m) high. There are 18 peaks of more than 9,800 ft (3,000 m) in the South Island. The tallest mountain on North Island is Mount Ruapehu, an active cone volcano, 9,176 ft (2,797 m) high. The dramatic and varied landscape of New Zealand has made it a popular location for filming, including the recent Lord of the Rings trilogy.

The Maori

The Maori were the first settlers. They arrived from Polynesia some time after the 13th century and established their own culture. New Zealand's Maori name is Aotearoa, and is usually translated as 'Land of the long white cloud', supposedly referring to the cloud the explorers saw on the horizon as they approached.

Why are New Zealanders called Kiwis?

The kiwi, a small flightless bird only found in New Zealand, has become the country's national symbol.

What is New Zealand's main team sport?

Rugby. New Zealand's world-beating international team is known as the 'All Blacks' due to their black shirts and shorts.

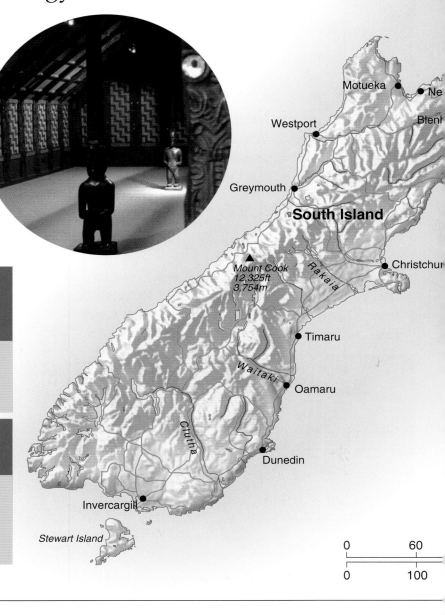

New Plym

Motueka · Ne

Westport · Blenl

Greymouth ·

South Island

▲ Mount Cook
12,325ft
3,754m

Rakaia

Christchur

Timaru ·

Waitaki

Oamaru

Clutha

Dunedin ·

Invercargill ·

Stewart Island

| 0 | 60 |
| 0 | 100 |

The Waimangu Geyser is the largest ever known. Scalding water is thrown up to 1,476 ft (450 m) into the air. In 1903 four people were killed when they were thrown 2,625 ft (800 m) by one eruption.

The four stars on the New Zealand flag stand for the Southern Cross constellation of stars as seen in the sky from New Zealand.

The Maori lived in fortified villages. The wood carvings used to decorate the buildings is their main art style. Over 1,000 Maori meeting houses with intricately carved designs are still in existence.

Colonial settlers

The first Europeans known to have reached New Zealand arrived in 1642. They developed commercial farming and the country's industrial base. Most people live in the cities of the warmer, volcanic North Island, where Auckland is the largest city and Wellington is the capital.

Flora and fauna

New Zealand is very isolated from other countries and therefore around 80% of the plants and trees are found only in New Zealand, such as the giant kauri and southern beech. Before the arrival of humans during the 1300s there were no land mammals in New Zealand. Birds, bats and sea creatures, some of which are now extinct, were the only animals to be found. It is still the case that some of the animals are found only on these islands. The weta is one such insect. There are about 70 varieties of weta; the largest of the species can grow to the size of a mouse and weigh more than 2.5 oz (70 gr). This is the heaviest insect in the world (it has a body length of around 8 inches (20 cm)).

There are four species of New Zealand primitive frogs but their conservation status is serious. Two of the species are classed as vulnerable, one as endangered and one as critical. There are no snakes in New Zealand.

The Takah – or South Island Takah – is a flightless bird found only in New Zealand. It was thought to be extinct but was rediscovered in 1948.

The world's longest name

Tetaumatawhakatangihangakoauaotamateaurehaeaturipuk apihimaungahoronukupokaiwhenuaakitanarahu is listed in the Guinness Book of Records as being the longest place name in the world. It's the name of a hill in Hawkes Bay in New Zealand. It means 'The brow of the hill, where Tamatea, the man with the big knees, who slid down, climbed up and swallowed'.

Map labels: angerei, Gt. Barrier Island, Tauranga, amilton, Rotorua, North Island, Gisborne, Wanganui, Napier, Hastings, anui, Palmerston North, Wellington

180   240 miles

300   400 kilometres

The Norman Conquest

The Battle of Hastings, in 1066, is one of the most famous battles fought on British soil, and changed English life forever. There were actually two invasions of England in 1066. Without the first one, the Norman Conquest might never have succeeded.

In 1066 the Anglo-Saxon King of England, Edward the Confessor, died without leaving any sons to inherit his throne. The kingship was then claimed by three men: Earl Harold Godwinson of Wessex, Duke William of Normandy, and Harald Hardrada, Viking King of Norway.

Earl Harold

Earl Harold was an adviser to Edward the Confessor, and the king's brother-in-law. He claimed that Edward had named Harold as his heir. The Anglo-Saxon high council, the Witan, preferred Harold to the foreign claimants, and Harold was crowned on the same day Edward was buried.

Duke William of Normandy

William was a distant blood relation of Edward the Confessor. He said Edward had chosen him as his heir a long time before. The Normans insisted Harold had sworn on holy relics to support William's claim to the throne.

Who were the Anglo-Saxons?

The Anglo-Saxons were the dominant people in England from 410 to 1066.

Who was the last Anglo-Saxon King of England?

King Harold was the last Anglo-Saxon King of England.

When Edward died childless and Harold took the English throne for himself, William considered Harold an oath-breaker.

Harald Hardrada

Harald became ruler of Norway after his nephew King Magnus died. Magnus had made a pact with King Harthacnut, a previous ruler of England, that if either one of them died childless then the other would inherit his kingdom. Harald claimed that as Magnus's heir, he was therefore the rightful King of England.

The Battle of Stamford Bridge

Almost as soon as King Harold was crowned, he had to get ready to fight for his new throne: news came that Harald Hardrada had landed with an army in the north of England.

King Harold rushed north with his hastily raised army, and on 25 September defeated the Vikings in a surprise attack at Stamford Bridge. Harald Hardrada was killed, and only 24 ships from his invasion fleet of 300 made it back to Norway.

While King Harold was defeating the Viking threat, Duke William had already started his own invasion. Harold's men were still celebrating their victory in the north when news came that William had invaded in the south, landing on 28 September.

The Battle of Hastings

To fight William, King Harold and his men had to march 250 miles from Stamford Bridge to Hastings. They did this in just nine days, but they were tired.

Harold took position with his army on top of a hill about five miles from Hastings. When William and his army arrived on 14 October, they saw that they would have to fight uphill.

The battle raged all day. During the afternoon a rumour spread that William had been killed, and his troops began to lose heart. William took off his helmet so that he could be seen, and rode up and down to show his men he was still alive. That put fresh heart into the invaders.

As evening approached, William's men made a rush at the Anglo-Saxon shield wall, and then pretended to retreat in order to draw their enemies away from their tightly held line. Harold's men broke ranks to pursue them, and were caught in William's trap. The Normans then rushed Harold's shield wall, and King Harold fell, with most of his Anglo-Saxon nobles.

William was crowned King in Westminster Abbey on Christmas Day 1066, becoming William I of England. He is more famously known by the name of William the Conqueror.

The Domesday Book

William wanted to know what his new kingdom was worth, who held what land, and how wealthy his subjects were. In 1086, he sent out agents to do a huge census of the whole population, and the results were recorded in the Domesday (Doomsday) Book.

The Bayeaux Tapestry

This embroidery is 270 feet (82.3 m) long and 20 inches (0.51 m) wide, and tells the story of the Battle of Hastings and events leading up to it from the Norman point of view.

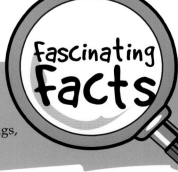

fascinating Facts

The Bayeaux Tapestry contains 50 scenes, 632 people, 202 horses, 55 dogs, 505 other animals, 37 buildings, 41 ships, 49 trees and almost 2000 Latin letters.

North America

North America is a continent bordered by the Arctic Ocean to the north and to the east, by the Caribbean Sea to the southeast and by the Pacific Ocean to the south and west. It covers almost 5% of the earth's surface – an area of about 9,450,000 sq miles (24,480,000 sq km). It is the third largest continent in area, with a population of more than 514,000,000.

The native people of North America originally came across the frozen Arctic Ocean from Asia, but centuries of immigration from Europe, Africa and south-east Asia have made the USA and Canada a multicultural society.

The American cordillera

This is a continuous string of mountains that stretches from Alaska to Antarctica. It includes ranges such as the Rocky Mountains in North America and the Andes in South America.

Rocky Mountains

The Rocky Mountains, or the Rockies, are part of a mountain chain that stretches more than 3,000 miles

ARCTIC OCEAN

ALASKA

C A

NORTH PACIFIC OCEAN

U N I T E D OF AM

Are the Great Lakes in the United States or Canada?

The five Great Lakes are on or near the United States / Canadian border. Lake Michigan is the only one entirely in the United States; it is the second largest in volume. The other four lakes are Lake Superior (the largest and deepest), Lake Huron (the second largest in area), Lake Erie (the smallest in volume and the shallowest) and Lake Ontario (the smallest in area). These four lakes form the border between the United States and Canada (the border runs roughly through the middle of the lakes).

Where is the coldest place in North America?

Yukon (Canada) and Greenland are among the world's coldest places, with temperatures reaching a low of −80°F (−62°C).

The world's biggest living tree is the giant Sequoia called General Sherman in the Sequoia National Park, California, standing 276 ft (84 m) tall, 36 ft (11 m) in diameter and with a girth of 102 ft (31 m).

In Canada the Inuit (formerly known as Eskimos) are able to govern themselves in the Nunavut province. They have adapted to the harsh environment and often combine modern technology with their traditional lifestyle.

Fascinating Facts

(4,800 km) from British Columbia in Canada to New Mexico in the United States. They contain ice caps, glaciers and volcanoes. The highest peak is Mount Elbert in Colorado, which is 14,440 ft (4,401 m) above sea level. Mount Robson, at 12,972 ft (3,954 m), is the highest peak in the Canadian Rockies.

Alaska

Alaska was part of Russia until 1867, when it was bought by the USA for US$7.2 million (3.9 million GBP). The America people thought it a waste of money, not knowing of the vast oil and gold reserves at the time!

Languages in Alaska

More than 90 languages are spoken in Alaska. About 20 of these are native to Alaska. The indigenous languages, known locally as Native languages, belong to two major language groups. These are the Aleut, or Eskimo group, and the Athabaksan group. A number of these languages are spoken by no more than a few hundred people. Most people, though, will speak two or three languages.

Greenland

Greenland is the world's largest island. Although it is geographically part of the Arctic nation and therefore associated with North America, it is actually part of Europe. The people from Greenland live mainly in the coastal region, as ice sheet covers 80% of the island. The Vikings landed on Greenland in the 10th century having sailed from Iceland. By the 18th century it had come under Danish rule and became fully integrated into Denmark in 1953. 1n 1979 it became self-governing and in 1997 Inuit place names superseded Danish ones.

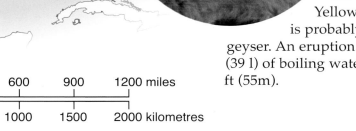

Old Faithful

The Old Faithful Geyser in Yellowstone National Park, USA, is probably the world's most famous geyser. An eruption can shoot up to 68 pints (39 l) of boiling water to a height of up to 180 ft (55m).

GREENLAND
(Kalaallit Nunaat)

Arctic Circle

● Nuuk (Godhaab)

A   D   A

St. John s ●

Ottawa
□

ATES

Washington ●

ICA

300	600	900	1200 miles
500	1000	1500	2000 kilometres

Numbers

When numbers could not be written down, the earliest counting device was the human hand and its fingers.

Counting devices

A counting board is a piece of wood, stone or metal with carved grooves or painted lines. Between the lines beads, pebbles or metal discs were moved.

The abacus is a device (usually wooden, more recently plastic), with a frame holding rods. Beads with holes in the middle are fitted on the rods. The beads slide along the rods. An abacus is not a calculator: the person operating the abacus performs calculations in their head and uses the abacus as a physical aid to keep track of the numbers.

Do you know how horses are measured?

Horses are measured in hands'. One hand measures 4 inches.

What is the Salamis tablet?

The Salamis tablet is the oldest surviving counting board. Originally thought to be a gaming board, it was used by the Babylonians about 300 BC. It was discovered in 1846 on the island of Salamis.

How the Incas counted

The Incas of South America developed a method of recording numbers which did not require writing. It involved knots in strings called quipu. The quipu consists of strings which were knotted to represent numbers. A number was represented by knots in the string. If the number 586 was to be recorded on the string then six touching knots were placed near the free end of the string, a space was left, then eight touching knots for the 10s, another space, and finally 5 touching knots for the 100s.

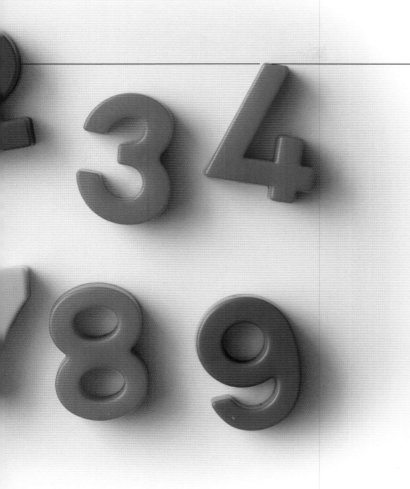

The money used by a quite a few of the countries in Europe is called the Euro. This is a decimal currency. There are 100 cents in one Euro.

History of numbers

From around 3,000 BC the Egyptians had a writing system based on pictures representing words (hieroglyphs). They had a base 10 system like the modern decimal system, but they used pictures instead of numbers. The number system of India (invented around 600 AD) was much better, and the system we use today is based on it. The ancient Roman number system is still used today: you can see Roman numbers on clock faces.

The decimal system

The decimal system we use today uses ten different numbers – 0, 1, 2, 3, 4, 5, 6, 7, 8 and 9 – plus a dot called the decimal point. This system is also called Hindu-Arabic or Arabic, or base 10 system. Ten is the base and the decimal point marks a place in the number.

Fascinating Facts

Arabic letters are written right-to-left, but numbers in Arabic are written left-to-right.

Tri- means three. So triangles have three sides, the French flag is a tricolore because it has three colours, and the dinosaur triceratops had three horns.

All US dollar bills have a portrait of a famous American on the front, and a decorative design on the back.

Olympic Games

In ancient times the Olympic Games were held in a place called Olympia, on the south-western Greek mainland. No one knows exactly when they were first held, but from 776 BC the Greeks started making a note of the date for the Games. The Olympic Games were held in honour of Zeus, the king of the gods.

At first only one race (the sprint) was run, and the Games lasted one day. Gradually more events were added, and by the end of the 5th century BC the Games lasted for five days. Only Greek male citizens were allowed to compete in the Games.

The Festival

By the 1st century AD, Olympia had been transformed by the construction of magnificent stone temples and sports facilities. Two days before the start of the Olympic festival all the participants set out from Elis to walk 58 km to Olympia. This route was called the Sacred Way.

There were no awards for second or third place, but the winner received a wreath woven from a branch of the sacred olive tree in the Altis. This holy place was where the ancient Greeks believed the god Zeus lived in his great

Q&A?

Do you know why the Olympic flag has five rings?

The rings on the Olympic flag stand for the world's five continents, which are linked together by competing in the multinational Games.

Which swimmer holds the record for winning the most gold medals at one Olympic Games?

The American Mark Spitz holds the record. He won seven golds in swimming events at the 1972 Munich Games.

temple. The religious ending to the festival was the sacrifice to Zeus of 100 oxen.

Banning the Games

The Games gradually became more about pleasing the spectators than the gods. The final Olympic festival was held when the Christian Emperor of Rome, Theodosius I, banned the worship of non-Christian gods.

The Olympics were revived in June 1896 by Baron Pierre de Coubertin, who believed passionately that international sports competitions were a way to build friendship between nations.

The Modern Games

In 1896 nearly 250 men from different countries completed against one another for ten days and in 43 events. The modern Olympics are not religious, and since 1900 women have been allowed to take part.

The Paralympics

Since 1960 there has been a third kind of Olympics – for less abled athletes. These Games are called the Paralympics, and they take place every four

years, about the same time as the Summer Olympics. Paralympic events include all sorts of sports, from basketball to rhythmic gymnastics.

The marathon

The longest Olympic running race is the marathon. Athletes have to complete a course of about 42 km. The event is named after a great Greek victory over Persian invaders in 490 BC. According to a later legend, a Greek messenger ran all the way from Marathon to Athens with the joyful news, then dropped dead.

At the 1988 Paralympic Games, held at Seoul in South Korea, Denmark's wheelchair athlete Connie Hansen won five events. She was first in the 400m, 800m, 1500m, 5,000m and wheelchair marathon races. At the next Paralympics in 1992, in Barcelona, Spain, she won the marathon again!

Since the Amsterdam Games in 1928, a special flame burns at all Olympic venues. Since 1936 this flame has been brought from Olympia in Greece, and is usually carried by torch-bearers.

Pacific Ocean

The Pacific Ocean is the largest ocean in the world, covering 65% of the Earth's surface. At almost 70 million sq miles (180 million sq km), it is considerably larger than the entire land area of the whole world!

The Pacific Ocean stretches from the Arctic Circle to Antarctica, and to the eastern coasts of North America and South America. In the centre and to the west are thousands of islands, mostly around the equator.

Q&A?

How deep is the Pacific Ocean?

The average depth of the Pacific Ocean is 15,215 ft (4,637.5 m) deep. At its deepest part, the Mariana Trench, it is 36,200 ft (11,034 m) deep.

Does the International Date Line change in the Pacific Ocean?

Yes, it travels roughly along 180° longitude, with diversions to pass around some countries or islands. The International Date Line is an imaginary line that separates two consecutive days. The date in the Eastern Hemisphere is always one day ahead of the date in the Western Hemisphere.

Peaceful sea?

Pacific is from the Latin words for 'Peace.' However the Pacific is not always peaceful. Many typhoons pound the islands of the Pacific. The area is full of volcanoes and often affected by earthquakes. Tsunamis, caused by underwater earthquakes, have damaged islands and destroyed entire towns and communities. Massive whirls, formed by ocean currents, are found in the area north and south of the equator.

Fishing

The main fishing areas in the Pacific are found in the more shallow waters of the continental shelf. The continental shelf is the extended land beyond each continent, which is relatively shallow. Then comes the continental slope, which eventually merges into the deep ocean floor. Salmon, halibut, herring, sardines and tuna are the chief catch.

Not all fishing communities have large commercial fleets, however. Small island communities fish nearer to home.

Exploration and settlement

The first people who lived on the islands were from Asia. They crossed the open seas in ancient boats. Europeans explorers arrived in the 16th century, people such as Vasco Núñez de Balboa from Spain. During the 17th century the Dutchman Abel Janszoon Tasman discovered Tasmania

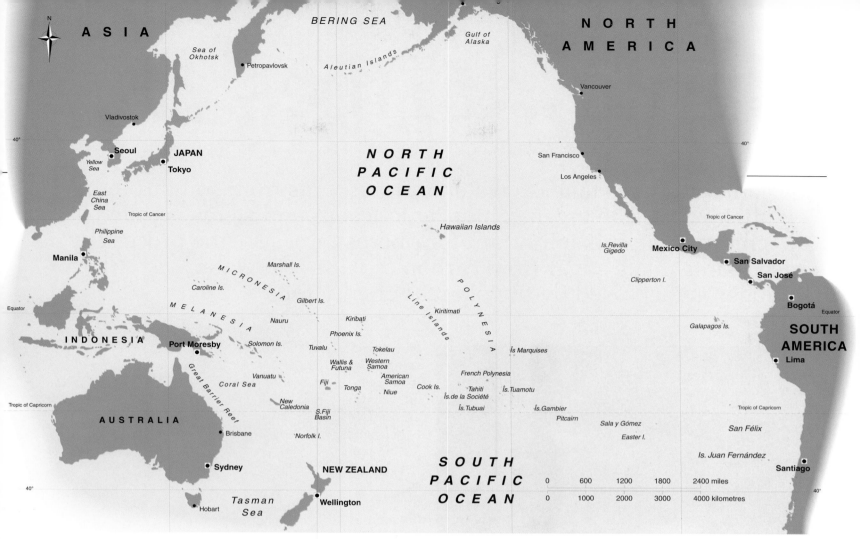

and New Zealand. Then the 18th century saw the Russians land in Alaska, and the French settle in Polynesia. The British sailed with Captain James Cook to Australia, the South Pacific, Hawaii, and North American.

studied can still be seen in the Pacific, in particular the turtles and tortoises of the Galapagos Islands.

The Pacific is rich in mineral wealth, but the ocean is so deep that mining would be very difficult and dangerous. In the shallower waters of the continental shelves off the coasts of Australia and New Zealand, petroleum and natural gas are extracted, and pearls are harvested along the coasts of Australia, Japan, Papua New Guinea and the Philippines.

During the 1800s Charles Darwin's research on his five-year voyage on the HMS Beagle brought him fame as a geologist and author. He studied the theory of evolution and natural selection. You can read more about this in the chapter about Charles Darwin. In 1859 he published the book On the Origin of Species. Many of the animals he

Fascinating Facts

90% of all volcanic activity occurs in the oceans.

If you placed Mt Everest in the Marianas Trench there would still be over a mile (1.6 km) of ocean above it.

Plants *and* Trees

Plants and trees take up water and nutrients from soil through their roots. The green colouring in leaves and stems is called chlorophyll. It is important for photosynthesis – the process by which plants make sugar from carbon dioxide and water. The sugar is then used by the plant as energy for growth.

Some trees and shrubs are evergreen – they keep their leaves all year.

Others are deciduous – their leaves fall off in autumn.

Many trees and plants are well adapted for the situation in which they grow. For example, fir trees have narrow, tough, needle-like leaves that can withstand very cold weather. Plants that grow in hot, dry places have small leaves or a very tough coating – like cacti. This ensures that they can live off small amounts of water.

Some plants are perennials, which means that they live for a long time. They usually die down in the winter and live off stored energy in their roots or bulbs in the ground. Other plants are annuals, which means that they grow, flower and set seed in one season. At the end of the summer the plant dies and the seeds are scattered.

New plants can be made in two ways – by vegetative propagation or by sowing seeds.

Trees and plants have many uses:

- Cereals such as wheat, rice, oats, barley and maize are grown around the world for food.

- Drinks; coffee comes from roasted coffee beans, chocolate from cacao seeds, and tea from dried leaves of the tea plant.

- Construction materials, such as wood from trees and thatch from reeds.

- Cotton fibres for cloth.

- Rope is made from hemp.

- Drugs and medicines – opium for controlling pain comes from poppies, digitalis for heart disease comes from foxgloves, and drugs from periwinkles and yew trees are used for cancer.

The tallest trees in the world are the giant redwoods of California which are more than 330 ft (100 m) metres tall.

Tree roots can be so strong that they can split rocks and sometime damage roads and walls.

Horsetail was around at the time of the dinosaurs. We know this because it's been found in dinosaur fossils. It grows almost everywhere in the world except Australia and Antarctica.

The biggest flower in the world is found in the Indonesian jungle (Rafflesia arnoldii). It can grow to be 3 ft (0.9 m) across and weigh up to 15 lb (6.8 kg). It smells of rotting meat and this attracts insects, which pollinate it when they walk across it searching for the meat which they think they can smell.

Dendrochronology is a method of finding out the age of a tree by tree-ring dating as they grow a new ring each year. Wide rings often show a year of good growth when water and nutrients were plentiful but a narrow ring indicates a difficult year, sometimes when there was a drought.

Fascinating Facts

Some plants protect themselves from being eaten by animals by growing thorns or spikes along their stems or having parts which are poisonous. Yew trees are poisonous in all parts except for the fleshy red coating of their berries.

The biggest flower in the world is found in the Indonesian jungle (Rafflesia arnoldii). It smells of rotting meat and this attracts insects, which pollinate it when they walk across it searching for the meat which they think they can smell.

Q&A?

Can plants be carnivorous?

Some plants live in such poor soil that they have become carnivorous like the Venus Fly Trap – they get some of their nutrients by catching and digesting insects.

What is a parasitic plant?

Mistletoe is a parasitic plant; it has no roots of its own, it grows on certain trees and sucks its nutrients from the host tree.

Politics

Politics is the study of how we are governed and how governments work. In the ancient world, Emperors ruled Empires, and ordinary people had no say in how they were ruled. Later, in the Middle Ages, countries were ruled by Kings and Queens. The King was very powerful, and made most of the decisions about a country himself, or with advice from a small group of people he trusted.

Democracy

Today many countries in the world are governed by a system we call democracy. This means that everyone has a say in how their government is run. People in a democracy also vote for leaders in an election. Democracy was invented in Ancient Greece, where leading citizens openly debated (that is, discussed and argued about) the best way to govern.

Parliament

Governments must decide how much to tax their citizens, what to spend the tax money on, and how to make the country run smoothly. One of the ways these decisions are made in the United Kingdom is through Parliament. Parliament is the place where laws are made and ministers try to solve the country's problems. There are two Houses of Parliament in Britain – the House of Commons and the House of Lords.

Parliamentary elections

Members of Parliament, or MPs, are chosen by a General Election. Each city or large area of the country has candidates, people who want to be elected and who usually belong to a political party. The main parties in the

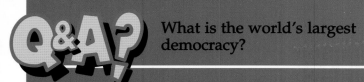
UK are the Labour Party the Conservative Party, and the Liberal Democrats. Every UK citizen over the age of 18 can vote for one of these candidates. Once the votes have been cast, they are counted and the candidate from each area with the most votes is elected to Parliament. The political party with the most MPs is asked to form the government, and the party's leader becomes the Prime Minister, sometimes known as the PM.

Equal voting rights

Not all elections have been open to everyone. For example, it was only in the last century that women won the right to vote. Early in the 20th century women called Suffragettes held many public protests to campaign for women's suffrage (the right to vote). Even so, women were not granted equal voting rights with men in the UK until 1928. In the United States of America, black people were not always guaranteed the right to vote until 1965. During the 1950s and 1960s, the Civil Rights Movement, led by Dr Martin Luther King Jr, held many protests. The Civil Rights Act of 1964 and the Voting Rights Act of 1965 guaranteed equal rights for minorities.

Democracy in the USA

The United States of America has a democratic system that is a bit different from the one in the UK. Each of the fifty states elects two Senators, who serve in the Senate, and Representatives, who serve in the House of Representatives (Congress). The more people who live in a state, the more Representatives it elects. For example, California, which has many people, elects more than fifty Representatives, but Alaska, which has few people, only has one.

Americans also elect a President. There are two main political parties in the USA, the Democratic Party and the Republican Party, and the President is usually a member of one of these. The seat of government in the USA is located in the capital city, Washington, D.C.

Making a difference

Politics are very important in today's world. People care deeply about how their children are educated, how good their hospitals are, how much money they will earn and how much tax they will have to pay. They worry about what others think of their country and whether they will ever go to war. Voting in an election is one of the most important things an adult can do.

Britain has a political party called The Monster Raving Loony Party.

A monarchy is a form of government that has a Monarch (a king or Queen) as Head of State. In such cases the Monarch usually rules for life. There are 29 existing monarchies in the world.

Fascinating Facts

Prehistory

Prehistory, or 'before history', is the period of human evolution before written records. The study of prehistory looks at the life of prehistoric animals such as dinosaurs and woolly mammoths, and prehistoric peoples, or cave dwellers. Palaeontologists study fossils, tools and paintings to work out how people lived.

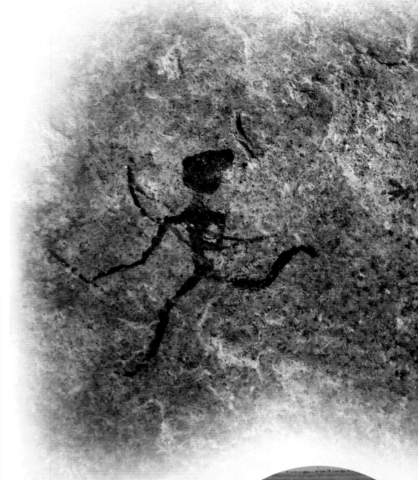

Prehistory is divided into three broad ages of prehistoric people: Stone Age, Bronze Age and Iron Age. These names are based on the technology used during the different periods. The categories were devised when a Danish museum curator needed to subdivide a large number of prehistoric exhibits. New artefacts (objects) are still being discovered, providing new information about what the world was like for early human beings.

The Stone Age

The Stone Age or 'Neolithic' period was 2 million years ago. Tools and weapons were made from stone, and people hunted animals, fished with simple weapons, gathered food such as berries from plants, and discovered fire. Humans were evolving during this period. The species that became Homo sapiens emerged at the end of this period. Before this were Homo habilis and Homo erectus.

Archaeologists have found cave paintings, which show that early people produced artwork, such as rock paintings called 'petroglyphs'. Early humans also used dyes to decorate their bodies, and there is evidence that some of them used copper ore to produce basic tools. Very hard rocks like flint were shaped to use as cutting tools or arrowheads. There was an increasing use of technology, and a gradual development of agriculture. Dogs were used for hunting, and lived with their masters.

People began to live in larger groups or settlements, to farm and to trade. Villages were based on the farming of cereals like wheat, barley and millet, and the raising of cattle, sheep, goats and pigs. People lived in simple shelters, such as caves or huts made from mammoth skins and bones.

The first use of iron occurred in Ancient Egypt around 4000 BC. Spear tips and beads were fashioned from iron found in meteorites.

Skara Brae on the island of Orkney, off the coast of Scotland, is a Neolithic village discovered by archaeologists. Here archaeologists found stone beds and shelves, and even an indoor toilet connected to a nearby stream.

The Bronze Age

Metalworking began during this period, and bronze tools were increasingly common and useful. There was skilled and detailed workmanship, producing many beautiful objects such as carved drinking horns and decorated pottery. There were also some early forms of writing, such as Egyptian hieroglyphs and Mayan symbols.

What was the most important invention of the Bronze age?

The wheel. This allowed people to make carts and transport goods.

How is bronze made?

Bronze is a mixture of copper, tin and other metals.

The search for more raw materials led to exploration and colonisation of new territories. Trade routes enabled travellers to reach other countries. Cities were formed and countries emerged, but traders became rivals and competition for raw materials led to wars. Communities built boats, developed farming techniques and invented new technology, for example the ox-drawn plough.

The Iron Age

Iron tools and weapons were made in this period, which ended with the development of written history. Different parts of the world advanced at different speeds. The Greek and Roman Empires and their great cultures were very advanced, but in Northern Europe the Iron Age lasted until the early Middle Ages.

Iron was hard, had a high melting point, and there was a

lot of iron ore available. So having once been rare and costly, iron was now a cheap and useful material, and became used for many different tasks.

Iron allowed warfare to become more sophisticated. Villages were strengthened, and hill forts and castles built. There was fighting on horseback and in horse-drawn chariots, and swords and arrows were produced from iron.

Coins were manufactured in bronze, making trade easier. Iron-made tools were stronger and better, and people's lives improved because of higher agricultural productivity. Iron-tipped ploughs were more efficient than wooden ones, and iron axes cut down trees quickly – clearing land for farming, and providing wood for building.

Rainforests

Rainforests are lush green jungles, with incredibly tall trees and hot, humid climates. They are called 'rainforests' because they get rain almost every single day. 50% of this rainfall is water that has evaporated from the rainforest itself and then cooled and condensed back into rain.

The animals and plants that live in the rainforests have adapted to the extremely hot and humid conditions there. Although rainforests cover only 6% of the Earth's surface, they are home to more than half the world's animal and plant species!

Plants in the rainforests grow in a system of layers:

Top layer – formed of giant trees up to 246 ft (75 m) tall. Only 1% of trees grow high enough to reach this layer. Animals here tend to be strong fliers like bats, macaws, eagles – even some butterflies!

Canopy layer – the main part of the rainforest, formed of smaller trees, 66–98 ft (20 –30 m) tall. It receives full sunlight, and in many places the branches form a leafy 'canopy' which prevents sunlight and rain getting to lower levels. This layer teems with life – good climbers such as monkeys, snakes and

Q&A?

Where are rainforests?

Rainforests are found in 85 countries near the equator – in Central America, Africa, Australia and Asia. Central America was once covered with rainforest, but large areas have now been cleared.

Which is the largest rainforest?

The world's largest rainforest is the Amazon jungle in South America, covering 2,700,000 sq miles (6,992,968 sq m).

lemurs, as well as birds like toucans and hornbills can be found here.

Understory – the dark layer beneath the canopy – only 2% of light gets through! Plants here are much smaller – woody vines, small trees and tall shrubs. Most animals here live on the trees, like spiders, insects, small mammals and frogs.

Forest floor – the lowest layer, the floor of the rainforest. Little vegetation grows here. The main animals down here are large mammals like gorillas, aardvarks and jaguars, and insects like ants and beetles.

Animal life

There are millions, perhaps billions, of animals living inside the rainforests. About 90% are insects. Other common animals are reptiles such as lizards and snakes, tropical birds such as toucans and parrots, and other mammals such as monkeys, leopards and sloths. Animals have adapted to live in the rainforests through camouflage, slowness, disguise and poison. Animals like chameleons and stick insects use camouflage to blend in with the leaves ands trees, making them hard to see.

Sloths have adapted to move slowly because that saves energy in the heat and make it harder for predators to see them. Animals use disguise to make predators think they are bigger or more dangerous than they really are – some butterflies have markings that look like eyes on their wings, to appear like the head of a bigger animal. Poison is used as a defence and for capturing prey. The poison-arrow frog has brightly coloured and patterned bodies as a warning to predators – which says 'don't eat me, I'm poisonous!'.

Rainforests at risk

Wide areas of rainforest are being cut down – the equivalent of 4,000 football pitches every hour! Rare animals and plants now face extinction and the tribes who live there may have lost their homes.

It's easy to forget that the rainforests are home to people too! Some 50,000,000 tribal people live there – for example, the Pygmies of Central America, the Huli of Papua New Guinea, and the Yanomami in South America.

If you have ever seen a film where Tarzan swings through the jungle, chances are he was using a liana.

Plant life

Rainforests teem with plant life – many plants have also adapted to thrive in their surroundings.

Rainforest plants

Lianas – these are rope-like vines which grow up trees towards the sunlight. Once at the top of the canopy, they spread to other trees.

'Pitcher' Plants – these carnivorous plants are named after their jug-shaped leaves. Inside these leaves is a strong smelling nectar that attracts insects, which get trapped inside the leaves and are then digested by the plant. Pitcher plants can be up to 30 ft (9 m) tall.

Bromeliads – these pineapple-like plants have thick waxy leaves which form a bowl shape and catch water. Some hold several gallons, and have been found with creatures like frogs and snails living inside them.

Plants that grow on

trees – many rainforest plants actually grow on the branches and trunks of trees, where there is more light and air than on the forest floor. These sunlight-loving plants are called epiphytes – some examples are orchids.

Recycling

R ecycling is making something new out of something old instead of just throwing it away. Recycling 'bins' where people can take old bottles, cans and paper are now a familiar sight

It's natural to recycle!

In nature, things are recycled all the time – when a tree dies, beetles will feast on the wood, and fungi will break it down, returning the nutrients from the dead tree to the soil for other plants to use.

A good deal of what we use in our human lives can also be recycled. Glass can be melted down and remade into new jars and bottles. Old newspapers and magazines can be turned into pulp using water, making a thin liquid mixture from which new sheets of paper can be made. Even plastic bags and bottles can be melted down and made into new things.

What do we mean by 'finite resources'?

This means that, once these materials are used up, they are gone for good! Examples of finite resources are fossil fuels such as coal and oil.

How long does it take plastic to break down naturally?

If a plastic bottle is simply thrown away, it will take 450 years to break down naturally.

Why is it important?

Recycling uses less energy and fewer raw materials than making new things 'from scratch'. When something is simply thrown away, all the energy and raw materials that went into making it are wasted.

Let's take glass as an example. To make glass, raw materials of sand, soda and lime all have to be mined. They must then be heated at 2372°F (1500°C), and the heat energy probably comes from a non-renewable resource, like coal or oil. Recycling 1 tonne of glass saves 1.2 tonnes of raw materials and the equivalent of 30 gallons (136 litres) of oil energy!

What can we recycle?

Glass – glass is 100% recyclable! We can keep melting it down and re-using it forever! If we throw it away, it will not 'break down' – archaeologists have found glass bottles from over 3000 years ago!

Plastic – plastic is harder to recycle than glass, but most plastic bottles and carrier bags can be recycled.

Paper and cardboard – recycling paper and cardboard saves trees, and reduces pollution. One tonne of recycled paper saves 17 trees and enough energy to heat a house for six months!

Cans – steel and aluminium cans are easy to recycle. One recycled aluminium can saves enough energy to run a television for three hours. Recycling one tonne of steel saves 1.5 tonnes of iron ore and 0.5 tonnes of coal – and uses only 25% of the energy that creating brand new steel would use.

What else can we do?

Even better for the environment than recycling are
• re-using items
• reducing the amount of energy we use and the amount of waste we produce!

How can we re-use?

Here are some everyday things that can easily be re-used.
• **Batteries** – It takes 50 times more energy to make a normal battery than we get out of it. Thrown away batteries can leak dangerous chemicals. Using re-chargeable batteries instead reduces pollution as well as saving money.
• **Plastic carrier bags** – keep them and re-use them for your next shopping trip.

How can we reduce waste?

• **Water waste** – don't leave the tap running while you clean your teeth. It wastes 9 pts (5 l) of water a minute.
• **Light** – change to energy-saving bulbs. They use less energy than normal ones, thus cutting carbon-dioxide emissions. And they last a lot longer.
• **Electric devices** – don't leave TVs and other devices on standby. It's the equivalent of about 15% of the world's electricity. Turn them off properly.

How much rubbish do we really produce?

Quite a lot!
• The volume of waste produced in one year in the UK would fill a line of dustbins stretching all the way to the moon and back.
• People in the UK throw away seven times their own body weight in rubbish every year.
• 8 billion plastic carrier bags are given away by UK shops every year. That's enough to cover all of London in a layer of plastic bags.
• 80 million food and drink cans end up going to waste in landfills each year.

Religion

A religion may be a belief in something spiritual – a God, or gods – or it may have more to do with the way that we live our lives. Most religions have teachers called priests, and celebrate special festivals.

Buddhism

Buddhism was founded in India over 2,500 years ago and is based on the teachings of Siddhartha Gautama, who became known as the Buddha. Buddhism has no supreme god or deity, but teaches its followers to live a thoughtful and balanced life. Buddha means 'enlightened' and Buddhism is all about attaining enlightenment, known as 'Nirvana'. To help with this, Buddhists practise meditation.

Buddhist symbol: the Wheel of Life, symbolising the cycle of life and rebirth.

Buddhist festival: Wesak, the celebration of the Buddha's birth, enlightenment and death.

Christianity

This religion originated in Palestine around 2,000 years ago. Christians believe in only one God, and that a man called Jesus was his son. The Christian holy book, the Bible, tells the story of Jesus. Christians are taught that God cares about people, and wishes them to try to behave like Jesus and live good lives. Sunday is the Christian holy day, when Christians meet and worship in buildings called churches.

Christian symbol: the Cross, symbolising the death and return to life of Jesus.

Christian festival: Easter, celebrating the death and return to life of Jesus.

Hinduism

Hinduism is considered the oldest religion in the world, dating back at least 4,000 years. Hindus believe that Brahman (the Universal Soul) can be worshipped in many different forms, such as Krishna, Rama and Shiva. Hindus believe in reincarnation – this means that

Q&A?

Which are the largest religions in the world?

The largest organised religions in the world today are Buddhism, Christianity, Hinduism, Islam, Judaism and Sikhism.

What are the five rules that Muslims live by?

Declaration of faith; praying five times a day; giving to the poor; fasting during daylight hours in the holy month of Ramadan; making a pilgrimage (the 'Hajj') to Mecca at least once during their lifetime.

Islam is founded on the teachings of Muhammad, 'peace be upon him'. Muhammad is so respected by Muslims that it is customary to say this whenever his name is mentioned.

A Sikh place of worship is called a Gurdwara, and is anywhere that the holy book (the Guru Granth Sahib) is kept.

people live many lives, one after another, until they become truly close to Brahman. Behaviour in one life affects what the next life will be – this is known as karma.
.

Hindu symbol: Aum (or 'Om') is the most sacred syllable in the world to Hindus, symbolising Brahman and the whole Universe.

Hindu festival: Janmaashtami, which celebrates the birth of Krishna.

Islam

Islam originated in Arabia some 1,400 years ago. Followers of Islam are called Muslims. Muslims believe in one true God called Allah. The Muslim holy book is called the Qur'an (Koran). A Muslim place of worship is called a mosque.

Islamic symbol: the crescent moon and star is often used as a symbol of Islam, but not all Muslims agree with this; historically the faith has no traditional holy symbols.

Islamic festival: Eid ul-Fitr, which marks the end of the holy month of Ramadan.

Judaism

Judaism originated in Israel around 4,000 years ago. Followers of Judaism are called Jews. They believe in one single God, called Yahweh, whom they worship in a building called a synagogue. Their most holy book is the Torah, which contains the first five books of the Hebrew bible. The Jewish holy day is Saturday, which they call the Shabbat (Sabbath). Jewish spiritual leaders are called rabbis.

Jewish symbol: the Menorah, a candelabrum with seven candle holders which symbolises the burning bush seen by Moses on Mount Sinai.

Jewish festival: Yom Kippur (the Day of Atonement).

Sikhism

Sikhism was founded in the Punjab (India) in the 15th century and is based on the teaching of Gurus (spiritual teachers). The first Guru was called Nanak. Followers of Sikhism are called Sikhs ('Sikh' means 'learner'). They believe in one God, and that he guides and protects his followers. Sikhs believe all people are equal in the eyes of God.

Sikh symbol: Ik Onkar – the first two words in the Guru Granth Sahib, which mean 'there is only one God'.

Sikh festival: Sikh festivals are called Gurpurbs, and on these days Sikhs celebrate in remembrance of particular Gurus.

Holy places of the world

Almost all religions have places in the world that have special significance for them:

Amritsar – *the site of the Golden Temple in Punjab, India, is sacred to Sikhs.*

Bodh Gaya *in Nepal is where the Buddha reached enlightenment, and is a place sacred to Buddhists.*

The Ganges River *in India is sacred to Hindus who drink from it, bathe in it and scatter the ashes of their dead upon it.*

The Holy Land – *Israel, Jordan and Egypt – is sacred to Muslims, Jews and Christians.*

Mecca – *the Sacred Mosque in Mecca is a place of pilgrimage for Muslims. All Muslims face in the direction of Mecca when they pray five times a day.*

Reptiles

Reptile comes from the Latin 'reper' meaning to creep. Historically, reptiles were defined as cold-blooded, scaled animals, but scientists have now replaced this definition with a broader one. The big difference is that birds are now seen as reptiles because they evolved from dinosaurs, which were reptiles.

There are four main groups of reptile: Crocodilia, Rhynchocephalia, Squamataand Testudines.

Crocodilia

This group includes crocodiles, caimans and alligators. Their name comes from the Greek krokodeilos, meaning pebble worm. The first crocodilians evolved 220 million years ago. Crocodilians, along with sharks, are sometimes referred to as 'living fossils' because unlike most other animals they have remained unchanged for millions of years.

Rhyncocephalia

The only surviving members of this group, the tuatara, are native to New Zealand. The name tuatara comes from the native Maori language and means 'peaks on the back', referring to the spiny ridges running down their back. The most striking difference from other reptiles is their teeth: tuatara have two rows of teeth in their upper jaw and a single row in their lower jaw which fits between the two upper rows. When the tuatara closes its mouth, the interlocking teeth enable it to tear apart hard insects and other prey.

Squamata

This is the largest group of modern reptiles, with over 7,600 known species. It includes snakes, lizards and limbless reptiles (amphisbaenia).

Snakes

'Snake' comes from the Old English 'snaca', meaning to crawl. They have long, narrow bodies covered in fine scales. As the snake grows it sheds its old skin in one piece, emerging with a fresh one.

Snakes' eyes are protected by transparent scales called 'spectacle' scales. They don't have ears but hear through small bones under the skin. They smell by flicking their

Today reptiles can be found on every continent except Antarctica.

Snakes are covered by a plates and scales that are nearly watertight. Even their eyes are covered by clear scales to keep the dirt out!

fascinating Facts

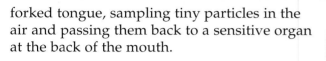

forked tongue, sampling tiny particles in the air and passing them back to a sensitive organ at the back of the mouth.

Some snakes, like the Black Mamba, have a poisonous bite. Others, like the boa constrictor, wrap themselves around their prey and crush it to death by squeezing or 'constricting' it. Others swallow their prey whole.

Snakes can swallow much larger creatures than seems possible, because they have a flexible lower jaw that allows them to open their mouths very wide.

Lizards

Lizards are scaled, usually four-legged, and have external ear openings and movable eyelids. Many can shed their tail when attacked, hopefully distracting the predator and allowing the lizard to escape. The tail later regrows. Some lizards, like the chameleon, can change colour in response to their surroundings. Most lizards feed on insects and rodents but some, like the iguana, are herbivores which only eat plants.

Amphisbaenia

These 'worm lizards' are a rare group of limbless reptiles which resemble scaly worms and live in warm or tropical regions. Their skulls are wide and blend seamlessly into the body, their eyes and ears are concealed under a covering of fine scales, and they have a short blunt tail.

Testudines

Testudines, or turtles, are a line of reptiles that dates back over 250 million years, much earlier than snakes and lizards. They have large, hard shells that protect their bodies leaving only their head, limbs and tail exposed. Today they include tortoises, marine turtles and terrapins.

Q&A?

What does cold-blooded mean?

The term cold-blooded is a bit misleading because a reptile's blood is not cold. But reptiles don't generate enough heat from their own bodies to maintain a constant blood temperature (as mammals, including humans, do). Instead reptiles rely on their environment and behaviour to maintain their body temperature. They bask in the sun to warm themselves up, and move into the shade to avoid overheating.

Which were the earliest reptiles?

The earliest reptiles are believed to be creatures called Hylonomus. They were a small, lizard-like creature that lived about 315 million years ago, long before the first dinosaurs.

Human reproduction

The first nine months of human life are spent inside the mother's womb. The womb is designed to provide the baby with everything it needs to grow and develop. It begins as a single cell and when it is born a healthy baby weighs about 7lb (3 kg).

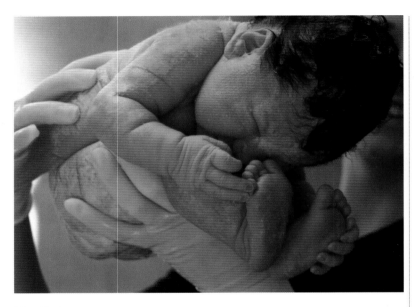

Babies

A baby starts to grow when two special cells – an egg cell (ovum) from the mother and a sperm cell from the father – meet and fuse together. This process is called fertilisation. A fertilised egg settles (implants) in the womb and grows. The growing baby gets everything it needs – oxygen and nutrients – from its mother's blood supply through the umbilical cord (the tube that links baby to mother) which has to be cut at birth after which it crinkles up and makes the tummy button.

When the baby is ready to be born (when it is about 39 weeks old), the womb starts to contract (squeeze) and the baby is pushed out. The baby has usually turned itself round so that it can be born head first. The first thing a baby has to do is to start breathing air by itself. Like other baby animals, human babies usually live off their mother's milk for the first few months of life.

After birth, babies grow quickly and steadily increase in height and weight. In the first year a baby will grow about 25 centimetres in length and triple his or her birth weight. After this, children grow at about 6 cm per year.

Babies start to grow their first set of teeth at about 6 months of age. By the time they are three years old they will have all 20 milk teeth or baby teeth. At about the age of 7 the first teeth begin to loosen and fall out. They are replaced by permanent teeth. Most people have their adult teeth by the age of 21, although the very back teeth – the wisdom teeth – sometimes erupt (come through) a bit later.

The next growth spurt occurs around the time of puberty between the ages of 8 to 13 years in girls and 10 to 15 years in boys. This growth spurt is associated with sexual development, which includes the appearance of pubic and underarm hair, the growth and development of sex organs, and in girls, the onset of menstruation.

How are twins made?

Identical twins are formed when a single fertilised egg develops into two embryos instead of one.

Why do babies always have big eyes?

Babies always look as if they have very big eyes as the eyes are almost adult size even though the baby has only recently been born.

Children grow faster in spring than at other times of the year.

At the age of three weeks the fertilised egg has become an embryo (future baby) and the heart, although not complete, has already started to beat.

fascinating Facts

In their mid or late teenage years girls boys will reach physical maturity.

Inheritance

Children inherit some characteristics from each of their parents. For example, if the mother is short with brown eyes and the father is tall with blue eyes, the child could be tall like the father with brown eyes like the mother. This is already fixed at the time when the egg and the sperm fuse because the egg carries information from the mother and the sperm carries information from the father. Another thing that is fixed at this time is whether the baby will be a boy or a girl.

The Romans

Around 2,000 years ago, the Roman Empire dominated Europe. It ruled lands around the Mediterranean from France to Turkey to North Africa. It came to an end in 476 AD.

The city of Rome

Rome was the capital city of the Roman Empire, and today is the capital city of Italy. It was famous for being built on seven hills. At first, Rome was ruled by kings, but the last king, Tarquin the Proud, was overthrown in 510 BC and Rome became a Republic. A republic is a form of government that is not ruled by a monarch (king or queen). The Republic was ruled for 400 years by a council called the Senate.

The Roman army

Over time, the generals of the Roman army became very powerful, and started to control government. However, they tended to argue among themselves, and eventually just one man took over – Rome had an Emperor.

The Romans were able to keep and expand their Empire thanks to their army. They had the first professional army of paid soldiers in the world. Soldiers were brought into the army from all parts of the Empire, and sent to fight far away from their homes.

The army was organised as follows:
- The army was divided into legions of 5,000 men. There were about 30 legions.
  - Each legion was divided into 10 cohorts.
  - Each cohort was divided into 6 centuries. A century contained 80 men and was commanded by an officer called a Centurion.
  - Each century was divided into 10 groups of 8 men who lived, travelled and fought together.

What did a Roman soldier wear?

The Roman soldiers were very well-equipped. Ordinary soldiers wore leather sandals, wool tunics and leather breeches. They had armour made from overlapping iron bands. They carried a curved shield (called a scutum) and had a bronze helmet. Each man carried a sword (called a gladius), two javelins and a dagger.

Roman towns

The Romans built towns in all the lands they conquered. They were all built to the same plan. Streets were arranged in a criss-cross pattern. Two main streets divided the town, with smaller streets built off them at right angles.

What did Roman women wear?

Roman women wore a garment called a Stola, a long dress of fine woollen cloth that came to their ankles. They often wore their hair curled and up on top of their heads, and were fond of jewellery.

What did the Roman men wear?

Roman men wore knee-length tunics, belted at the waist and sandals. For important occasions he would wear a Toga, a drape of fine wool cloth that went around and over the body, covering the right shoulder.

fascinating facts

The first Roman Emperor was called Augustus. He came to power in 27 BC.

Walls were built round the town for protection, and people could only enter or leave by gates.

Rich people lived in well-built town houses, but poor people lived in cheap blocks of apartments, some up to four storeys high. Rich houses had central heating, plumbing, gardens and lovely decorations like mosaic floors.

The Roman town

You could find the following buildings in any Roman town:

Forum – Important buildings like offices and law courts were built around this 'town square', and a market was often held here.

Baths – the Romans built large public bathhouses called thermae. People went there to get clean but also to relax and meet friends. As well as bathing, they could exercise there in the gymnasium.

Amphitheatre – where public entertainments like gladiator contests and chariot races were held.

Basilica – this was something like the town hall, where government took place.

Roman engineering

Central heating – public baths and the houses of rich people had central heating! Floors were built on top of a series of 'tunnels' called a hypocaust – hot air from a furnace travelled through these tunnels, heating the floors and rooms above.

Plumbing – Roman houses had the best drains in the ancient world. Underground drains took away waste water and sewage, and were flushed through with water from the baths.

Aqueducts – Roman towns had piped water. If water had to be brought from a long way away, they would build huge aqueducts (a kind of bridge that carried water on the top of it) across valleys.

Roads – long, straight 'Roman roads' were built wherever the Romans went, and many can still be seen today.

Russia

All of Russia that is east of the Ural Mountain range is known as the Russian Federation. This part of Russia is the largest country on Earth, spanning over 6.5 million sq miles (17 million sq km).

European Russia, to the west of the Ural Mountains, contains the major cities and industries of the former communist Soviet Union. Since 1991, when communism collapsed, the western regions of Ukraine, Belarus, Estonia and Latvia have become independent nations and Russia has struggled to improve the standard of living for the majority of its citizens. The country has cold winters, but is a fertile agricultural region and is rich in natural resources. This former superpower controls much of Europe's natural gas supplies.

Bordered by the Arctic Ocean to the north, the climate is harsh, and even on the southern borders with China and Outer Mongolia farming is limited to keeping a few animals. Despite the fact that the area has large amounts of oil, gas, uranium, coal and timber, living standards are low, hampered by the vast distances to markets in the west, the frozen ground, and years of communist rule. Kazakhstan, on its southern border, is a huge country which covers a territory equivalent to the whole of Western Europe and has vast mineral resources and enormous economic potential.

The Aral Sea, straddling the Uzbekistan and Kazakhstan border, has decreased in volume by 80% since 1960. Much of the water flowing into the lake was diverted by the Soviet

Where does the name Red Square come from?

The name of Red Square in Russian is Krasnaya ploshchad. Originally krasnaya or krasniy translated as 'red' or 'beautiful' and so Krasnaya ploshchad meant Beautiful Square. Over many years the Russian word krasnaya ceased to be used for beautiful and so Krasnaya ploshchad now means Red Square.

Which is the longest railway in the world?

The Trans-Siberian railway is 5,771 miles (9,288 km) long and runs between Moscow and Vladivostok on the Pacific coast. It was constructed between 1891 and 1916.

St Petersburg is sometimes called the 'Venice of the North' as it has many canals and hundreds of bridges.

Rasputin, called the Mad Monk, was never really a monk. He gained influence over the Czar and Czarina by seeming to cure their son of a blood disorder. He was unpopular with many people and was eventually assassinated. There are various stories about his death but nobody really knows what happened.

based on the Greek alphabet, with about a dozen additional letters invented to represent Slavic sounds not found in Greek. Changes were made up to 1918, leaving the alphabet as it is today.

Wildlife

The mountains bordering Mongolia are home to the rare Siberian Ibex, whose front legs are shorter than its back ones, enabling it to climb mountains easily. Its hooves give it exceptional balance. The male has horns that can be as long as 5 ft (1.5 m).

The extensive forest and tundra of the Russian Far East are home to numerous species of wildlife, including tigers, leopards, lynx and brown bears. These large carnivores require vast areas of suitable land to survive. A large number of people living in this region rely on harvesting natural resources to provide food and income. If too much of the forests disappear the animal population will be under threat.

Russia is famous for caviar – the eggs from the sturgeon fish. In Russia, caviar is eaten on blinis (thin buckwheat pancakes), or on toast, often accompanied by vodka. The international demand for caviar is so great that it is now a luxury item, and due to dam building, poaching and pollution, the sturgeon could become extinct.

government to irrigate farmland. Not only did the lake shrink, but the remaining water became very salty, killing off many fish, so that by 1979 the commercial fishing industry closed.

Russian alphabet

The Russian Cyrillic alphabet is thought to have been devised by Greek missionaries 1,000 years ago. It is closely

Russian culture

Dance is an important part of Russian culture. There are many famous Russian dance groups including the Bolshoi ballet, the Cossacks and the Georgian folk dancers.

Giving Easter eggs is a Russian tradition. Some are made of chocolate, some are real eggs, but the most famous are those designed by Fabergé for the Russian Royal family 100 years ago. These were made out of fine porcelain and painted and decorated with gold and jewels.

Seashore *and Coastal Erosion*

We usually picture sandy beaches when we think of the coast, but actually a coast is any land that borders the sea. The place where land and sea meet is usually called the shoreline or seashore.

Beaches

A beach is a sloping area of sand, pebbles or shingle along the very edge of the sea. Most beaches are made of sand, though some are rocky. Some are even made from broken seashells! Rock pools are pools of sea water that are trapped in rocks on the beach when the tide goes out, and are home to a wide variety of tiny wildlife.

Some coastline features to look for:

Bay – A bay is a wide indent in the coast, between two headlands. Bays are usually sheltered spots. A small bay is called a cove. A huge bay is called a bight, and a gulf is a long, narrow bight.

Cliff – Cliffs are formed over millions of years by waves wearing away the edge of the land.

Estuary – An estuary is an area where the mouth of a river widens out and meets the sea coming in causing fresh and salt water mix.

Headland – These are long tongues of land sticking out into the sea. Headlands are created over millions of years, as waves strike rocky shores, wearing away the softer kinds of rock and leaving the harder ones.

Spit – Also called sandbars, spits occur when sand and debris are washed out across bays by waves, creating tongues of sand that run out into the sea.

Why does seaweed float?

Seaweed needs to be on or near the sea's surface because further down in the water there is not enough light for it to thrive. Seaweed uses trapped air in 'pods' to make it float.

How is sand produced?

Sand is produced as waves grind down rocks and cliffs into smaller and smaller pieces.

Features created by coastal erosion

The coastline is always changing, very slowly, due to natural processes like the rise of sea levels, the pounding of the waves, and weather. In most cases, the result is that the coast is gradually being worn away. We call this wearing away erosion. Coastal erosion can create many spectacular features in places where the coast is made up of different types of rock.
Sea caves are formed when waves wash away an area of softer rock at the base of a cliff, making a

hollow inside harder rock.

Sea arches are produced when two sea caves are worn away from different directions and then meet when the rock separating them is worn away.

Sea stacks are formed from sea arches, when erosion finally causes the top of the arch to collapse. This leaves only a pillar of rock standing alone in the sea.

What lives on the seashore?

Sea anemones are brightly coloured creatures that look like flowers when the many tentacles that surround their mouths are extended. These tentacles are used to capture prey and to sting anything that attacks the anemone. They have no skeleton and can only move very slowly.

Starfish have no bones. Most have five arms – if an arm is cut off, the starfish will grow another! Their mouths are underneath their bodies – a starfish that wants to eat especially large prey can actually push its stomach out of its mouth to catch and digest the prey.

Sea urchins are spiny, hard-shelled creatures which are often found washed up on beaches. They have spines all over their shell for protection, and some urchins have venomous spines.

Crabs have five sets of limbs and can move in any direction. A crab keeps its skeleton on the outside of its body, which is called a carapace. Hermit crabs cannot grow their own carapaces and so move into empty seashells.

Limpets are shellfish with flattened, cone-shaped shells. They have a muscular 'foot' which allows them to seal themselves to the rocks and cling on to avoid being washed away by the tide.

Shellfish such as mussels, clams and winkles live inside shells and attach themselves to rocks with the 'foot' underneath the shell. Many shellfish are edible.

The UK and Ireland together have 8,618 miles (13,870 km) of coastline.

Sea anemones can live for up to 100 years!

Coral is built from skeletons of tiny animals called polyps. Polyps use their tentacles to capture food by special stinging cells in their tentacles that numb their prey. Then the tentacles pass it to the polyp's mouth.

Fascinating Facts

Shakespeare

William Shakespeare (1564–1616) is one of the most famous writers in history. He lived in England during the reigns of Queen Elizabeth I and King James I. He wrote thirty-eight plays and lots of poems, including the famous sonnets. His plays were first performed in the Globe Theatre in London, England. Since then, they have been translated into many languages and have been read and seen all over the world.

Histories and comedies

Shakespeare wrote lots of different sorts of plays. He wrote plays about the Kings and Queens of England, about their

battles and struggles for power. He also wrote comedies, and famous tragedies. A famous comedy written by Shakespeare is *A Midsummer Night's Dream*. This tells the story of a group of people who get lost in the woods, and who have tricks played on them by the fairies. In one of the funniest scenes, a weaver called Bottom has his head turned into a donkey's head and the Queen of the fairies, called Titania, is tricked into falling in love with him!

Tragedies

Many of Shakespeare's plays are called tragedies, because one or more of the main characters dies in the end. Perhaps the most famous of these is *Romeo and Juliet*, which tells the story of a young boy and girl living in Verona. They love each other, but their

families are at war so they cannot be together. At the end of the play they die in a very sad way, and their families finally make peace. Other famous tragedies by Shakespeare are *King Lear*, *Othello* and *Hamlet*.

Words we remember

Shakespeare is famous for his stories, but also for the words he uses. Many lines from Shakespeare have become very famous. Even if you have not read the plays, you might know lines like 'To be or not to be, that is the question' from *Hamlet*, or 'Romeo, Romeo, wherefore art thou Romeo?' from Romeo and Juliet. Some lines from

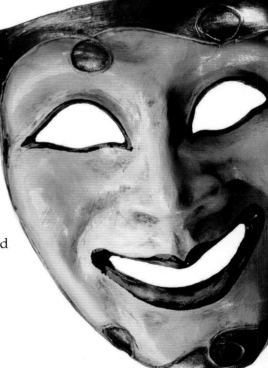

Shakespeare is buried near the altar in Holy Trinity Church beside the river in Stratford-upon-Avon. Nobody has ever dared to disturb his grave as it bears an inscription cursing anybody who does.

Shakespeare made up over 1,700 words, including birthplace, champion, fashionable, generous, gossip, leapfrog, luggage, moonbeam and zany.

Shakespeare's plays are so famous that they have become part of everyday speech. If you say that something has 'vanished into thin air', that you will not 'budge an inch', or that you are 'in a pickle', you are using phrases that Shakespeare invented.

What was Shakespeare like?

We are still not certain what Shakespeare was really like. Although there is lots of evidence about where he was born, what his family did and what he did during his life, there is not much about what he said, thought or felt. We do not even know what he really looked like, because all the famous portraits of him were painted from the artist's memory after Shakespeare's death, or copied from another picture. Some of the pictures of him are just guesswork.

Did he write his own plays?

Some people think there are no portraits of Shakespeare the playwright because they think he was not a playwright at all! These people believe that a poor boy from Stratford-upon-Avon who did not have the finest schooling available could not have written the greatest plays known to mankind. They say that other famous writers, such as the playwright Christopher Marlowe, or Sir Francis Bacon, wrote the plays, or even that Queen Elizabeth I did! Other people think that no one person could have written so many great works of literature. But as historians find out more and more about Shakespeare's life, it seems more and more likely that Shakespeare himself wrote all his plays.

made about his life. His picture is all around us, and he even appears as a hologram on plastic bankcards. It seems that Shakespeare will be with us for many years to come!

A lasting legacy

Today, the name William Shakespeare is known all over the world. His plays are still performed regularly, and there are hundreds of books being written about him every year. His plays are made into films, and sometimes films are

Q&A?

Did both men and women act in Shakespeare's plays?

Not at first. In Shakespeare's time, women were not allowed to be actors. To play a female character, a young boy would dress up in women's clothes and speak in a high voice!

What is a sonnet?

A sonnet is a fourteen-line poem. All of Shakespeare's sonnets end with what is called a rhyming couplet (when the last word of each of the last two lines rhymes with the other).

The Solar System

The Sun, the centre of our solar system, is a giant, spinning ball of very hot gas. The light from the Sun heats our world and makes life possible. The solar system consists of the sun and nine planets (and their moons) which orbit the Sun. Scientists study the planets and stars with very sophisticated equipment, such as radio telescopes and satellites.

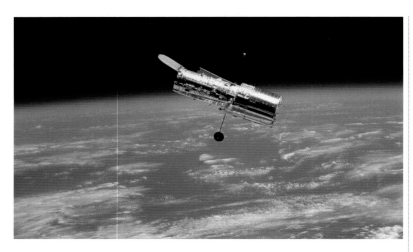

The planets

The inner planets (those planets that orbit close to the Sun) are quite different from the outer planets (those planets that orbit far away from the Sun).

The inner planets

Mercury, Venus, Earth and Mars are the inner planets. They are relatively small, composed mostly of rock, and have few or no moons.

Mercury is the closest planet to the Sun and is the fastest-moving planet. Temperatures on Mercury range between 750°F and –274°F (400°C and –170°C).

Venus is a similar size to the Earth; it is the brightest and, at 887°F (475°C), the hottest of the planets, due to its atmosphere of carbon dioxide gas which traps the Sun's energy. Scientists have tried to send probes onto this scorching planet, but the atmosphere has proved too hot.

Earth looks blue and white from space due to the oceans and clouds which cover its surface. It consists of a solid crust above a molten layer, at the centre of which is a solid iron core. Earth is surrounded by a layer of gases which form an atmosphere, and 71% of its surface is covered with liquid water – a property unique in the Solar System and which has enabled life to develop. The Earth is 94.5 million miles (152 million km) from the Sun.

Mars also has an atmosphere and has, in the past, had water, leading to theories that there might be life on Mars. Space probes have tested the surface and found no trace of life.

The outer planets are Jupiter, Saturn, Uranus, Neptune and Pluto. They are mostly very large, mostly gaseous, ringed and have many moons. Pluto is the exception – it is small, rocky and has one moon.

The largest planet, **Jupiter,** consists of hydrogen and helium and is covered by clouds.

Saturn is famous for its rings, which are 167,000 miles (270,000 km) across but only 660 ft (200 m) thick. The rings are made of chunks of ice varying from snowball to iceberg size.

Uranus is a very cold planet, as it is 20 times further from the heat of the Sun than the Earth.

Very little was known about **Neptune** until the Voyager 2 spacecraft showed pictures of its blue-green clouds.

Pluto is the smallest, coldest and most distant planet in the Solar System. It was only discovered in 1930. Surface temperatures are –387.5°F (–233°C).

Stars

A star is an enormous ball of gas. It generates energy and therefore emits light. All stars except the Sun appear as tiny shining points in the night sky that twinkle

Is the moon a planet?

No. The moon is Earth's natural satellite. It is a cold, dry orb whose surface is covered with craters and scattered with rocks and dust. The moon has no atmosphere. It is possible that there is some frozen ice on the moon.

Do stars last forever?

The average life span of a yellow star, like our Sun, is about 10 billion years. The Sun will eventually burn out in about 5 to 6 billion years.

because of the effect of the Earth's atmosphere and their distance from us. The Sun is also a star and although only a medium sized one it is close enough to Earth to appear as a disk and to provide daylight.

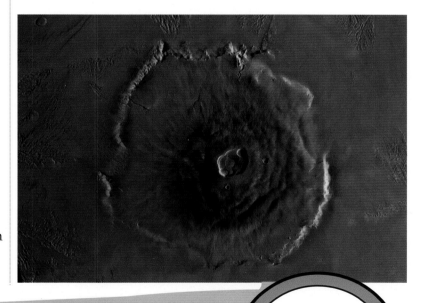

Fascinating Facts

Saturn's rings are around 155,000 miles (250,000 km) wide but less than 0.6 mile (1 km) thick. Viewed edge-on, its rings seem to disappear. Jupiter, Uranus and Neptune also have rings, but these are much fainter.

Mars is the home of Olympus Mons, the largest volcano found in the solar system. It stands about 17 miles (27 km) high with a crater 50 miles (81 km) wide.

Sound *and* Light

Sound is a form of energy which causes tiny particles to vibrate. As they do this, they bump into their neighbours, causing them to vibrate, and so on. This 'knock-on' effect is how sound travels.

The vibrating particles 'push' against their neighbours and form a region of higher pressure, which then moves away from the source of the sound. This movement is a sound wave. It's like dropping a bar of soap into water – the splash sends out ripples.

How sound travels

Where the particles are close together – in a solid or a liquid – it's easy for particles to bump into one another and cause sound to travel quickly. In the air, where particles may be far apart, the sound travels more slowly. If there are no particles near the vibrating particles, the sound will not travel at all!

Frequency and wavelength

Every sound has a frequency, which means the number of times the sound causes particles to vibrate in a second. This is measured in Hertz (Hz) – 1 Hertz = 1 vibration per second. Different creatures' ears can hear different sound frequencies. Humans can hear sounds as low as 30 Hz or as high as 20,000 Hz.

How we hear

This is how we hear things – a noise makes the air vibrate, and the vibration ripples through the air. This makes the tiny bones in our ears vibrate, which sends a signal to our brain and we 'hear' the sound.

Sonar

Although many creatures hear sounds, some use it to find their way around. Bats send out high frequency squeaks and then listen for the echoes as the sound waves bounce off objects and other creatures. Their brains use this information to pinpoint where things are.

Q&A? How is sonar used in submarines?

The submarine emits (sends out) sound waves and receivers 'listen' for the echoes. The information is fed into a computer, which determines where objects are.

Dogs can hear sounds of much higher frequencies than humans, up to about 65,000 Hz. That is why they can hear a dog whistle even though humans can't. Bats can hear sounds of more than 100,000 Hz!

The furthest detected galaxies are more than 6 billion light years away, so the Earth didn't even exist when the light we see from them was produced!

Light is a form of energy caused by the vibrations of electrically charged particles. Like sound this energy is transmitted in a wave that has a frequency and a wavelength. The faster the charged particle vibrates the higher the frequency and the smaller the wavelength of the light it produces.

Humans can only 'see' light from a tiny portion of the electromagnetic spectrum (visible light), but we use many different forms of light such as radio waves, microwaves and x-rays.

How we see colours

When light strikes an object it can be reflected, be absorbed or pass straight through, depending on what the object is made of and the wavelength of the light. Different materials reflect and absorb different kinds of light. This makes things appear to be different colours – if something reflects only green light then it looks green to us, because the other visible light striking it has been absorbed. Some objects appear black because they absorb nearly all visible light. Objects that appear white absorb almost none, so all colours are reflected back.

The speed of light

Light does not travel instantly but it does travel very, very quickly. In space it travels at 186,000 miles (300,000 km) every second – that's about 874,000 times faster than

sound travels in the air, or 130,000 times faster than the fastest planes!

Very distant light

Even travelling at this terrific speed light takes about 8 minutes to travel to the Earth from the sun – so when you look at the sun you're actually seeing where it was about 8 minutes ago! Light from the stars takes much longer. You may have heard of 'light years'. A light year is the distance light travels in a year and is used to measure the distances between stars and galaxies. One light year is 5,865,696,000,000 miles (9,460,800,000,000 km). Proxima Centauri, our nearest star, is 4.24 light years away, so light from it takes more than 4 years to reach us!

Seeing and hearing

Because light travels so much faster than sound, you sometimes see something before you hear its noise. If you see a lightning flash and then count the seconds until you hear the thunder, you can tell how far away the storm is. Every 3 seconds you count means the storm is roughly 0.6 miles (1 km) away.

Q&A?

What is an incandescent light bulb?

The word incandescent means to give off visible light. Most of the energy, however, is used in raising sufficient heat to make the light visible, so it is very wasteful of energy. The new energy saving light bulbs use up to four times less electricity to generate the same amount of light.

Space Travel

Rockets have interested scientists and amateurs for at least 2,100 years. The Chinese used them as weapons as early as the 11th century.

In the 1880s Russian scientist Konstantin Tsiolkovsky worked out that for a rocket to escape earth's gravity (the force that pulls objects back to the ground), it would have to travel at a speed of 8 km a second and that to achieve this, a multi-stage rocket fuelled by liquid oxygen and liquid hydrogen was needed.

However, it was not until 1926 that the American Robert Goddard designed a liquid fuel rocket that would actually work. At the time, though, Goddard's work was laughed at. It was only later, when people realised that rocket technology could be used in weapons, that his work was taken seriously.

Sputnik means 'satellite' (an object that circles the earth, as the moon does) and also 'fellow traveller' in Russian.

During the Apollo 14 mission, astronaut Alan Shepard hit three golf balls on the surface of the moon – they are still there!

Why were the first American spaceships called Apollo?

They were named after Apollo, the Greek and Roman god of the sun.

What is the International Space Station?

The space station that is being built in space allows people to live and study for long periods in a "weightless" environment, and to understand the effects of gravity on plants, animals, and humans. It isn't finished yet, but it's already the largest man-made object in space, measuring about 390 ft x 315 ft (120 m x 96 m) and has lots of solar panels to provide electricity.

The Space Race

Both Russia and America wanted to be the first to send satellites, rockets, and men into space. The Russians had the first successes. On 4 October 1957, they successfully launched Sputnik 1 and the Space Race began. Because it showed that the Russians might be capable of using space technology to make weapons, and because it showed that their country had enough money to build expensive spacecraft, Sputnik caused fear in the United States. At the same time, the Sputnik launch was seen in the Soviet Union as an important sign of the strength of the nation. Before Sputnik, America had assumed that it was better than other countries at everything. After Sputnik, they launched a huge effort to get ahead in the Space Race.

The imagination of the American public was captured by the American space projects. School children followed the launches, and making model rockets became a popular hobby. President

Kennedy gave speeches encouraging people to support the space programme. Nearly four months after the launch of Sputnik 1, the US launched its first satellite, Explorer I. But before this there were lots of embarrassing launch failures at Cape Canaveral!

Animals and humans in space

In 1957 the dog Laika was sent into orbit in the USSR's Sputnik 2. The technology to bring her back did not exist, so she died in space. The American space program then sent chimpanzees into space before launching their first human orbiter. The cosmonaut (Russian astronaut) Yuri Gagarin became the first man in space when he entered orbit in Russia's Vostok 1 on April 12 1961, and 23 days later, Alan Shepard first entered space for the United States. John Glenn, in Friendship 7, became the first American to successfully orbit Earth, completing three orbits on February 20 1962. Soviet Valentina Tereshkova became the first woman in space on June 16 1963 in Vostok 6.

Man on the moon

The Americans felt that the only way to win the Space Race was to put a man on the moon. President John Kennedy said, 'We choose to go to the moon. We choose to go to the moon in this decade and do the other things, not because they are easy, but because they are hard.' It was an American, Neil Armstrong, who became the first person to set foot on the moon's surface on 21 July 1969, after landing in Apollo 11 the previous day. It was an event watched on television by over 500 million people around the world. It was one of the finest moments of the 20th century, and Armstrong's words on his first touching the moon's surface have become very famous:

'That's one small step for man, one giant leap for mankind.'

Advances in space

There have been many missions into space and to the moon since Neil Armstrong took his famous first steps. America and Russia have launched space stations into Earth's orbit, and there are plans for an international space station. The Hubble Space Telescope was launched in 1990 and the pictures it has taken of deep space are very clear and have shown many exciting new things. Astronauts also carry out lots of new experiments on every mission to see how things react differently in space than here on earth.

Spiders *and* Scorpions

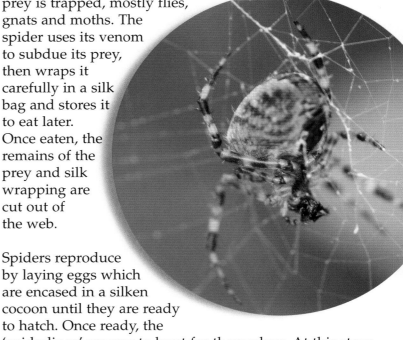

Spiders are often mistaken for insects, but actually belong to another group of animals called arachnids. Insects only have six legs, whereas arachnids have eight legs on two-part bodies. Spiders, ticks, mites and scorpions are all arachnids.

Scorpions

Scorpions tend to live in warm areas of the world, usually on rocks or in cracks between them. They eat insects and spiders, hunting mostly at night. Famous for the sting on the end of its tail, the scorpion uses this for self-defence and subduing its prey by injecting poison from special glands. The scorpion crushes its prey with its pedipalps (large pincers), before taking it into its jaws.

Where do spiders live?

Spiders are found throughout the world, and there are 35,000 different types. They are carnivores (meat eaters), catching their prey in different ways. Most familiar to us is the spider's web which it spins to trap flying insects, which it then eats. Some spiders create a net of silk which they drop on their prey, whilst others lie in wait in burrows.

Common garden spiders spin large webs called orb webs. Some spiders wait at the centre of the web. Other spiders wait near their webs until the prey is trapped, mostly flies, gnats and moths. The spider uses its venom to subdue its prey, then wraps it carefully in a silk bag and stores it to eat later. Once eaten, the remains of the prey and silk wrapping are cut out of the web.

Spiders reproduce by laying eggs which are encased in a silken cocoon until they are ready to hatch. Once ready, the 'spiderlings' emerge to hunt for themselves. At this stage they look exactly like miniature versions of their parents, quickly growing to full size.

Tarantulas are very large spiders, but not as dangerous as the Black Widow. Their bite may be painful to humans, but is less poisonous.

Baby scorpions are born fully formed and are carried on their mother's back until they moult (shed their skin), after which they live their adult lives alone.

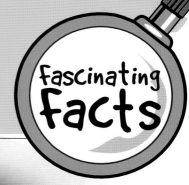

Q&A?

How do spiders make their webs?

Spiders spin their webs using a special silken thread which is produced in glands at the rear of their body.

What is the most venomous spider?

Three spiders are often quoted as the most venomous – the Black Widow spider, and the Sydney funnel spider; but according to the Guinness Book of Records the world's most venomous spider is the Brazilian wandering spider.

Sports

Before the Victorian era sport was brutal, and football in particular was vicious. Before the 1800s there were no game rules or referees to provide order or protection. This changed during the course of the Victorian period, when a more civilised and controlled society was created. Sport acquired rules and regulations, and the emphasis changed from 'manly' physical pursuits to enjoyable exercises with a spirit of fair play.

Football

In public schools the aristocratic pupils held sway over their middle-class teachers, and were free to play as they pleased. However, parents started complaining about the treatment of youngsters who were put in goal and suffered the brunt of the violence. Schools had to take action or face the prospect of parents removing their children.

Thomas Arnold, headmaster of Rugby School, wanted his pupils to grow up into moral Christian gentlemen. He encouraged regulated sports which provided exercise and encouraged healthy competition. By 1845, the pupils at Rugby recorded their version of the rules of football, which included allowing handling of the ball. In 1849, pupils at Eton created a rival game, restricting the use of the hands. The game spread, and a common set of rules was needed. At Cambridge University in 1863 a set of rules was devised in which handling the ball was outlawed.

At the end of that year, players from around the country came together to form the Football Association, and the Cambridge rules were adopted. With the formation of the FA, other sports soon followed suit – the Amateur Athletic Club was formed in 1866, the Rugby Football Union in 1871, and the Lawn Tennis Association in 1888. They enabled the establishment of rules and the arrangement of competitions.

The 20th century

British settlers spread the news about football wherever they went. Even today, many Argentine and Brazilian football sides reveal their roots with English names. Closer to home, Italian clubs such as AC Milan and Juventus, who got their famous playing strip from Notts County, also have English connections. But it was not just football that the English migrants have taken with them. Rugby and cricket flourished in Australia and New Zealand, while India and Pakistan took cricket to their hearts. Sport entered the 20th century with a new image. Tennis and golf went from strength to strength while athletics flourished, particularly with the establishment of the Olympic Games.

Boxing champion Muhammed Ali's real name is Cassius Marcellus Clay.

The talented and controversial football player Diego Maradona is famous for the 'Hand of God' incident. During the 1986 World Cup, he scored a goal with his hand and claimed that God had done it.

Tennis

London is famous for the Lawn Tennis Championships held at Wimbledon, but the first Wimbledon championships were held in 1877, 11 years before the launch of the Lawn Tennis Association. The game's birth can be traced back to 1858 when Major Henry Gem marked out the first court on a lawn in Edgbaston, Birmingham. But it was Major Walter Wingfield who developed the modern game of tennis.

Cricket

Cricket rules had been laid down as early as 1744, but in 1814 the game was first played at Lord's Cricket Ground, London. Lord's is known as the home of cricket. The first official Test match was not until 1877, when Australia beat England in Melbourne. When Australia won a Test in England for the first time in 1882, the competition for the Ashes began.

Q&A?

What was Steffi Graf's nickname?

'Fraulein Forehand', for her powerful serve and even more powerful forehand.

What sports are popular in Asian countries?

Chinese people are good at badminton and table tennis, whereas the Japanese excel at sumo wrestling – the first wrestler who touches the floor with any part of his body other than the soles of his feet loses. The fights themselves usually last only a few seconds and only in rare cases up to one minute or longer.

Golf

As with cricket, golf rules were first laid down in the 18th century, but it is the Victorians we have to thank for the Open Championship which was first played in 1861. The four golf majors now are the British Open, the US Open, the US Masters, and the US PGA. No man has won all four Majors in one year.

Boxing

Although Ancient Greek boxers used leather hand coverings, bare-knuckle fighting was popular and serious injuries and even death were common. The Marquess of Queensberry devised new rules, under which gloves became compulsory.

Technology

Technology means all the tools, machines, inventions and discoveries that we use to make the things we do easier. Technology includes the machinery that helped build your house, the electricity that makes your lights work and even the bulbs that give you light.

Technology makes things happen, and modern technology makes things happen faster, better, cheaper or easier than before.

The first technology included all the tools and techniques devised by prehistoric man. We now take for granted some of these. People discovered how to make fire over 500,000 years ago and made clothes 100,000 years ago. They made dishes to eat from, produced bows and arrows to hunt with, and invented the plough in order to farm crops.

What did the Egyptians invent?

The Ancient Egyptians invented the ramp and the lever, making it easier to build their great pyramids and temples. They also found a way of making paper using papyrus reeds, and devised methods of farming in wet areas such as next to the Nile.

What did the Romans invent?

The Ancient Romans invented the arch and the vault, both used to create bigger buildings, and the building material concrete. They also developed aqueducts (to provide cities with water), indoor plumbing, and under-floor heating.

What did the Chinese invent?

The list of Chinese inventions is very long! Lots of items assumed to be invented by Europeans were actually invented much earlier by people in China. Chinese inventions include matches, cast iron, the wheelbarrow, the parachute, gunpowder, the magnetic compass and spectacles.

Over the centuries mathematicians, scientists and engineers discovered many more processes and created many more inventions. For example, sailing ships became bigger and faster, allowing European explorers like Columbus and Magellan to sail the oceans, and new devices like the sextant and the marine chronometer helped them to navigate (find their way). Inventions like the pendulum clock in 1656 (replacing water clocks or sand-timers) and the printing press (spreading information) had a huge impact on the way people lived their lives. So did inventions like gas lighting (1792) and the flushing toilet (1775). Changes in technology continued even before the Industrial Revolution.

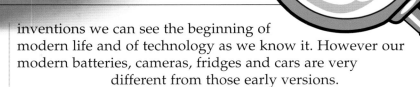

Thomas Alva Edison who developed the electric lightbulb has nearly 1300 patents to his name.

inventions we can see the beginning of modern life and of technology as we know it. However our modern batteries, cameras, fridges and cars are very different from those early versions.

Important modern inventions include the frozen food process (1923), television (1939), the electronic computer (1946), the computer microchip (1959), cellular (mobile) phones (1979), and the Internet (1990). There is more technology available to us now than ever before, and new machines and techniques are being invented all the time!

What was the Industrial Revolution?

The Industrial Revolution happened in the 1800s in Britain and elsewhere in Europe. It was a time of great invention. New processes – especially with the use of steam power – meant people could make products much more quickly and cheaply. For example, the invention of the power loom in 1785 speeded up the making of cotton. Many factories were built, and the invention of the steam train by Trevithick and Stevenson meant that materials could be taken speedily to the factories, and goods to cities and ports.

Technology has built the world we are part of, and most technology has been helpful. It has made our lives more pleasant and convenient, and helped the growth of business and industry. Unfortunately, there are some negative aspects of technology. Workers have lost their jobs as machines have been introduced to do such jobs more quickly. Also, people are worried about the damage to the environment caused by factories and cars, which cause pollution.

What other technology was invented during the 19th century?

Nineteenth-century inventions include the battery (1800), photography (1816), the typewriter (1829), the refrigerator (1834), the improved electric lightbulb (1879), and the car (1885). In these

In what year was the telephone invented?

1876.

In what year did the first underground railways in London start operation?

1863.

Towns *and* Cities

In ancient times, people lived mainly in small communities in villages or hamlets. The earliest towns were often built near rivers so that people could get water to drink and fish to eat. When the Romans occupied Britain and other countries, they built towns, castles and walls for protection. They linked towns by building straight roads, some of which still exist today!

Early towns

In many countries, the rich and wealthy lords and landowners lived in castles or manor houses. Other people lived in small houses, and would sell their goods in local markets. Early towns began to develop around these markets, and people would buy and sell the things they could not make or grow themselves.

Where does the word 'city' come from?

It comes from the Latin word civitas, meaning 'citizenship or community of citizens'. The Latin word for city was urbs, and a resident of a city was a civis.

What is the largest capital city in Europe?

Moscow (Russia) is the largest, with more than 8 million people.

The growth of the towns

Towns often developed around ports and harbours, where people traded by boat and ship. Some of these harbour towns exist today, and trade still goes on in them. Other early towns were built on hilltops so that people could watch out for any approaching enemy. Many medieval towns had walls, and people could live inside the walls for safety. Originally, the word town meant a fortified place (somewhere with a wall or some defences). Most walled towns were dirty and smelly places – there was little sanitation (ways to make things clean) and no running water or soap. That caused disease and illness, and people in those days did not live very long.

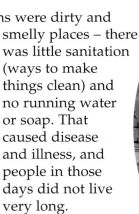

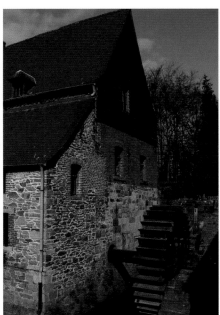

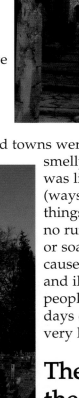

The move to the cities

Early methods of farming were fairly basic and did not produce much food. Then as farming methods improved more food could be grown on the same amount of land. Better farming methods meant that fewer people were needed and so people moved to the cities. This trend is still continuing today in some countries.

Town or city?

A city is usually a big urban area with a large population, but in some countries the word 'city' has a particular meaning. In Britain, for example, a place with a cathedral is a city, even if it is quite small. In medieval times, many British cities, including York, Lincoln and Canterbury, became important because of their cathedrals. In the United States, many small population areas are also called 'cities' because they have been given the legal status of cities by the government. In most countries, however, a city means a place with a very big urban core and large population. .

The Industrial Revolution

Up until the 1800s, people in most countries produced goods by hand, using skills learnt from their elders. After the Industrial Revolution, which began in Britain and spread throughout the world, goods could be produced cheaply and quickly in factories because newly developed machinery could do the work of many people. This caused anger among craftsmen because it took work away from them. But it also meant that the towns and cities grew in size as people moved there to work in the factories.

Cities today

Today there are many big cities in the world. Some of the largest are Mumbai, Tokyo, Shanghai and Seoul in Asia; Cairo and Lagos in Africa; Moscow and London in Europe; Mexico City and New York in North America; and Sao Paulo in South America. Modern methods of transport have made it easier to travel quickly between cities. Also, modern methods of communication such as telephone and email allow people to communicate instantly. Nowadays fewer people have to go into a town to work than in the recent past – some people can even stay at home and work

through the Internet! Modern working methods have meant that many people no longer have to live in towns or cities. Despite these advances, however, many of the world's great cities will probably remain large and crowded for a long time to come.

The most populous city (the one with the largest number of people) in the world is Shanghai, China, with a population of more than 15 million!

The term 'City of London' refers to a small area in central London. It is approximately 1 sq mile (2.6 sq km) and is London's main financial centre. Modern London developed from the original City of London and the nearby City of Westminster, where the royal government was located.

The city of Istanbul, in Turkey, has had several different names, including Byzantium and Constantinople. It was the capital of the Byzantine Empire and, later, the Ottoman Empire.

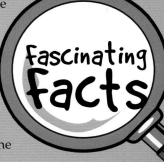

Fascinating Facts

Travel and Transport

Before the invention of the wheel, people had to carry their belongings themselves, or pull them on wooden sledges. Carts with stone wheels arrived around 3,500 BC, and later horses pulled the carts. Iron horseshoes weren't developed until around 770 AD. This made horse power much more efficient as the iron shoes prevented the horse's hooves from being worn away by walking over rough roads.

The Romans built roads – some of the routes of the Roman roads are still in use today! Having good roads helped the Romans in their military campaigns as the soldiers could travel more quickly to the battlefields. They also used chariots when fighting battles.

Over the centuries farmers and merchants continued to use carts to transport goods, and people began to use four-wheeled carriages, however these were only available to the rich until the arrival of the omnibus, or bus as we call them today. The first bus route, schedule (timetable) and fare system was invented in France in 1662 by the mathematician Blaise Pascal, but buses did not become common until the late 1700s.

People travelled by water along rivers over seas and lakes. This was done by wind power (using sails) and people power (using oars). The first canoes were invented around 3,500 BC and the Ancient Egyptians used large boats to move goods down the Nile. The Romans used ships to travel to other lands and expand their empire, using slaves for their rowing power. Over time bigger and better sailing ships were designed. During the Age of Discovery in the 15th and 16th centuries, European explorers sailed across the oceans in huge galleons. Inland, miles and miles of canals (man-made waterways) were built throughout Europe to transport goods to and from the coast and between cities.

Great changes came when people began to invent machine-powered transportation. Using steam power from burning wood or coal. Now people could transport goods much more quickly, which was good for business. Later, mechanical means of transportation meant that individual people could travel from place to place and could see the world easily and affordably.

The first steamboat with a regular passenger service was invented by Robert Fulton in 1807. Nowadays steam power has been replaced by diesel fuel, and passenger ships are mostly car ferries or holiday cruise ships. Ships still transport goods across the oceans, but mostly in containers. The first steam powered locomotive (train) was invented by Richard Trevithick in 1801 but it was designed to go on the roads! The first steam-powered railroad locomotive was George Stevenson's Rocket, invented in 1814.

The 19th century was the age of railroad building in Europe and America. The railway took over from the canals as the main method for transporting heavy goods such as coal.

The artist and inventor Leonardo da Vinci sketched a bicycle as early as 1490. He also made over 100 drawings of his theories of flight, sketching flying machines like the ornithopter, and drew a design for a motorised carriage.

An early bicycle was invented in 1790 by Comte Mede de Sivrac, but unfortunately it had no steering!

Although a clockwork-powered carriage was invented in 1740, the world's first practical automobile was built in 1867. Henry Ford started the Ford Motor Company in 1903 wanting to make a car for the everyonr, not just a luxury item for the extremely rich. Since then the car has become the most popular type of transport, as it is affordable and available to virtually everyone.

 **What was the Tin Lizzie?**

It was a nickname for the Ford Model T. This car was launched in 1908 and during over 19 years nearly 15,500,000 were sold in the USA alone!

Who invented the hot–air balloon?

Joseph and Jacques Etienne Montgolfier were two French brothers who made the first successful hot-air balloon. Their first balloon was launched in December 1783, and ascended to an altitude of 985 ft (300 m). This type of hot-air balloon was called the Montgolfiére; it was made of paper and used air heated by burning wool and moist straw.

A timeline of transport:

1783 ➜ The first hot-air balloon invented by the Montgolfier brothers.
1895 ➜ First human glider flown by Otto Lilienthal.
1899 ➜ The first successful airship, the Zeppelin, invented by Ferdinand von Zeppelin.
1903 ➜ The first airplane flown by the Wright brothers (first powered flight).
1907 ➜ First helicopter invented by Paul Cornu.
1926 ➜ First liquid-propelled rocket launched by Robert H. Goddard.
1940 ➜ Modern helicopters invented by Igor Sirkorsky.
1947 ➜ First supersonic (faster than the speed of sound) flight.
1967 ➜ First successful supersonic passenger jet (Concorde).
1969 ➜ First manned mission to the Moon (Apollo 11).
1981 ➜ Space shuttle launched.

United Kingdom

60°
58°
56°
54°
C
Ir
52°
50°

The United Kingdom comprises Great Britain and Northern Ireland. Great Britain is Europe's largest island and for the last 500 years has been one of the world's most influential and richest countries. At its height the British Empire stretched over 25% of the Earth's surface, ruling countries such as Canada, South Africa, India and Australia, which is why so many nations in the world speak English. The Empire is no more, and even Scotland, Wales and Northern Ireland now have their own parliaments.

The UK was a world leader in shipbuilding, steel making, car manufacturing and coal mining, but these have declined, with most people now employed in finance, health care, education, retail and tourism.

Languages

The language of the UK is predominantly English, although Welsh is spoken by 25% of the Welsh people and Gaelic is spoken to a lesser extent in Western Scotland and the Hebrides. Cornish is spoken in small areas of Cornwall. The UK is a multicultural society and many languages are spoken, mainly from the Indian subcontinent and Africa.

England

England is the largest of the British nations and has in London one of the most cosmopolitan capital cities in the world. It is home to both the government and the monarchy and the headquarters of many national institutions and companies. This combination of royalty and national monuments attracts tourists from around the

world. The most visited sights are Westminster Abbey, Downing Street and St Paul's Cathedral.

Northern Ireland

Northern Ireland consists of the six counties of Ulster and is situated in the north-east of Ireland. It covers 5,459 sq miles (14,139 sq km), about a sixth of the total area of the island. It is mostly rural with industry centred around the capital Belfast.

Northern Ireland's most spectacular feature is the Giant's Causeway (a causeway is a path). The unique rock formations have withstood Atlantic storms for millions of years. This feature is the result of volcanic activity. The Causeway itself is made up of hexagonal columns of differing heights. There are over 40,000 of these columns. The story is that the giant stepped from Ireland and over to Scotland, using the columns

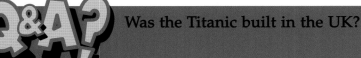

Was the Titanic built in the UK?

The Titanic was built at the Harland and Wolff shipyard in Belfast, Northern Ireland. She was the largest passenger ship in the world. On April 14, 1912, she broke into two pieces, and sank two hours and forty minutes later at 2:20 a.m. Monday morning.

Why doesn't the Queen rule England?

England (and the rest of the UK) has been ruled by a parliament of elected officials since the mid-13th century.

Wall between the River Solway and River Tyne, to try and keep them out. The two countries became unified in 1707. The Scots achieved their own parliament in 1998 and elected representatives who have total control over issues such as education, health, agriculture and justice. The parliament is in the capital city of Edinburgh, which has many fine buildings such as Edinburgh Castle and Holyrood House.

Wales

Successive English Kings tried to integrate Wales into England. King Edward I ordered a ring of castles to be built to circle the land but it was not until the reign of Henry VIII that Wales was fully under control. The castles today remain as magnificent tourist attractions. Wales is a rugged country; in the North are the magnificent mountains of Snowdonia. Mid Wales has a more rolling countryside but is very sparsely populated, while in the south are the Black Mountains and the coal-rich Welsh Valleys. It is in this region that the capital, Cardiff, is situated and where most of the people live.

on Staffa (near Mull in the Scottish Highlands) as a stepping stone.

Scotland

The Celts of Scotland have always fiercely defended their homeland. The Romans could not defeat them and built two walls, the Antonne Wall between the River Clyde and the Firth of Forth and Hadrian's

Stonehenge is a megalithic monument located in the English county of Wiltshire. It is composed of earthworks surrounding a circular setting of large standing stones and is one of the most famous prehistoric sites in the world. Archaeologists think the standing stones were erected between 2500 and 2000 BC.

Britain is the home to the world's most poisonous fungus, the yellowish olive Death Cap.

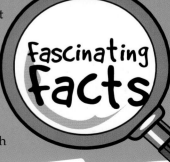
Fascinating Facts

The USA

The USA stretches from the Arctic Ocean to tropical Hawaii and includes the massive Rocky Mountains as well as fertile lowlands. Vast natural resources and culture of enterprise make the USA one of the world's richest nations, the home of many global businesses such as Ford, MacDonald's, Microsoft and Disney.

The people

The United States has one of the world's most diverse populations, with immigrants from all over the world. Thousands of years ago, Asians crossed the Bering Strait from Asia and populated both North and South America. Their descendants are the Native Americans. Spanish, French and English settlers colonized in the 1600s, and slaves from Africa were brought to the country later. The Industrial Revolution attracted millions of European immigrants from Ireland, Britain and Italy, and the last 50 years have brought migrants from Mexico.

Western USA

Here the nation's most dramatic landscapes can be found. The Rocky Mountains form several large mountain ranges.

Q&A?

What do the stars and stripes mean on the United States flag?

The flag of the United States has 13 horizontal red stripes, which represent the 13 original colonies. In the top left corner of the flag is a blue rectangle with 50 small, white stars. These represent the 50 states in the United States of America. The flag is known as 'the Stars and Stripes'.

Did the Mayflower take the first settlers to America?

No. The first settlers are thought to have been a group of English traders who landed in Virginia in 1607. But the Mayflower, which sailed in 1620, is probably the most famous of the early ships to go to America. Those on board included 102 passengers from Holland and Britain. A replica of the Mayflower can be seen at Plymouth, Massachusetts.

Vast quantities of powder snow make this one of the world's biggest winter skiing areas, the main centres being near Aspen in Colorado and Lake Tahoe in California. As the traditional coal, steel and automobile industries of the Eastern USA declined, many people moved to the West Coast where new industries were growing. Aircraft and

software development in Seattle, computer component development and manufacture in 'Silicon Valley' San Francisco, and the music, movie and entertainment industries of Los Angeles have built one of the richest regions in the world.

Television and film dominate American culture and spread it throughout the world. Hollywood movies are viewed worldwide, as are such long-running television programs as 'The Simpsons'.

Southern California, Nevada and Arizona are desert, the driest place being in Death Valley. Water from the River Colorado has cut the deep gorges of the Grand Canyon and Bryce Canyon, and provides much needed water for the farmers and cities of California.

Eastern USA

Europeans have settled the eastern half of the USA since 1613, and many towns are named after the places from which these colonists came. People who migrated to settle permanently in colonies controlled by their country of origin were called colonists or settlers. Sometimes the settlers formed the colony themselves if they settled in an unpopulated area. A colony is the territory where the people settle.

New Orleans

New Orleans, called the Big Easy due to its relaxed life style, is the world's jazz capital, and the Mardis Gras festival attracts millions of visitors. In August 2005, Hurricane Katrina, the largest hurricane ever recorded over the USA, flooded over 80% of New Orleans.

Washington, D.C.

Washington, D.C., named after President George Washington, is the capital city and home to the President of the United States and to the Senate buildings. It was designed in 1791 by a French architect and was the world's first planned capital. Washington, D.C., is one of America's most visited sites.

The world's largest silver nugget, weighing 1,840 lbs (835 kg) was found in 1894 near Aspen, Colerado.

Disney World, near Orlando, Florida is the world's largest tourist attraction, covering an area of 30,000 acres (12,140 hectares).

The Vikings

The Vikings lived in Scandinavia (Denmark, Norway and Sweden) around 750-1100 AD. Villages all round the coasts of Europe lived in terror of their raids, but they also travelled in peace. Vikings were traders, selling weapons, timber, jewels, pottery, spices and honey in their impressive ships.

What has been written about the Vikings?

Much of what we know about the Vikings comes from their sagas (stories), which were written in Iceland in the 13th and 14th centuries. The Vikings themselves did not write things down, though they did carve 'picture words' called runes into wood and stone.

Written stories we have about the Vikings were provided by English and French monks, whose settlements were often attacked by the Vikings. These accounts describe Vikings as terrifying savages.

Viking ships

The Vikings built wonderful ships, called longships. They had a high prow (front) and stern (back) to help them glide through rough waters. The prow was often decorated with a fearsome carved dragon's head.

The ships were built of wood. Tar from pine trees was used to waterproof them. They had square sails, and could be rowed by oarsmen if there was no wind. A large oar at the back of the ship was used for steering.

Longships could sail up shallow rivers, and could be run right up onto the beach at the start of a raid so that the Vikings could leap straight out, ready to fight.

What was everyday life like for a Viking?

The Vikings weren't just warriors and explorers – they were also settlers and farmers. Most of them lived on farms. Their chiefs lived in huge longhouses with wood or stone walls and straw-covered roofs. Families and servants all shared one big room. A hole in the roof was the only way to let smoke escape, and the longhouses would have been very dark as they had no windows.

In the cold of winter, even farm animals would be kept inside the longhouse.

The Vikings' clothes were made from wool, linen and leather. They loved bright colours, and made red and green dyes from berries, and yellow and green dyes from vegetables.

They loved jewellery and dressed up their outfits with rings, arm rings, brooches, fancy buckles and necklaces.

Were the Vikings the first Europeans to discover America?

Their sagas (stories) tell us that they were! They tell the story of the hero Leif Ericsson, who discovered a new and rich land by sailing far to the West from his home in Greenland. He called it Vinland.

How did the Vikings find their way across the seas?

They had to make their way using the position of the sun and stars and the direction of the wind, and by keeping an eye out for familiar landmarks on the shore.

What sort of weapons did the Vikings have?

Vikings treasured their weapons. In the sagas, Viking warriors give their heavy swords, spears and battle-axes special names, like 'Leg Biter' and 'War flame'.

What's the story?

In 986 AD, a Viking trader named Bjarni Herjollfsson set sail from Iceland to Greenland. He was blown off course, and after many days sighted unfamiliar land, covered in forest, to the West. This could not be Greenland, which was always covered with ice. When he finally got home to Greenland, Bjarni told stories about the strange land he had seen.

Leif was determined to find this new land, and he set off westward with 35 men. By winter they had arrived, and become the first Europeans to set foot on the continent of North America.

What's the evidence?

In the 1960s, archaeologists excavated a typical Viking settlement camp at the tip of Newfoundland, in Canada. We cannot say for certain that this is the place found by Leif, but it

certainly proves that the Vikings were on American soil more than 1000 years ago.

Fascinating Facts

'Viking' comes from the Old Norse word vika, which means 'to go off'. They are also called the Norse, or Norsemen.

People in Iceland today can still read the Viking sagas, because the Icelandic language has stayed the same for hundreds of years.

Many people believe they were also the first Europeans to discover America – 500 years before Columbus ever got there!

Silver jewellery was used in place of money. A Viking buying a pig from his neighbour would take off his silver arm ring, and break off a piece to pay for the pig.

Volcanoes

Deep under the earth is very hot runny liquid called 'magma'. Sometimes the magma rises to the surface, building up great pressure, and than an eruption occurs. When this happens, a volcano is formed. Gases and lava shoot up through the opening and spill out, causing lava flows, mudslides and falling ash. Large pieces of lava are called lava bombs. An erupting volcano can also cause earthquakes and tsunamis.

Active volcanoes

A volcano is considered 'active' if lava comes out of the top. When this happens, the volcano is 'erupting'. If volcanoes have been quiet for a long time they are 'inactive'. Some inactive volcanoes suddenly become active.

Dormant and extinct volcanoes

Some volcanoes have not erupted for at least 10,000 years. These volcanoes are described as dormant, since they have the potential to erupt again. Some volcanoes only erupt once, and these are called 'extinct', because they will not erupt again.

Cone shapes

The volcano's eruptions can create cone-shaped accumulations of volcanic material. The thickness of the underground magma determines how a volcano will erupt, and what kind of cone will form. There are three cone shapes: cinder cones, shield cones, and stratovolcanoes cones.

Cinder shapes

Cinder cones have straight sides with steep slopes and a large, bowl-shaped crater at the summit. They rarely rise to more than 1,000 feet (304 m) above the surrounding landscape. They are known for their very violent, explosive, exciting eruptions. Paricutin in Mexico and Mount Vesuvius in Italy are famous cinder cones.

Shield shapes

Shield cones have very gentle slopes. They were named by Icelandic people because the cones' shape reminded them of a warrior's shield laid down. These volcanoes erupt many times over the same area forming huge, thick lava plateaus. The Columbia Plateau of the western United States is the largest lava plateau in the world. It covers almost 100,000 square miles (259,000 sq kms) and is almost a mile thick in places.

Every day, ten volcanoes erupt somewhere on Earth. Most of these are small eruptions, but they may be followed by larger ones.

Stratovolcanoes shapes

Stratovolcanoes cones have gentle lower slopes, but steep upper slopes. They are formed from a combination of eruptions. First the volcano has an explosive eruption that ejects huge amounts of steam, gas and ash. This is followed by the ejection of lava. A large cone is built up with many layers of ash and lava. These are the most common volcanic cones, and famous examples include Mount St Helens in Washington and Mount Pinatubo in the Philippines.

Underwater volcanoes

Many volcanoes are born on the sea floor. Etna and Vesuvius began as underwater volcanoes, as did the vast cones of the Hawaiian islands and many other volcanic islands in the Pacific Ocean.

Worst eruptions

There have been many cataclysmic eruptions. After a series of eruptions over the course of several days (26–27 August 1883), the uninhabited island of Krakatoa in Sumatra/Java exploded with probably the loudest

What is 'The Lighthouse of the Mediterranean'?

Stromboli, off the coast of Italy, has erupted repeatedly over many centuries. The volcano has been called 'The Lighthouse of the Mediterranean' because it erupts every 20 minutes or so.

bang ever heard by humans, audible up to 4,800 km (3,000 miles) away. About 200,000 people died, most of them killed by subsequent tsunamis with waves up to 30 m (98.5 ft).

When Vesuvius erupted suddenly, the town of Pompeii was buried under a vast layer of rock and volcanic ash. The town was preserved in a near-perfect state, and uncovered by archeological excavations that began in 1738.

The word volcano comes from the Roman god of fire, Vulcan. Vulcan was said to have had a forge (a place to melt and shape iron) on Vulcano, an active volcano on the Lipari Islands in Italy.

Mauna Loa, Hawaii, is the tallest mountain in the world if measured from the floor of the ocean where it was formed. It is 13,677 feet (4165 m) above sea level, but over 17,000 feet (5177 m) lies under the water. So this volcanic mountain is over 30,000 feet (9137 m) tall!

fascinaTing FacT

Water

W ater has the chemical formula H_2O, which means each water molecule is made of two hydrogen atoms and one oxygen atom. Water is the only substance that naturally occurs in solid, liquid and gaseous forms on the Earth.

Water is very important to life. Roughly 97% of the Earth's water is held in the oceans, which cover approximately 70% of the Earth's surface.

Water has the following physical properties:

- Its freezing point is 0°C (32°F) and its boiling point is 100°C (21°F).
- A litre of water weighs 1 kg (2.2 lbs).
- Its pH is 7, meaning it is neutral (see Acids and Alkalis, page 12 for more on this).
- It is an excellent solvent, meaning lots of things, particularly salts, will dissolve very well in it.
- It absorbs more red light (and infra-red) than blue light, so large bodies of pure water appear blue.

How is water vapour important?

Water vapour in the atmosphere is a greenhouse gas – it helps to reduce the amount of heat escaping from the planet into space. If there were no water vapour in the atmosphere the average temperature on the Earth would be –18°C (0.4°F)!

How are polar ice caps important?

The polar ice caps are extremely important to the global climate. They reflect heat more efficiently than the oceans or land and so help to regulate the amount of heat the Earth absorbs from the sun. They also lock away vast quantities of water that would otherwise be part of the oceans – if all the ice in the world were to melt the average sea level would rise by 70 m! (See Global Warming, page 92, for more about this.)

The Water cycle

- Water in the oceans evaporates as it is heated by the sun's heat, forming water vapour.
- This vapour rises into the atmosphere where it cools and condenses to form clouds of tiny water droplets.
- As these clouds encounter turbulence (rough, windy weather), the tiny water droplets collide and merge into larger droplets.
- These fall as precipitation (rain, sleet, hail or snow).
- This water collects on land into streams and rivers both above and underground. Eventually most of it flows back into the sea, where it will evaporate once more.

Of course, water doesn't always follow the cycle in order – some water will fall directly back into the oceans as rain, and some evaporates from rivers and streams before it gets back to the sea.

How do we use water?

Industry uses large amounts of water in a variety of ways including as a coolant in power stations, or as a solvent or chemical agent in many manufacturing and refining processes. Water has many industrial uses, such as irrigation, transportation and power generation.

Irrigation to water the plants

Irrigation is where water from another source (such as a nearby river) is diverted into fields along a series of channels. In some places this is essential to allow crops to be grown at all.

Transportation

Since the invention of boats and ships water has been used to transport goods and people from place to place – first along rivers and later over the seas and oceans. Ships remain a vital component of world trade.

Power generation

Hydroelectric power stations use moving water to turn turbines that generate electricity. There are two basic types – dams and tidal. In a hydroelectric dam a river is blocked by building a large dam across it (causing a reservoir of water to build up behind the dam). The water in the reservoir is at a much higher level than the water on the other side, so when it is allowed to flow it has a lot of force behind it. This force is used to drive the water through a turbine, causing it to spin and generate electricity. In a tidal hydroelectric station the force to drive the turbines comes from the ebb and flow of the tides.

Fact – people can usually go without food for weeks if necessary but can only survive for about 3 days without water.

Every living thing on Earth still needs liquid water to survive. Humans are roughly 70% water and need to drink water regularly to stay healthy.

fascinating
Facts

The Wheel

Imagine living in a world without wheels! That's exactly what people did until the Bronze Age. They had no wheeled carts to carry themselves or their things, no machinery run by wheels, and all their pottery was made without that crucial tool, the potter's wheel.

In the Bronze Age, horses and oxen began to be used as 'pulling' animals (we call these 'draft animals') and wheeled carts were developed. People also discovered how to use wheels in making pottery at this time.

The wheel was probably the greatest mechanical invention ever. Nearly every machine ever built – from tiny watch gears to engines and computer disk drives – makes some use of the wheel.

Invention

The earliest known examples of the wheel date from 3,500 BC. They were used in Ancient Mesopotamia and were rather clumsy solid disks of solid wood.

By 2,000 BC the ancient Egyptians were using a more advanced design – they developed spoked wheels to use on their chariots. These were much lighter (so the chariots could go faster), and could be repaired instead of discarded if they got damaged.

What did people use before the wheel?

Before they had wheeled carts, people used to move things by dragging them along. On smooth surfaces like ice and snow, this worked just fine – sledges are still popular forms of transport in cold areas. On rougher ground, though, dragging things was very hard work.

Sometimes logs were cut and used as rollers – heavy items like building blocks could be pushed forward more easily on a bed of rollers.

The potter's wheel

The potter's wheel came into use around 3,500 BC in Mesopotamia. Now potters could easily turn the pot they

Q&A?

How do wheels turn in a car?

Pistons in the engine are connected to a pole called the crankshaft. The pistons go up and down, turning the crankshaft. The crankshaft turns the driveshaft to which the front wheels are attached, making them turn.

How do we turn a wheel if we can't reach it?

A shaft or handle can be attached to the axle. Making the axle turn automatically turns the wheel – the wheel itself might be out of reach inside a piece of machinery, but we can still make it turn from outside.

were making, instead of having to move around it themselves or keep picking it up to turn it.

Think about what happens when you push a wheelbarrow – you don't have to touch the wheel to move it. An axle runs through the middle of the wheel. When you push your wheelbarrow, the axle transmits your forward movement to the wheel, which turns.

Here are just a few uses of the wheel throughout history:

The waterwheel

The waterwheel uses flowing or falling water to create power. The water hits a set of paddles on the wheel, causing it to turn. The movement energy of the wheel is carried to machinery by the shaft of the wheel.

Spinning wheel

A spinning wheel is a simple machine designed to twist wool or cotton into long lengths of thread. It is usually turned by hand or by a foot pedal. the person spinning working the spinning wheel is called the 'spinster'.

Cogwheel

A cogwheel, or gear wheel, a toothed wheel that engages with another toothed wheel in order to change the speed or direction of something

The turbine – a modern waterwheel

The modern turbine works in a similar way to the ancient waterwheel. A turbine is an engine that uses a fluid (gas or liquid) to drive machinery. Hydraulic, or water, turbines are used to drive electric generators in hydroelectric power stations. They use a flow of liquid to turn a shaft that drives an electric generator.

Having fun with wheels

As well as making our lives much easier, the wheel crops up in many of our leisure activities. Biking, roller-blading and skate-boarding are obvious fun uses of the wheel. We also see it in fairground rides, and even as a spinning firework, the Catherine Wheel.

Fascinating Facts

Some archaeologists think the potter's wheel was actually the first use of the wheel, before wheels were ever put onto carts!

A water wheel was described as early as 4000 BC by a Greek writer.

Wilderness

We usually think of wilderness as an area of land unchanged by people. Many areas of wilderness or near-wilderness exist around the world and form an important part of the Earth's ecosystem.

The word wilderness comes from the Old English 'wildeornes', which means wild beast.

Throughout history, the majority of our planet has been wilderness, because humans only settled in particular areas. However, in the 19th century it was realised that wild areas in many countries were disappearing fast, or were in danger of disappearing. This led to the creation of a conservation movement, initially in the United States, to reduce the impact of human activity on the landscape.

The Wilderness Act

The United States passed The Wilderness Act in 1964, which designated certain areas of land as 'wilderness'. This provided the first official protection for wilderness areas, although there had been ideas about

protecting them much earlier in the 20th century. The Wilderness Act restricts the building and leisure activities that can take place in these areas, which helps to conserve the animals and plants that live there. There are a wide variety of wilderness areas, some being mountainous whereas others are wetlands.

National Parks and Forests

Many countries have national parks and forests where human activity is limited. Whilst some people may live and work in the area, there are very strict rules about building and industry. There is often limited farming in these areas and people are encouraged to visit

them to pursue leisure activities such as walking, mountain-climbing or water sports.

In the UK the oldest nature reserve is Wicken Fen in Cambridgeshire, a vast wetland area which was established in 1899. The fens have been changing since Roman times, and this area was the only part which remained of the original landscape.

What is the oldest national park in the world?

Yellowstone National Park in the US.

In what year was the WorldWide Fund for Nature (World Wildlife Fund in the US) formed?

1961.

Hunting reserves

In many areas of the world, wildlife reserves have been set up to conserve animals just so that they can be hunted. This is how many of the big game reserves in Africa first came into being. However, ideas of making areas into natural hunting reserves date back much earlier, to the hunting reserves created by the kings of England in the Middle Ages.

Wonders *of the* World

The Seven Wonders of the World are famous structures built many years ago. The list was made in the 2nd century BC, and only includes the Mediterranean part of the world. Six out of the seven ancient wonders have been destroyed, but fragments remain, and there are descriptions of them in old books.

The Pyramids at Giza

This is the oldest ancient wonder, and the only one existing. There are three pyramids near Cairo in Egypt, the largest of which is 450 feet high, containing 2,300,000 stone blocks each weighing about 2.5 tons. They were built by the Egyptian pharaoh Khufu, and finished in 2680 BC. The Great Pyramid, the oldest and largest of the three, was built as Khufu's tomb. The other two large pyramids are the Pyramid of Khafre and the Pyramid of Menkaure. Khafre is now the tallest, as Khufu has been eroded and the topmost stone, the pyramidion, has been stolen. It was the world's tallest building for 4,000 years.

The Hanging Gardens of Babylon

We don't know if these really existed. They were supposedly built in present-day Iraq by King Nebuchadnezzer in 600 BC to please his queen, and were thought to have been terraced gardens on top of a building, between 75 and 300 feet high. Greek historians wrote about the gardens, but otherwise there is little evidence for their existence. Archaeologists have found ruined foundations of a large palace that could have been the building the gardens were built upon.

The Statue of Zeus at Olympia

This was 40 feet high and was made from ivory and gold by a famous Greek sculptor called Phidias in about 435 BC. It was lost (probably in a fire) but was pictured on old Greek coins. The statue is of the Greek god Zeus.

The Temple of Artemis at Ephesus

This was built in 350 BC, with columns 60 feet high, for the goddess Artemis (also known as Diana, the goddess of the moon). It took 120 years to build, and was a large marble temple with much fine artwork and sculpture inside. The beauty of the temple attracted many tourists and worshippers. It was destroyed by fire when the Goths invaded in AD 262. Only a single column remains from the original temple.

The Mausoleum at Halicarnassus

This was a huge white marble tomb built at Halicarnassus in about 355 BC by Queen Artemisia. It was a shrine in memory of her husband, and also held his remains. It was designed by Greek architects and was 135 feet high with an ornamental frieze around the outside. The King and Queen were great admirers of Greek civilization, and for much of

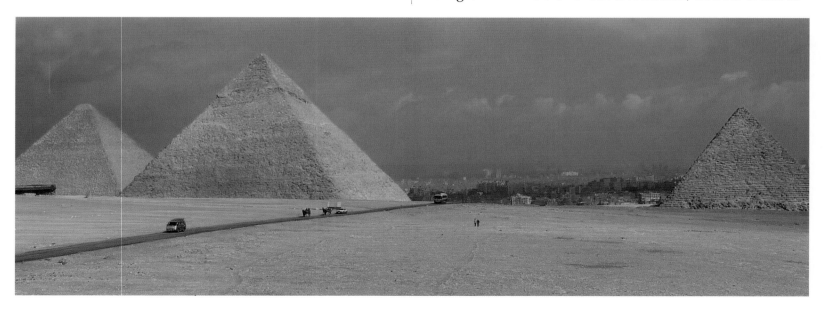

Modern wonders of the world include great architectural and engineering feats such as:
The Empire State Building in New York
The Taj Mahal in India
Stonehenge in England

their reign they used money from taxes to build beautiful Greek architecture. The shrine was destroyed by an earthquake, but some of its fragments are in the British Museum, London.

The Colossus at Rhodes

This was a bronze statue of the god Helios (Apollo). It took 12 years to build and was finished in 280 BC. We don't know what the Colossus looked like, but it was probably a statue near the entrance to the harbour. It broke at the knees during an earthquake in 224 BC and was not rebuilt, but the remains lay on the ground for over 800 years. A Roman writer, Pliny the Elder, wrote that each of the fingers of Colossus were larger than most Roman statues.

The Pharos (Lighthouse) of Alexandria

This was built during the third century BC on the island of Pharos off the coast of Alexandria, Egypt. It was first intended as a landmark for the port, to be seen by ships from a distance. Later it became a lighthouse, which was destroyed by an earthquake in the 13th century. A mirror reflected sunlight during the day and at night a large fire was lit for ships to see.

Which modern wonder of the world can be seen from space?

The Great Wall of China is the only structure of its kind visible from space.

Can you think of any natural wonders of the world?

Victoria Falls in Zimbabwe, the Great Barrier Reef in Australia, and the Grand Canyon in the USA.

Zoology

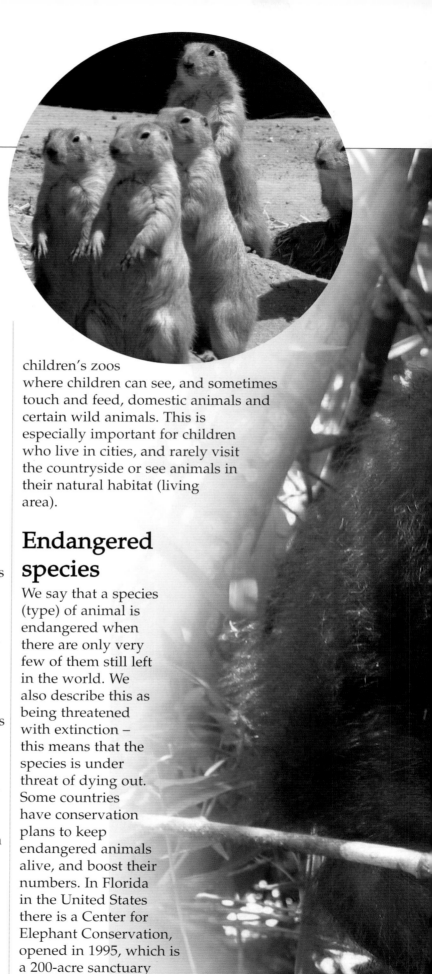

Zoology is the study of animals. The word zoology is taken from 'zoon', the Greek word for animal, and 'logy' meaning to study.

The ancient Greek philosopher Aristotle was one of the first zoologists, but it was not until the Middle Ages that zoology became widely studied. The English scientist Edward Wootton wrote *De differentiis animalium* in 1552. Through his study of Aristotle's earlier work and close observation of nature, Wootton's work extended knowledge about animals.

In Britain the term 'zoology' became well-known through the opening of zoological gardens in the 19th century. The name was soon shortened, and today there are zoos in most big cities. Visitors go there to observe wild animals, though many are in cages. Although the first zoos were intended for the entertainment of visitors, in recent years zoos have also focused on conservation (protecting animals from extinction) and education.

Modern zoos

Modern zoos often keep animals in enclosures designed to be like their natural surroundings. Nocturnal animals, which are only active at night, are seen during the day with dim artificial lighting. At night, when the visitors have gone, the animals are exposed to bright lighting. They think this is daylight, so they rest. Modern zoos often include children's zoos where children can see, and sometimes touch and feed, domestic animals and certain wild animals. This is especially important for children who live in cities, and rarely visit the countryside or see animals in their natural habitat (living area).

Endangered species

We say that a species (type) of animal is endangered when there are only very few of them still left in the world. We also describe this as being threatened with extinction – this means that the species is under threat of dying out. Some countries have conservation plans to keep endangered animals alive, and boost their numbers. In Florida in the United States there is a Center for Elephant Conservation, opened in 1995, which is a 200-acre sanctuary (resting-place) for retired circus elephants. Dedicated to just one

The oldest zoo which is still open today is the Vienna Zoo in Austria, which opened in 1752. The Vienna Zoo today has a red panda.

Giant pandas are the most expensive animals to keep in captivity, costing five times more than an elephant!

species, this centre has the largest gene pool for the Asian Elephant outside Southeast Asia.

Many animals around the world are in danger of extinction because they have been killed by hunters for their meat, skins, teeth or tusks. Others have lost their natural habitat when forests have been cleared for farming or building. Programmes of breeding these animals in captivity, and sometimes returning them to the wild, are well developed in a number of zoos around the world.

Giant pandas are an endangered species whose numbers have diminished through loss of their natural habitat, and very low birth rate. Although it is very rare for giant pandas to be born in captivity, two cubs were born in different zoos in the US in 2005. A male cub, Tai Shan, was born in July 2005 at the National Zoo in Washington, followed quickly by the birth of a female cub, Su Lin, in August at San Diego Zoo in California.

Q&A?

What is the Ménagerie du Jardin des Plantes?

The Ménagerie du Jardin des Plantes is the first zoo which was created specifically for scientific and educational purposes. It opened in 1794 in Paris, France, and is still open today.

Who is Jing Jing?

Jing Jing is a giant panda and mascot for the 2008 Olympic Games in Beijing, China.

General History

BC

c.9000	First walled city founded at Jericho
c.3500	First Chinese cities
c.2500	Use of papyrus by the Egyptians
c.2000	Completion of Stonehenge, England
c.1260	Trojan War
776	First Olympic Games in Greece
753	Foundation of Rome. Italy
c.550	Abacus developed, for counting, in China
509	Roman Republic established
221	Start of the Great Wall of China
c.5	Birth of Jesus

AD

27	Baptism of Jesus
65	Glastonbury Abbey, England built
105	Paper making started in China
122	Hadrian starts building defensive wall in northern England
350	Gothic bible produced
350	London, England, fortified
393	Final Olympic Games held until modern times
730	Printing starts in China
787	Vikings attack in Britain
871	King Alfred the Great takes the throne in England
1000	Iron Age settlements in Zimbabwe, Africa
1000	Inca empire growing in south America

1065	Westminster Abbey consecrated (declared a holy place) in London, England
1066	Norman Conquest in England
1086	Domesday Book completed in England
1155	Start of first university in Paris, France
1163	Notre Dame cathedral started in Paris, France
1215	King John signs Magna Carta at Runneymede, England
1290	Spectacles invented
1337	Start of Hundred Years War between England and France
1339	Kremlin constructed in Moscow, Russia
1350	Black Death in Europe
1400	Chaucer dies
1431	Joan of Arc dies
1453	Hundred Years War ends
1445	Gutenberg starts printing in Europe
1475	First book in English printed by Caxton
1509	First watch invented in Germany
1512	Michelangelo finishes painting the Sistine Chapel at the Vatican in Rome, Italy
1521	First books printed in Cambridge, England
1536	England and Wales unify

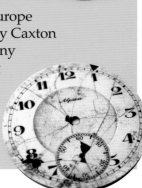

1558	Elizabeth 1 takes the throne in England
1564	Shakespeare is born
1576	First theatre opens in London, England
1587	Mary, Queen of Scots is killed
1588	England defeats the Spanish Armada
1610	Galileo writes about the moons of Jupiter and the rings of Saturn

1610	Tea first imported into Europe from China
1616	Shakespeare dies
1636	Harvard University founded
1638	First printing in America
1642	English Civil War starts
1649	Charles, King of England, executed
1653	Oliver Cromwell becomes Lord Protector of England
1660	Monarchy restored in England
1660s	Samuel Pepys compiles his diary
1665	Great Plague in London, England
1666	Great Fire of London, England
1679	Niagara Falls discovered
1681	First street lamps in London, England
1694	Bank of England established
1701	Yale University founded

1702	First daily newspaper in England circulated
1703	St Petersburg in Russia established
1705	Ships wheel replaces tiller
1710	Christopher Wren completes St Paul's cathedral in London
1715	Jacobite Rebellion in England
1721	Rifle first introduced in America
1741	First iron bridge constructed
1752	Gregorian calendar started in Britain
1756	Carbon dioxide discovered
1760	Discovery of hydrogen
1764	Invention of steam engine
1771	Discovery of oxygen
1774	Rules of cricket established

1789	Start of French Revolution
1789	George Washington becomes the first president of the USA
1796	Vaccine for smallpox discovered
1800	Union between England and Northern Ireland
1804	Napoleon Bonaparte becomes emperor
1807	Slave trade ended in British Empire
1815	Napoleon defeated at Waterloo
1825	Start of first passenger railway in England
1829	Braille system invented
1832	First railway built in USA
1835	Telegraph system invented in USA
1840	Queen Victoria marries Prince Albert
1851	Great Exhibition takes place in London
1861-65	American Civil War
1865	Abraham Lincoln assassinated
1867	Typewriter invented

General History *(cont)*

1919	Atlantic first crossed by air
1920	Start of radio broadcasting
1922	Discovery of tomb of Tutankhamun in Egypt
1926	General Strike in Britain
1926	Early television created
1928	Mickey Mouse is born
1931	Construction of Empire State Building in New York
1933	Polythene invented
1934	Nuclear fission discovered
1936	First television transmissions in Britain
1938	Nylon invented
1938	Ball point pen invented
1939-45	Second World War
1942	First nuclear reactor built
1945	United Nations created
1945	Microwave oven invented
1947	First supersonic flight
1952	Coronation of Elizabeth II in Britain
1953	DNA structure discovered

1867	Typewriter invented
1876	Invention of telephone
1885	First cars built by Karl Benz in Germany
1887	Pneumatic tyre invented
1889	Eiffel Tower in Paris, France finished
1901	Blood groups discovered
1901	First Nobel prize awarded
1903	Frst flight by Wright brothers
1908	Model T Ford car first made
1909	First cross-Channel flight between England and France
1912	Titanic sinks
1914-18	First World War in Europe
1917	Russian Revolution
1918	Women in Britain first given limited voting rights
1919	Soviet Republic founded

1956   Video recorder invented

1959   First motorway opened in Britain
1959   micro chip invented
1963   US President John F. Kennedy assassinated

1963   First woman in space
1967   First heart transplant
1969   First man lands on the moon
1972   Pocket calculator invented

1976   Concorde goes
        into service across
        the Atlantic
1977   Elvis Presley dies
1979   Margaret Thatcher becomes
        Britain's first woman prime
        minister
1980   John Lennon killed in New York
1981   Personal computer invented
1982   CDs introduced
1986   Mobile phone invented
1989   Berlin Wall falls
1990   Germany reunified
1991   Start of World Wide Web
1991   Nelson Mandela becomes president of South Africa
1997   Dolly the sheep cloned
2001   Terrorist attack destroys the World Trade Center in
        New York
2002   Queen Elizabeth II celebrates her golden jubilee in
        Britain

2002   Euro currency introduced
2003   First Chinese astronaut in space
2004   Indian Ocean tsunami hits southern Asia
2005   Hurricane Katrina devastates New Orleans
2005   London awarded 2012 Olympic Games

The world around us

Largest/highest/longest/deepest

The largest lake – Caspian Sea, Iran –
371,000 sq km/143,240 sq miles

The largest desert – Sahara, North Africa –
8,600,000 sq km/3,320,000 sq miles

The highest waterfall – Angel, Venezuela –
807 metre/2,648 feet

The longest river – River Nile, North Africa – 6,690 km/4,160 miles

The highest mountain – Everest, China and Nepal –
8,850 metres/29,035 feet

The largest sea – Coral Sea –
4,791,000 sq km/1,850,200 sq miles

The largest island – Greenland –
2.175,600 sq km/830,780 sq miles

The deepest cave – Jean Bernard, France –
1,494 metres/4,900 feet

The world around us

Seven wonders of the Ancient World

Egyptian Pyramids – Tombs built for Egyptian pharaohs more than 4000 years ago

Colossus of Rhodes – Bronze statue of the god Helius constructed in 300 BC

Hanging Gardens of Babylon – Terraced gardens along the River Euphrates created by Nebuchadnezzar in 6th century BC

Temple of Artemis at Ephesus – A marble temple built in the 6th century BC

Statue of Zeus at Olympia – A huge golden statue created in the 5th century BC

Pharos of Alexandria – The world's first lighthouse constructed at the entrance to the harbour at Alexandria in Egypt in around 300 BC

Mausoleum at Halicarnassus – Tomb for Mausolus built in the 4th century BC

General History, People

UK Kings & Queens

1603-1625	James I
1625-1649	Charles I
1649-1660	Republic
1660-1685	Charles II
1685-1688	James II

1760-1820	George III
1820-1830	George IV
1830-1837	William IV

1689-1702	William III
1689-1694	Mary II
1702-1714	Anne
1714-1727	George I
1727-1760	George II

1837-1901	Victoria
1901-1910	Edward VII
1910-1936	George V
1936	Edward VIII
1936-1952	George VI

1841	W. H. Harrison
1841-1845	John Tyler
1845-1849	James K. Polk
1849-1850	Zachary Taylor
1850-1853	Millard Fillmore
1853-1857	Franklin Pierce
1857-1861	James Buchanan
1861-1865	Abraham Lincoln
1865-1869	Andrew Johnson
1869-1877	Ulysses Grant
1877-1881	Rutherford Hayes
1881	James Garfield

1881-1885	Chester Arthur
1885-1889	Grover Cleveland
1889-1893	Benjamin Harrison
1893-1897	Grover Cleveland
1897-1901	William McKinley
1901-1909	Theodore Roosevelt

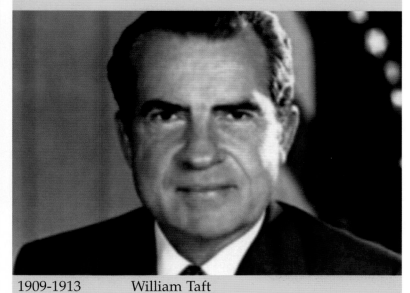

1909-1913	William Taft
1913-1921	Woodrow Wilson
1921-1923	Warren Harding
1923-1929	Calvin Coolidge
1933-1945	Franklin Roosevelt
1945-1952	Harry Truman
1953-1961	Dwight Eisenhower
1961-1963	John F. Kennedy
1963-1969	Lyndon Johnson
1969-1974	Richard Nixon
1974-1977	Gerald Ford
1977-1981	Jimmy Carter
1981-1989	Ronald Reagan
1989-1993	George Bush
1993-2000	Bill Clinton
2000- present	George W. Bush

Nature

Fastest/largest/biggest/longest/heaviest creatures

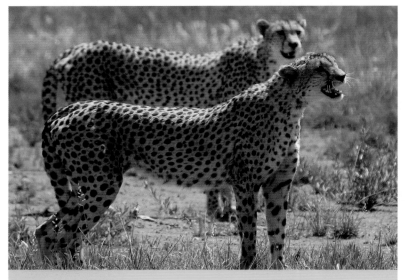

The fastest animal – cheetah – 110 km/h or 68mph

The fastest bird – peregrine falcon – 200 km/h or 125 mph

The fastest in the water – dolphin – 64 km/h or 40 mph

The fastest insect – dragonfly – 75 km/h or 45 mph

The largest land mammal – African elephant – 3 metres/10 feet tall

The biggest bird – ostrich – 2.75 metres/9 feet tall

The tallest land mammal – giraffe – 5.5 metres/18 feet tall

The fastest fish – sailfish – 110 km/h or 68 mph
The heaviest in the water – blue whale – 120 tonnes
The largest animal ever – blue whale – 35 metres/115 feet long
The longest snake – anaconda – 8.5 metres/28 feet long
The largest spider – Goliath bird-eating spider 0.25 metres/10 inches across
The largest insect – Goliath beetle – 0.11 metres/5 inches long

The largest wing span – wandering albatross – 3.5 metres/12 feet

Countries

Largest countries

6,601,668 sq miles (17,098,242 sq km) Russia

3,849,674 sq miles (9,970,610 sq km) Canada

3,717,812 sq miles (9,629,091 sq km) Unites States of America

3,705,841 sq miles (9,598,086 sq km) China

3,287,612 sq miles (8,514,877 sq km) Brazil

Biggest populations

6,464,750,000 world   1,315,844,000 China

| 1,103,371,000 | India | 222,781,000 | Indonesia |
| 298,213,000 | USA | 186,405,000 | Brazil |

Countries

Languages

Top 10 languages spoken around the world

1 Mandarin Chinese
2 English
3 Spanish
4 Hindi
5 Arabic

6 Portuguese
7 Bengali
8 Russian
9 Japanese
10 German

The world's tallest buildings

1,667 ft/508 m **Taipei 101 Tower,** Taipei, Taiwan

629 m/2,063 ft KVLY-TV mast, Blanchard, North Dakota, USA
610 m/2,001 ft Petronius Platform, Gulf of Mexico

558 m/1,830 ft Jakarta Tower, Jakarta, Indonesia

553 m/1,815 ft CN Tower, Toronto, Canada

The world's longest tunnels

53.9 km/33.5 miles	Seikan Tunnel, Tsugaru Strait, Japan
50 km/31 miles	Channel Tunnel, UK-France
26.5 km/16.5 miles	Hakkoda Tunnel, Hakkoda Mountains, Japan
25.8 km/16 miles	Daishimizu Tunnel, Mikuni Mounatains, Japan
20 km/12 miles	Wushaoling Tunnel, China

Flags *of the* World

AFGHANISTAN

ALBANIA

ALGERIA

ANDORRA

ANGOLA

ANGUILLA

ANTARCTICA

ANTIGUA

ARGENTINA

ARMENIA

AUSTRALIA

AUSTRIA

AZERBAIJAN

BAHAMAS

BAHRAIN

BANGLADESH

BARBADOS

BELARUS

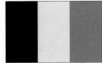
BELGIUM

BELIZE

BENIN

BERMUDA

BHUTAN

BOLIVIA

BOPHUTHATSWANA

BOSNIA &
HERZEGOVINA

BOTSWANA

BRAZIL

BRITISH VIRGIN
ISLANDS

BRUNEI

BULGARIA

BUKINA FASO

BURUNDI

CAMBODIA

CAMEROON

CANADA

CAPE VERDE

CAYMAN ISLANDS

CENTRAL AFRICAN
REPUBLIC

CHAD

CHILE

CHINA

CISKEI

COLOMBIA

COMOROS

CONGO, DEMOCRATIC
REPUBLIC OF

CONGO, REPUBLIC
OF

COOK ISLANDS

COSTA RICA

COTE D'IVOIRE

CROATIA

CUBA

CYPRUS

CZECH REPUBLIC

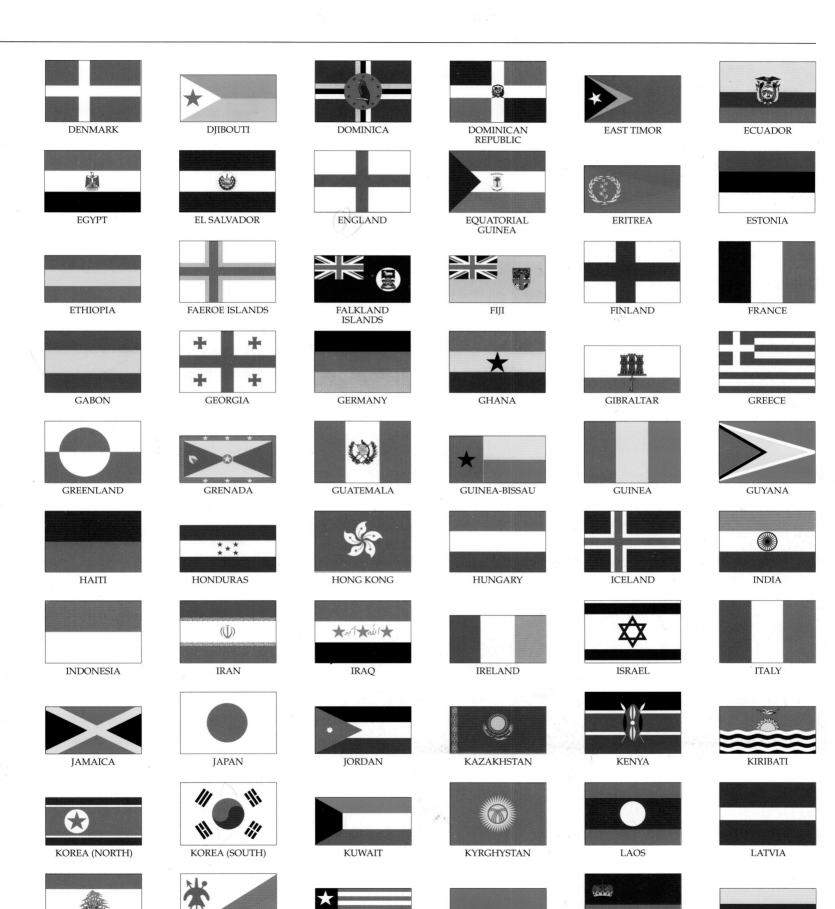

DENMARK	DJIBOUTI	DOMINICA	DOMINICAN REPUBLIC	EAST TIMOR	ECUADOR
EGYPT	EL SALVADOR	ENGLAND	EQUATORIAL GUINEA	ERITREA	ESTONIA
ETHIOPIA	FAEROE ISLANDS	FALKLAND ISLANDS	FIJI	FINLAND	FRANCE
GABON	GEORGIA	GERMANY	GHANA	GIBRALTAR	GREECE
GREENLAND	GRENADA	GUATEMALA	GUINEA-BISSAU	GUINEA	GUYANA
HAITI	HONDURAS	HONG KONG	HUNGARY	ICELAND	INDIA
INDONESIA	IRAN	IRAQ	IRELAND	ISRAEL	ITALY
JAMAICA	JAPAN	JORDAN	KAZAKHSTAN	KENYA	KIRIBATI
KOREA (NORTH)	KOREA (SOUTH)	KUWAIT	KYRGHYSTAN	LAOS	LATVIA
LEBANON	LESOTHO	LIBERIA	LIBYA	LIECHTENSTEIN	LITHUANIA

KEY FACTS

 LUXEMBOURG

 MACEDONIA

 MADAGASCAR

 MALAWI

 MALAYSIA

 MALDIVES

 MALI

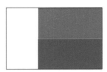 MALTA

 MARSHALL ISLANDS

 MAURITANIA

 MAURITIUS

 MEXICO

 MICRONESIA

 MOLDOVA

 MONACO

 MONGOLIA

 MONTENEGRO

 MONSERRAT

 MOROCCO

 MOZAMBIQUE

 MYANMAR

 NAMIBIA

 NAURU

 NEPAL

 NETHERLAND ANTILLES

 NETHERLANDS

 NEW ZEALAND

 NICARAGUA

 NIGER

 NIGERIA

 NIUE

 NORTHERN CYPRUS

 NORTHERN IRELAND

 NORWAY

 OMAN

 PAKISTAN

 PALESTINE

 PANAMA

 PAPUA NEW GUINEA

 PARAGUAY

 PERU

 PHILIPPINES

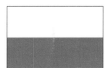 POLAND

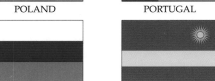 PORTUGAL

 PUERTO RICO

 QATAR

 RÉUNION

 ROMANIA

 RUSSIA

 RWANDA

 SAMOA (WESTERN)

SAN MARINO

 SÃO TOMÉ AND PRINCIPE

SAUDI ARABIA

SCOTLAND

SENEGAL

SERBIA

SEYCHELLES

SIERRA LEONE

SINGAPORE

 SLOVAKIA

 SLOVENIA

 SOLOMAN ISLANDS

 SOMALIA

 SOMALILAND

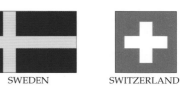 SOUTH AFRICA

 SPAIN

 SRI LANKA

 ST HELENA

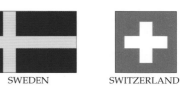 ST KITTS & NEVIS

 ST LUCIA

 ST PIERRE & MIQUELON

 ST CHRISTOPHER

 ST VINCENT

 SURINAME

 SWAZILAND

 SWEDEN

 SWITZERLAND

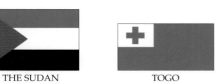 SYRIA

 TAIWAN

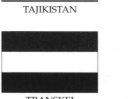 TAJIKISTAN

 TANZANIA

THAILAND

THE GAMBIA

 THE SUDAN

 TOGO

 TRANSKEI

 TRINIDAD

 TUNISIA

 TURKEY

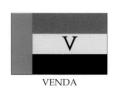 TURKMENISTAN

 TURKS & CAICOS

 TUVALU

 UGANDA

UKRAINE

 UNITED ARAB EMIRATES

 UNITED KINGDOM

 URUGUAY

 UNITED STATES OF AMERICA

 UZBEKISTAN

VANUATU

VATICAN CITY

VENDA

VENEZUELA

 VIETNAM

VIRGIN ISLANDS

WALES

WESTERN SAHARA

WESTERN SAMOA

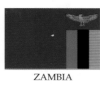 YEMEN

ZAMBIA

ZIMBABWE

Culture

Sport – Olympic Games

Since 1896 the Olympic Games have been held in many countries around the world (except during World War I and World War II).

1896	Athens, Greece
1900	Paris, France
1904	St Louis, USA
1908	London, UK
1912	Stockholm, Sweden
1920	Antwerp, Belgium
1924	Paris, France
1928	Amsterdam, Netherlands
1932	Los Angeles, USA
1936	Berlin, Germany
1948	London, UK
1952	Helsinki, Finland
1956	Melbourne, Australia
1960	Rome, Italy
1964	Tokyo, Japan
1968	Mexico City, Mexico
1972	Munich, Germany
1976	Montreal, Canada
1980	Moscow, Russia
1984	Los Angeles, USA
1988	Seoul, South Korea
1992	Barcelona, Spain
1996	Atlanta, USA
2000	Sydney, Australia
2004	Athens, Greece
2008	Beijing, China
2012	London, UK

Music – famous composers

1685-1750	Johann Sebastian Bach
1685-1759	George F. Haydn
1756-1791	Wolfgang Mozart
1770-1827	Ludwig van Beethoven
1833-1897	Johannes Brahms
1860-1911	Gustav Mahler
1873-1943	Sergei Rachmaninov
1898-1937	George Gerschwin
1900-1990	Aaron Copeland
1918-1990	Leonard Bernstein

Musical Instruments

Brass	French horn, trumpet, cornet, trombone, tuba
String	violin, viola, violoncello, double bass
Woodwind	piccolo, flute, oboe, clarinet, cor anglais, bassoon
Percussion	timpani, side drum, bass drum, cymbals, triangle, tam-tam, tubular bells, xylophone

Famous Artists

1452-1519	Leonardo da Vinci
1475-1564	Michelangelo
1606-1669	Rijn van Rembrandt
1760-1849	Hokusai
1840-1926	Auguste Rodin
1853-1890	Vincent van Gogh
1864-1954	Toulouse Lautrec
1881-1973	Pablo Picasso
1903-1970	Mark Rothko
1928-1987	Andy Warhol

Famous Writers

1340-1400	Geoffrey Chaucer
1564-1616	William Shakespeare
1770-1850	William Wordsworth
1812-1870	Charles Dickens
1828-1906	Henrik Ibsen
1830-1886	Emily Dickinson
1860-1904	Anton Chekov
1888-1965	T. S. Eliot
1899-1961	Ernest Hemingway
1944	Alice Walker

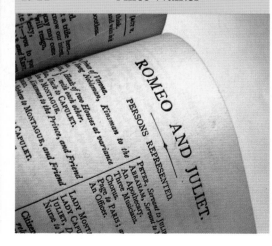

Dancers

1872-1929	Sergei Diaghilev
1888-1982	Marie Rambert
1898-2001	Ninette Valois
1904-1983	George Balanchine
1906-1988	Frederick Ashton
1919-1991	Margot Fonteyn
1929-1992	Kenneth Macmillan
1938-1993	Rudolf Nureyev
1948	Mikhail Baryshnikov
1969	Darcey Bussell

Designers

1833-1898	Edward Burne-Jones
1834-1896	William Morris
1839-1896	William de Morgan
1846-1920	Peter Carl Fabergé
1848-1933	Louis Comfort Tiffany
1855-1940	Carlo Bugatti
1860-1945	Rene Lalique
1868-1928	Charles Rennie Mackintosh
1899-1972	Clarice Cliff
1931	Terence Conran

Fashion designers

Cristobal Balenciaga
Pierre Balmain
Jean Cacharel
Coco Chanel
Christian Dior
Mariano Fortuny
Jean-Paul Gaultier
Donna Karan
Takada Kenzo
Karl Lagerfeld

INDEX

A

A Midsummer Night's Dream 170

aardvarks 10, 11

abacus 119, 142

Aborigines 36-37

acid rain 13

acids 12-13

actors 97, 171

aerial surveys 25

Africa 14-15, 49, 82, 201

Age of Discovery 68

agriculture 30, 76-77, 97, 118, 185

aircraft 74-75, 102-103, 187

airships 74

Alaska 141, 189

albatross 219

alchemy 118

Alexander the Great 16-17

Alexandria 15

alkalis 12-13

allergies 78, 79

alphabets 46, 108, 167

Alps 122, 123

aluminium cans 156

Amazon rainforest 154

America, discovering 69, 193

American Indians 53, 68, 128-129

amphisbaenia 161

amphitheatres 165

amps 62

Amristar 159

Amundsen, Roald 23

Ancient Egypt 25, 91, 116, 117, 143, 153, 199

    pyramids 24, 26, 202, 212

Ancient Greece 16, 26, 43, 96-97, 98, 150

    gods 97, 124, 144-145, 202, 213

    mythology 74, 97, 124

    Olympic Games 144-145

theatre 70, 96, 97, 124

Andes Mountains 122

Anglo-Saxons 138

animals 10-11, 20-21, 137, 167, 218-219

    Antarctica 22

    Arctic 29

    bison 128

    desert 56-57

    dogs 175, 177

    dolphins 20, 37, 218

    endangered species 123, 137, 204-205

    extinct 21

    mountain 123,

    rainforest 154, 155

    squirrels 121

    whales 20, 21, 22, 23, 37, 113, 219

    zoology 204-205

Ankylosaurus 58, 59

Antarctica 22-23, 49, 161

anteaters 10

Apollo missions 176-177

apprentices 19

aquatic life 22, 23, 28, 37, 72-73, 169

    see also dolphins; fish; turtles; whales

aqueducts 165

Arabic numbers 143

arachnids 178-179, 219

Aral Sea 166-167

Arc de Triomphe 81

archaeologists 24-25

archaeology 24-25

arches 182

architects 26

architecture 26-27, 91

Arctic 28-29

Arctic foxes 29

Arctic terns 29

Aristotle 17, 93

Arkwright's spinning frame 133

Armstrong, Neil 177

arrowheads 24

art 18-19

Art Deco 27

Art Nouveau 27

artists 18-19, 229

Arts and Crafts movement 27

Asia 30-31

    see also China; India; Indonesia; Japan; Russia

Asian tsunami 131

asteroids 59

astrology 32-33

astronauts 69, 95, 177

astronomers 34, 35, 102

astronomy 34-35, 60, 102

Athens 96

atomic clocks 51

Aurora Australis 22-23

Aurora Borealis 112

Australia 36-37, 72, 132, 179

authors 229

autobahns 88

Aztecs 38-39

B

babies 162-163

Babylonians 32, 142, 202, 212

balanced diet 78

balloon flight 74, 187

Baroque 27

basilicas 165

baths 165

bats 20, 21, 175

batteries 157, 183

Battle of Hastings 138-139

Battle of Stamford Bridge 138

Battle of Trafalgar 126

Battle of Waterloo 127

INDEX

INDEX

INDEX

INDEX

Acknowledgements

The authors and publishers would like to thank the following people who played such a significant role in creating this Children's Encyclopedia:

Illustration
HL Studios

Page Design
HL Studios

Editorial
Jennifer Clark, Ros Morley, Lucie Williams

Photo research
Ros Morley

Project management
HL Studios

Jacket Design
JPX

Production
Elaine Ward

All photographs are copyright of Jupiterimages.com, Ros Morley Editing, USGS, NASA, WWF, istockphoto, stockphoto, stockxchnge, www.imageafter.com, Flickr.com, except where stated below:

Bayeux Tapestry © GEORGE BERNARD / SCIENCE PHOTO LIBRARY
Dolly, the world's first adult sheep clone © PH. PLAILLY / EURELIOS / SCIENCE PHOTO LIBRARY
Artwork of the death of the dinosaurs © D. VAN RAVENSWAAY / SCIENCE PHOTO LIBRARY
Rodolfo Coria dusting fossil jaw of giant dinosaur © CARLOS GOLDIN / SCIENCE PHOTO LIBRARY
Hubble Space Telescope image of the Einstein cross © NASA / ESA / STScI / SCIENCE PHOTO LIBRARY
Roman glass jewellery bead, SEM © STEVE GSCHMEISSNER / SCIENCE PHOTO LIBRARY
Seahorse © Frank Burgey; Aztec Waterway © Ben Earwicker; Rainforest sunlight © Rolf Esslinger; Totem pole © Dale Eurenius; Dinosaur bones © Kim Fawcett; Fish Market Lake Baikal © Enrique Galindo; Bromeliad © Stacy Graff; Wires Tacoma © Mel Guknes (Singingbarista); Prayer mat © Alaaeddin Hammoudeh; Helicopter © Dave Johnson www.tollbarstudio.co.uk; Ford T1 © www.khaane.com; Ancient Architecture © Marius Largu; Jade mask © Michel Meynsbrughen (Clafouti); Venus Fly Trap © Dr. David Midgley, Berowra, NSW, Australia; Waterwheel Arkansas © Bill Sarver;